KT-154-478

95p

INTERCOMMUNION AND CHURCH
MEMBERSHIP

J.M. Turner.
1975.

INTERCOMMUNION AND CHURCH MEMBERSHIP

Edited by John Kent
and
Robert Murray S.J.

Darton, Longman & Todd
London

Dimension Books, Inc.
Denville, New Jersey

First published in 1973 by
Darton, Longman & Todd Limited
85 Gloucester Road, London SW7 4SU
England

and

Dimension Books, Inc.
Denville, New Jersey
USA

© 1973 John Kent and Robert Murray.
All rights reserved. No portion of this book
may be reproduced in any form without
written permission from the publisher, except
for brief passages included in a review appearing
in a newspaper or magazine.
Printed in Great Britain at
The Pitman Press, Bath
ISBN 0 232 51201 9

This Symposium was held as a service to the Roman Catholic Theological Commission for England and Wales. The papers here printed, therefore, have been circulated to members of the Commission, who have also received a report, and expressed their gratitude for this ecumenical contribution to the continuing discussion. It must be emphasised that all contributions, including notes, represent the opinions of their authors only.

Contents

INTRODUCTION

THE PAPERS ON CHURCH MEMBERSHIP AND INTERCOM-
MUNION which are gathered here were presented at the 10th
Downside Symposium, which took place in Bristol in April, 1972, at
Burwalls, a hostel belonging to Bristol University. This particular
subject had been suggested to the Symposium Group by the Theological Commission of the Roman Catholic Bishops of England and
Wales. The papers have been presented to the Commission. The
subject was handled in the now traditional manner, by discussion
within the group and by holding the Symposium to which a wide
range of contributors were invited, the problem of membership being
kept in view as well as that of intercommunion.

Of the members of the Group responsible for the Symposium,
especial thanks are due to Nicholas Lash, to John M. Todd (chairman, 1971), to Ian McNeill (secretary and treasurer), who has been
greatly assisted by his wife, Sally, and to John Coulson (chairman,
1972, and of the meetings at Burwalls). The Downside Centre for
Religious Studies, of which John Coulson is Warden, made a generous
grant towards the cost of the symposium itself; a grant was also made
by the Theology Commission; and the symposium was held in
association with the Department of Theology and Religious Studies,
Bristol.

Three of the founding members of the Group are now dead, and it
is with an especial sense of loss that the members wish to record the
deaths of Dom Ralph Russell, their chaplain, and of Lancelot
Sheppard. John Todd writes of them: 'Like his lifelong friend Reg
Trevett, Fr Ralph was a westcountryman by birth. He was practically always present at meetings of the group and remained one of
its essential animateurs to the end. His qualities are well known,
those of a specially kind and warm heart wedded to an alert and
understanding mind. There was a recognisable holiness about him.
His special charity prevented him from indulging in the cutting wit
which is, to some extent, part of the human stuff of meetings of
civilised westerners. Put that alongside a distinct loyalty to the

Roman Catholic Church in a slightly old fashioned sense, and you have a perhaps unexpected but important ingredient of both our early and later days. Ralph's contribution always tended towards compromise or to some kind of 'comprehensive' solution to problems. But he never shirked intellectual confrontation and always contributed real insights. Lancelot Sheppard was also a specially faithful member of the group, very seldom absent. His was that kind of constant reliability which is a primary constituent of any group of friends meeting together for a purpose. He edited the fifth symposium, entitled *True Worship*, the meeting having been held appropriately at the Benedictine Abbey of Bec in Normandy, a place to delight Lance's sense of the Benedictine life, of liturgy and of history. Appropriately too it was the shortest of the symposia. Lance only spoke when he had something specific to say. 'His' Symposium provided a concise, meaty book, likely to be an important reference point for many years to come. The deaths of Ralph and Lance following on that of Reg Trevett put a mark of finality against this our twentieth year.'

It only remains to be said that during those twenty years the Downside Symposium Group has made a unique contribution to modern theological thinking, and has constantly fostered the growth, on an ecumenical basis, of the lay theology which is one of Christianity's greatest needs in our time.

John Kent
Robert Murray S.J.

PART ONE

PART ONE

INTRODUCTION

The opening section deals with the problem of intercommunion and church membership in the context of history, ecclesiastical law and creed. Professor Fransen of Louvain submits traditional Roman Catholic attitudes to intercommunion to a careful examination, balancing the impatience which many ecumenical enthusiasts feel in the present situation against the statement that according to tradition some visible unity of life and communion seems necessary to intercommunion as such. Pastoral decisions are dependent on the mentality of the faithful in the countries affected by them, but the episcopate should be encouraged to look for ways of widening the occasions of intercommunion. Professor Wiles' paper covers one aspect of Professor Fransen's survey, the view that the Eucharist is primarily the sacrament of unity, and does so from the angle of Early Church history. He argues that it is important to remember that in the Early Church the Eucharist was a sacrament of unity in a *local* setting and in a *local* congregation, rather than a symbol of the oneness of the Christian congregations as a whole.

Dr. Lash's paper, which, like Professor Fransen's, is written with the Roman Catholic position very much in mind, takes up the question of the importance, for intercommunion, of confessional differences of belief. If 'complete agreement' in belief is an illusion, what attainable goal is there at this theological level which would either justify or perhaps compel a common celebration of the Eucharist? Dr. Lash suggests that a solution may be found in the idea of 'mutual recognition'. There are grounds for suggesting that Christians who use what they mutually recognize to be the same creed are not sufficiently divided in belief to require absolute eucharistic separation. These papers should be compared with Dr. Murray's essay on 'Tradition as a Criterion of Unity' in the third section of the symposium.

BIOGRAPHICAL NOTE

PIET FRANSEN S.J. *is Professor of Dogmatic Theology in the Jesuit Faculty of Theology, Heverlee, Louvain and at the University of Innsbruck. His books to appear in English include* Intelligent Theology *(1967) published in three volumes, the second of which was written with Professor T. F. Torrence ; and* The New Life of Grace *(1969). He has also contributed to several of the previous Downside Symposia.*

1 *Intercommunion*

PIET FRANSEN, s.j.

I. *Introduction*

J. H. NEWMAN ONCE SAID THAT THE MOST SERIOUS THREAT to the Church's existence and life comes when three important functions within the Church's communion are confused with one another. The first of these is the task of the scientific theologian, which he carries out either by research into the historical sources of the faith, that is, the Bible as the Word of God, or by philosophical and sometimes speculative reinterpretation of the divine message. The second is the practical investigation of the moral and pastoral theologian with the help of sociology, psychology and the other human experimental sciences. Last but not least, in the Roman Church there is the teaching and leading office and ministry of the episcopate, first in their own dioceses, and then in union with the Pope on behalf of the whole Church. If the theologians possess the 'clavis scientiae', the key of knowledge, as Gratian put it in the most important collection of Canon Law in the Middle Ages, the bishops receive the 'clavis auctoritatis', the ministry of authority by which, after discussion and reflection, decisions are made.[1] It is very difficult for one person to combine the functions of theologian, moralist and bishop, though St Augustine showed that a great philosopher and theologian

---

[1] 'Sed alius est causis terminum imponere, aliud scripturas sacras diligenter exponere. Negotiis diffiniendis non solum est necessaria scientia, sed etiam potentas.' Introductio in Dcst. XX, Pars I Sect. 1; ed. Friedberg, I, 65.

could become an even greater bishop – unless one agrees with those of his modern biographers who argue that his episcopal commitment, especially in such a puritan and fanatical Church as that of Africa seems to have been, narrowed and even hardened the broader approach to problems which he showed before his ordination to the episcopate.[2] St Charles Borromeo was a remarkable reformer of his Church in Milan, and therefore a qualified pastoral specialist in his own right.

Normally, however, a bishop has no time for protracted theological work, and is not generally appointed because of his outstanding scholarly accomplishment. The theologian, however, has to be faithful to the methods of his own science, which would otherwise have no authority at all. This does not mean that he can afford not to familiarise himself with what is happening among ordinary Church people: he should not be allowed to use his theoretical academic freedom as a way of exonerating himself from having any responsibility to the laity. The propensity of some present-day theologians to air their own views with an 'après moi le déluge' mentality denies what was said at the beginning of this paper; the importance of these functions within the Church's communion.

Much greater danger, however, originates in a prophetic conception of the role of the bishop, which may have existed in the oldest traditions of the Church, but has often taken a specious form in modern times. On the basis of this understanding of tradition, linked to some quotations from the documents of Vatican II, bishops all over the world tend to consider themselves not only as the leaders of their dioceses, but as the principal theologians and pastoral specialists of their dioceses as well. To defend this attitude they appeal to the special guidance of the Holy Spirit which was granted to them at their ordination. All this can undoubtedly be found in the Vatican II documents, but the problem is how to interpret what is implied there. It is a dangerous illusion to imagine that the guidance of the Holy Spirit will compensate for a lack of theological and pastoral information and insight. The official declaration of Mgr Gasser, president of the Theological Commission, clearly stated that the

---

[2] EUGENE TESELLE, *Augustine, The Theologian*, New York/London, 1970; JAROSLAV PELIKAN, *The Christian Tradition*, vol. I, *The Emergence of the Catholic Tradition*, Chicago/London, 1971, 308–18.

guidance of the Holy Spirit, promised and imparted to the teaching authority of the Church, was never to be identified with any form of supernatural private revelation, and even less with the special form of inspiration which allows us to consider the words of the New Testament to be the Word of God. Whenever the guidance of the Spirit is opposed to the theological or pastoral information and studies of other members of the Church, there is no escaping the accusation that one is implicitly referring to a kind of revelation, or supernatural illumination of the mind.

These basic considerations have been presented so as to define clearly my own task in this introductory paper. I am neither a bishop nor a pastoral specialist, and I am not going to talk as though I were. Let me therefore indicate what line I am going to take in a more positive way. The task of the theologian who is really committed to his own faith and Church, and who is not entirely absorbed by re-search or abstruse speculation, is to free his contemporaries from the 'conventional wisdom' which John Kenneth Galbraith, the famous economist, so convincingly described and attacked in his book, *The Affluent Society*. The Church as a human society cannot escape the different psychological and sociological human laws which emprison any community in such a 'conventional wisdom', which in its turn threatens to obscure the realities of the Christian faith. I am con-vinced that the Church is even more subject to this kind of tempta-tion because she is concerned with eternal truths and realities. It is so easy, and it has been done throughout the history of the Church, to invest her language, doctrine and practice with a divine authority which belongs exclusively to God Himself. There is present through-out Church history a tendency to enhance the truth and the value of the Church's statements and practices. Thus what starts as a com-mon opinion soon becomes an evident truth; a decree of a local council is quickly changed into a solemn definition of faith (especi-ally if a Pope writes an encyclical about it); a timely formulation of the faith suddenly turns into a timeless statement, valid for all times and places; any practice which we knew when we were young is changed miraculously into an age-old tradition. Vatican I drew the limits of pontifical infallibility so tightly that a theologian like René Laurentin was able to write in 'Le Figaro' a year or two ago that the definition was almost useless; nevertheless, the generation which knew all about the Council at first hand found no difficulty in quickly extending the idea of infallibility to other forms of pontifical authority and government. It seems, especially in the Roman Catholic Church, to be a sign and guarantee of one's own faith and loyal acceptance of the Church's doctrine to amplify, extend and enhance it as much as possible. Indeed, what I really enjoy about the work of a theologian is the sense that theology, especially historical theology, liberates the student from many of the narrow and even sectarian conceptions which he has assimilated under the influence of the so-called 'common opinion' of the local Church. Only the freedom of the Spirit is able to open a way to greater creativity, to open our hearts to the spiritual guidance which reaches out to us in the 'kairos' of the present world. Certainly, we have to look back to the past in order to keep in communion with the whole Church, but this also means a serious danger of freezing our religious life into a legalistic, ritualistic or dogmatic immobility.

My purpose, therefore, in this introductory paper, is to foster, as far as possible, greater openness and a spirit of freedom, in order to enable us all to meet the exigencies of our time and to listen to the guidance of God in our hearts as well as in the communion of our Church.

What can a theologian say about Intercommunion? I want to divide my answer into two sections. In the first section I shall analyse the meaning and the validity, and eventually the workability of the criteria which are officially acknowledged by the different Churches in relation to Intercommunion. In the second section I shall attempt to see whether there exist some serious possibilities for a greater creativity and flexibility in this matter.

II. *The Official Criteria of the Churches*
The Churches which use the clearest criteria in the matter of Intercommunion are the Eastern Churches and the Church of Rome.[3] The other Churches, especially those stemming from the Reformation, seem to refer to the same criteria, though they accept a greater flexibility, even on the doctrinal level. The reason is evident. The Reformation objected from its very beginning to any form of

---

[3] NICHOLAS LASH, *His Presence in the World*, Chapter 6. Priesthood, Ministry and Intercommunion, Dayton, Ohio/London, 1968, 168-201.

absolute human authority which came between the authority of God and of his Word in the Bible and one's own conscience. It would be unjust, however, to accuse the Eastern Churches or the Church of Rome of absolute rigidity. The Eastern Churches accept what they call 'economy'. The principle of 'economy', that is of right stewardship, does not belong to any particular Church tradition. It belongs to the core of Orthodox doctrine about the nature of the Church within the divine dispensation. *Oikonomia* is primarily and basically the whole reality of our salvation, as manifested in Christ and operated by His Spirit. In a more technical, ecclesiastical, and therefore more particularised sense it expresses the competence of the Church as a body to adapt her teaching, her administration of the sacraments and her laws to particular situations of spiritual need.

The Roman Catholic Church generally looks askance at this Eastern doctrine and practice, seemingly so foreign to the Roman conception of law and government; but this suggests ignorance, as a matter of fact, of the Roman tradition itself during the Patristic period and the Middle Ages. It was Tertullian who coined the words *dispensatio* and *dispositio* as a translation for *oikonomia*.[4] The word has now lost its original meaning, except for a few traces still to be found in French and English theological terminology.

We even find a remarkable description of *dispensatio* in the decree on Communion under the two kinds of the Council of Trent.[5] After the Council, however, this theological insight disappeared almost completely from books about the Church and the sacraments, though

---

[4] RENÉ BRAUN, *'Deus christianorum'*. Recherches sur le vocabulaire doctrinal de Tertullien (*Publications de la Fac. des Lettres et des Sciences Humaines*, vol. XLI), Paris, 1962, 158–67. STEPHAN OTTO, *'Natura' und 'Dispositio'*. Untersuchung zum Naturbegriff und zur Denkform Tertullians (*Münchener Theol. Studien*, 19, Band), München, 1960.

[5] 'Praeterea declarat, hanc potestatem perpetuo in Ecclesia fuisse, ut in sacramentorum dispensatione, salva illorum substantia, ea statueret und mutaret, quae suscipientium utilitati seu ipsorum sacramentorum venerationi pro rerum, temporum et locorum varietati, magis expedire iudicaret.' For the meaning of the important restriction 'salva illorum substantia', see H. LENNERZ, 'Salva illorum substantia', *Gregorianum*, 3, (1922), 385–419. The conclusions of this study were practically endorsed by Pius XII, when he defined 'substantia', in the beginning of his Apostolic Constitution 'Sacramentum ordinis' in the following way: '. . . ea quae teste divinae revelationis fontibus, ipse Christus dominus in signo sacramentali servanda statuit'. Denzinger-Schönmetzer, Nr. 3857.

it continued to exist at the practical level. One could say that Vatican II restored awareness that the Church possesses a wide power to adapt her laws, her doctrine and the administration of the sacraments to the religious needs of the people.

The reason for this greater Roman doctrinal rigidity is to be traced back to a general hardening of sacramental theology as a reaction against the positions of the Reformation. For the practical flexibility I see many reasons, especially the Italian mentality which, because of the growing centralisation of the Roman Church, exerted a deep influence upon its policies. If I may express a personal opinion, based upon experience, I am convinced that this attitude is characteristic of the Italian ethos, in secular as well as religious affairs. They enjoy putting up a splendid doctrinal and canonical façade, but at the same time they are fully prepared to tolerate, behind this façade, and in an unofficial way, many divergencies which they attribute to human frailty. What we 'northern barbarians' call 'triumphalism' looks to any Italian a proper and civilised way of expressing love and fidelity towards the Church. The Italian mentality shows something of the 'face saving' moral obligations we know so well from Asian countries and cultures, while remaining in practice very pragmatic, and sometimes even rather cynical. One cannot understand Rome's reactions if one is not aware of the southern idiosyncrasies which so often appear to us to be sheer dishonesty. This misunderstanding shows itself even within the Roman Church itself when strangers to Italy take this 'façade-dressing' too seriously.

Whatever the truth of this may be, let us look first of all at the criteria for intercommunion as they have been formulated since Vatican II. I have chosen a series of documents from the Roman Church, first because they are available, and second because I am increasingly convinced that real ecumenism starts at home. If the ecumenical movement seems to have come to a standstill at many points, it seems to me that the deepest reason for this is that we still refuse to accept the urgent need for a critical analysis of our own Church's traditions and doctrines.[6]

---

[6] P. FRANSEN, 'Unity and Confessional Statements, Historical and Theological Inquiry of R.C. Traditional Conceptions', *Bijdragen*, 33, (1972), 2–38.

On 28 April, 1965, the Secretariat for Christian Unity published an *Ecumenical Directory* for the implementation of the Decree on Ecumenism and on the Eastern Churches issued by Vatican II. This *Directory* had a special chapter devoted to the subject of intercommunion, divided into two parts, the first one considering relations with the Eastern Churches and the second relations with 'the other Christian Churches'. This division into two parts already depended on the criteria set out in the document itself. The Roman Church recognises unity in faith and validity of ministry as existing in the Eastern Churches.[7] Under the pressure of circumstances the Secretariat felt obliged to repeat these instructions, especially those on eucharistic communion, in a *Declaration*, written in French and published on 7 January, 1970, by Cardinal J. Willebrands.[8] The doctrine of this *Declaration* is perfectly traditional. The principal criteria for intercommunion are laid down as unity of faith, a consensus on eucharistic theology, the possession of the Apostolic Succession, and the validity of ministerial ordination.

Some room for 'economy' is explicitly left open, especially in relations with the Eastern Churches: in special circumstances some forms of intercommunion are allowed. The *Directory* enumerates as special circumstances those already well known in Canon Law: in the face of death, in situations of persecution and of emprisonment. In some earlier documents, issued under Pius XII, the case of war was also mentioned. The basic consideration is always that there should be real urgency and that a minister of the man's own confession is not available.

We shall now analyse the value of the several theological criteria, and conclude our survey with an analysis of the authority of these Roman decisions.

1. *Unity in Faith*

The criterion of unity in faith is one of the oldest in the Church. In the Early Church no traveller was allowed to attend the Eucharist in

---

[7] *Unitatis Redintegratio*, nn. 8, 14, 15 and 22; Orientalium Ecclesiarum, nn. 27 and 29. See *The Documents of Vatican II*, ed. by Walter M. Abbott, New York, 1966, 352, 357–64 and 383–5. *Directorium AAS*, 59, (1967), 574–92, and 'Note sur l'application du Directoire oecuménique', *Osservatore Romano* of 6 October 1968.

[8] 'Déclaration sur la position de l'Eglise Catholique en matière d'Eucharistie commune entre chrétiens de diverses confessions', *AAS*, 62, (1970), 184–8.

another town without some attestation, the so-called 'litterae pacis' from his own bishop or church community.[9] 'Heresy', which had at that time a larger meaning than today, excluded one from participation in the Church's liturgical life. History tells of a priest who was punished because he admitted a foreign person to the Eucharist without sufficient examination.

Our question is how far this criterion can be used today. St Thomas stated that faith is primarily about reality, and only subsidiarily about statements of faith. Real unity of faith, therefore, consists in a common commitment to Christ as our Saviour and to His Spirit. On the other hand we don't want to minimise the importance of the ecclesial visibility of this common commitment. I think that there are very few Christian Churches today which accept a purely spiritual unity of faith. Some visible signs and bonds of unity are a human and an ecclesial necessity as well.

A real problem arises, however, as soon as we try to use this unity of faith as a criterion for concrete forms of Intercommunion. A criterion inevitably means something which can be controlled by any responsible authority, and therefore established by law and custom. At the same time it is clear that what may be considered as a valid sign of unity of faith is something which has varied considerably from time to time. The Roman Church itself gradually developed a pronounced preference for criteria established by law (de jure). I have nothing in principle against Church order and Canon Law in this respect, but it is only honest to admit that one is dealing with legal regulations, and not to behave as though this legal structure had transformed itself into a set of permanent theological principles.

Moreover, the situation in the Christian Churches has become more delicate in modern times. In the past a viable conception of the unity of faith was not so difficult to agree about. In the present theological crisis, however, which affects all Christian bodies, it

9 LUDWIG VON HERTLING, 'Communio und Primat', Miscellanea Historiae Pontificiae, 7, (1943), 1–48, reprinted in Una Sancta, 17, (1962), 91–125. The English translation planned by Corpus Books, Washington, seems to have been cancelled. See further w. ELERT, Abendmahl und Kirchengemeinschaft in der alten Kirche, hauptsächlich des Ostens, Berlin, 1954, and A. VÖLKER, Einheit der Kirche und Gemeinschaft des Kultes (Analecta Gregoriana, 171), Rome, 1969; Des chrétiens s'interrogent: Eucharistie-Eglise-Unité, Paris, 1969.

frequently happens that one feels more in common with some members of another confession than one does with particular groups within one's own. What is the real unity of faith in such a case? There is a remarkable historical analogy to our present situation. North Africa was radically divided during the Donatist controversy. In many small towns and villages one church was built in opposition to another, one bishop was ordained against another. That is why at that time there were more than four hundred bishops in north Africa. The visible unity of the one faith had suddenly broken down. This tragedy caused St Augustine to elaborate for the first time his own views about the spiritual unity of grace and faith, views which were misused at a later date by the spiritualist movements. Nevertheless, no one would dare to accuse Augustine of ignoring or neglecting the visible unity of the Church. By this I want only to emphasise how, in particular circumstances, the inevitable tension between the invisible unity of grace and faith and the visible unity of the body can be strained almost intolerably. Of course, theology knows neat distinctions for use in such circumstances. One distinguishes between the substance of faith and its many varied theological, pastoral, liturgical and canonical expressions.[10] Vatican II introduced the notion of a hierarchy of truths as a necessary condition for ecumenical dialogue.[11] Not every truth has the same value in the dispensation of our salvation. The same principle applies to statements of faith, to regulations of Canon Law, to liturgical rites. The Patristic Church knew of the difference between the ecumenical symbols of faith and other doctrines. The Middle Ages applied the same distinction, using 'articuli fidei et sacramenta' as the central core of the larger reality they called 'fides et mores', which as such were not irreformable. These distinctions disappeared from later Roman Catholic theology.

Modern hermeneutics, however, insists upon the fact that these distinctions, though neat in theory, are often useless in practice.[12] In relation to the most important of them, the so-called 'substance of

[10] At the opening of Vatican II John XXIII shocked some conservative minds referring to this distinction: 'The substance of the ancient doctrine of the deposit of faith is one thing and the way it is presented is another', Abbott, op. cit., 715.

[11] *Unitatis Redintegratio*, n. 11; Abbott, op. cit., 354.

[12] E. SCHILLEBEECKX, Towards a Catholic Use of Hermeneutics, in: *God, the Future of Man* (*Theological Soundings*, 5/1), London, 1969, 1–49, esp. 10–13.

faith', we are now more deeply aware that to formulate the 'substance', one has to come down to the use of a particular language, and therefore to accept a certain way of thought, an approach and concern which are by no means timeless. There is no possibility of establishing a chemically pure 'substance' in matters of faith.

Modern hermeneutics prefers to distinguish between 'the intended meaning' (*das gemeinte*) and its actual expression in any given language and context of thought (*das gesagte*). But here, too, modern theologians refuse to segregate artificially 'any aimed-at meaning' from its chosen linguistic expression, which would mean that one was still trying to escape into a purely spiritual faith. Words and thought are inseparably united in human existence; one never exists without the other. And so modern theology is continually brought back to the decisive role of a personal commitment in faith.[13] I don't want to confuse the issue at this point by piling up one philosophical subtlety on another. There is no question of confusing the issues, but of looking at the facts properly and soberly. We know that no human authority, not even that of the Church, is qualified to judge the sinful nature of one's activity. The Church is similarly not qualified to pronounce any final judgment on the authenticity of one's personal faith in Christ. The Church can only form a prudential judgment about the probability of either, and act according to the best of her ability. That is where her pastoral ministry and responsibility come in. She is only competent in judging the *public* use of language in describing the content of one's faith.

The point I am trying to make is that the Church's judgment is of a prudential nature. Only in this context is she allowed to use her canonical authority and jurisdiction. I am not saying that the Church is not empowered to define a proper formulation of the faith in given circumstances of doubt and controversy – what we call dogma – and to issue a statement about the relative importance of this dogmatic definition within the hierarchy of truths. Personally,

[13] B. LONERGAN, *Method in Theology*, London, 1972, emphasises the need to distinguish between the different realms and stages of meanings, whose deeper intended aim can only be discovered after a real 'conversion' of the theologians. This 'conversion' practically aims at a profound purification of his attitude of faith and love. See for a less technical exposition of the same topics, *Doctrinal Pluralism*, Milwaukee, Marquette, 1971.

I think that in this ministry of teaching, the Church has also to appeal to her pastoral responsibility, but I would prefer not to be lead astray into the rather different question of the Church's infallibility in defining a dogmatic truth.[14]

Intercommunion, looked at in this way, is largely a question of pastoral care and government. Of course, some central truths are inevitably involved. To decide whether a certain form of Intercommunion can be tolerated, explicitly permitted or even encouraged belongs to the sphere of decisions about concrete forms of public ecclesiastical life. In this particular context the Church can only issue guidelines and regulations which are valid 'ut in pluribus', that is in normal circumstances. We would therefore no doubt agree that the unity of faith is a very important matter in relation to any form of Intercommunion, so long as all parties concerned agree that this notion of the unity of faith has to be handled carefully and prudently, and with a sense of its serious limitations.

2. The Common Faith in the Eucharist

Another criterion of intercommunion which has been accepted since the XVIth century is that of theological agreement about the Eucharist itself. Two points are generally stressed by Roman Catholics in this particular context: the real presence of our Lord in the celebration of the Eucharist, and that the Eucharist is a 'true sacrifice'. Both these were established by the Council of Trent. In other articles I have pointed out that the definitions of Trent are usually interpreted in a more absolute way than the Council itself intended.[15] I am leaving those considerations aside in this paper, however. One can safely say that for a Roman Catholic (and in a quite different way for any member of the Eastern Churches), the real presence and the sacrificial nature of the Mass are among the most cherished traditional beliefs, as one can see in the discussion aroused by the Anglican-Roman Catholic Statement on the Eucharist issued in 1972.[16]

[14] *The Infallibility Debate*, ed. by JOHN J. KIRVAN, New York, 1971, see also my article 'Unity and Confessional Statements', quoted in note 6.

[15] P. FRANSEN, 'On the Need for the Study of the Historical Sense of Conciliar Texts', in: *Problems of Authority*, ed. by JOHN M. TODD, London, 1962, 72–8. See for the first synthesis of our studies in that matter our article 'Unity and Confessional Statements', as quoted in note 6.

[16] For instance in *The Clergy Review*, 57, (1972), 163–73 and 250–62.

But what do we mean by 'real presence'? I don't think I should have to prove that 'transubstantiation' is not the only possible theoretical formulation of our faith in the real presence. Trent itself never went any further than saying, in its 2nd canon of the XIIIth Session, that the bread and wine are changed into the body and the blood of Christ, 'which change the Catholic Church most aptly calls "transubstantiation"'.[17] Faith in the real presence may be described as meaning that the Risen Lord is giving Himself for our salvation and our unity in the celebration of the memory of His Passion and Resurrection.

The problem of fixing the substance of the faith becomes even more delicate when we describe our faith in the Eucharist as being a true sacrifice. Trent refused to give any definition of what it intended by the words 'a true sacrifice'. The context on the Constitution shows only that Trent wanted this 'sacrifice' to be seen in connexion with the unique sacrifice of Christ. Even nowadays it is not easy to find a universally accepted definition of this theological notion.[18] The definition I learned from my professors in Louvain during the second world war, and therefore many years before our recent controversies, would doubtless be accepted by many Protestants. A sacrifice is a public act of worship, expressed in a liturgical celebration, in which the ecclesial community acknowledges God in adoration, thankfulness and propitiation as Creator and Saviour. I don't think that the notion Fr Congar uses, and which is so important for the understanding of his notion of the ministry, is so different from mine. There are, of course, many other definitions accepted and advocated inside the Roman Catholic communion. Nobody has therefore any right to impose his own view and definition upon others, and least of all, upon other Christians outside his own communion. In this matter some people are rather easily upset. They feel nervous as soon as they miss the word 'sacrifice' in a particular text, as is the case in some new liturgical prefaces and canons. Is faith only a question of words, or is it a basic question of a belief in realities? Before we condemn fellow Christians, we have first to discover what they really intend to say by means of their particular words and expressions. Again, I don't mean that some common

---

[17] D-S n. 1652. See *The Teaching of the Catholic Church*, ed. by K. RAHNER, n. 493.
[18] N. LASH, *His Presence in the World*, op. cit., 170–7.

expressions cannot be used precisely to manifest and consolidate our unity in faith, but this is a question of pastoral advisability. The Ecumenical Council of Florence in matters of much greater importance, namely in the confession of our faith in the Trinity, accepted explicitly differences in formulation and theology between East and West.[19]

Again the Church may properly select a specific formulation for any point of faith, as she did at the council of Trent in connexion with the word 'transubstantiation'. There was no other formulation available in the current theological tradition. It becomes more difficult and hazardous to do so in a situation where there is no background of this kind to which to refer.

3. The Apostolic Succession

The Apostolic Succession is a very old criterion of the Church's unity. Historical research, however, has shown that this expression has been used in the past with quite different meanings. In former times it was conceived chiefly as the dependence of any newly founded Church upon an already existing Church, founded in turn by an Apostle. One of the best modern ecclesiologists, Fr Y.-M. Congar states that Apostolic Succession should not be thought of in a purely juridical sense; that it entails continuity in the same faith as well.[20]

The Apostolic Succession is very broad and complex. One may choose to limit oneself to its purely juridical aspect, as the transmission of authority by means of valid ordination. One must then be honest enough to realise that this juridical and almost hereditary succession is not always as evident as one might think it is. We shall touch on this point in what follows about the validity of orders. If one uses the idea of Apostolic Succession in its richer meaning then there are, of course, more unsolved problems on the practical level.

It belongs to the peculiar nature of the Church's authority to be able to put an end to a state of uncertainty which may threaten communion within the Church: this is the very core and essence of her

---

[19] D-S n. 1300-2, the Bull 'Laetentur coeli' of the 6 July 1439.

[20] Y.-M. CONGAR, 'Apostolicité de ministère et Apostolicité de doctrine', in: Ministères et communion ecclésiale, Paris, 1971, 51-94. See N. LASH, His Presence in the World, op. cit., 187-94.

ministry. Such an authoritative decision is a prudential one, not a dogmatic definition.

One of the crucial points about Apostolic Succession is the validity of ordination. This is the fourth and last criterion officially established for permitting Intercommunion.

4. The Validity of Ordination

It belongs to the jurisdictional and pastoral competence of the Church to determine what kind of ordination she accepts as valid, that is, to establish the conditions of validity without which there is no security. I don't pretend that this is the first task of the Church, but that it is a necessary task in view of the hazardous conditions of human life.

In matters of ordination such decisions are acts of jurisdiction of a prudential and tutioristic nature. This may easily be shown by historical example. The Ecumenical Council of Florence, for example, in its Decree for the Armenians, stipulated that the only valid 'matter' of ordination was 'the handing over of the chalice with the wine and the paten with the bread'. The 'form' of the same ordination, that is, the words of consecration, was the prayers at the end of the ordination service: 'Receive the power of offering sacrifice in the Church for the living and the dead. . . .'[21] The Council of Florence simply endorsed the common theological tradition of the Middle Ages since St Thomas, and therefore drew its formulation of the decree from a small work of his called *De Articulis fidei et Ecclesiae sacramentis*.

During the first half of this century many theologians tried to prove that this decree of the Council of Florence was no more than a practical instruction for the benefit of the Armenians, not a real decree issued by an Ecumenical Council on a point of doctrine. They were disturbed by the fact that an ecumenical council had simply ignored not only the patristic and liturgical, but also the Pauline tradition, according to which christian ministers were to be ordained by the laying on of hands and the words of the Preface for ordination. This view of the Council of Florence can no longer be maintained. The title of St Thomas' booklet speaks for itself as soon as one

---

[21] D-S n. 1326; *The Teaching of the Catholic Church*, n. 625.

realises the real force of 'articuli fidei' and of the connexion with the sacraments which the formula implied. In medieval language 'articuli fidei et sacramenta' was a formula expressing the core of the Christian faith. Moreover, the short description of the proceedings we possess in the official Acts of the Council itself, the introductory and concluding words which begin and end the series of documents sent to the Armenians, make it clear that the Council was thinking of an exposition of a 'doctrine of faith'.[22]

It has also to be remembered that at that time 'fides' had a broader meaning than it has now. It included the common doctrine of the Church and also its common practices, especially those touching the sacramental dispensation. Even at the Council of Trent some bishops saw no objection to the fact that this 'fides' might be changed and adapted in later times. 'Dogma', too, possessed a larger meaning.[23]

The Council of Trent in its exposition of the Sacrament of Order avoided the issue, though it tried to leave the question open, by quoting simply 2 Tim. 1, 6, 7; and 1 Tim. 4, 14.[24] For political and theological reasons Trent retained the medieval conception of a cultic ministry, ordained for the service of the Eucharist and the administration of Penance, but excluding the idea of some Reformers that it consisted uniquely in the preaching of the Gospel.[25] This typical medieval view of the Priesthood had motivated the changes in ritual which the Church had accepted in the XIIIth century, and which we have described above.

When Pius XII in his Apostolic Constitution 'Sacramentum ordinis' of 30 November, 1947, returned to the older practice of the Church, the laying on of hands and the words of the Preface, and stipulated that these were to be the essential rites of ordination, he made clear that he did not want to solve the dogmatic question as to whether this ritual had been instituted by Christ Himself, and

[22] *Harduinus*, IX. See the Introduction, 435A and the Conclusion, 441-2. The Decree itself is said to be 'about the truth of the sacraments', to which is added that the text presents a short and easier exposition of the doctrine; D-S 1310.

[23] See 'Unity and Confessional Statements', as quoted in note 6, where all those points are exposed and proven with an ample bibliography.

[24] D-S 1766; *The Teaching of the Catholic Church*, n. 628.

[25] P. FRANSEN, 'Le Concile de Trente et le sacerdoce', in: *Le Prêtre, Foi et Contestation*, ed. by Mgr A. Descamps, Gembloux, 1969, 106-42.

therefore belonged to the 'substance' of the ordination.[26] To understand what I mean by a prudential decision of the Church, one has only to read the arguments put forward by the Pope, and the quasi-official commentary published by F. X. Hürth, who was then one of the personal theologians of the Pope, and who probably wrote the draft of the Constitution.[27]

This historical survey of salient points in the evolution of the rite of ordination in the Roman Catholic Church shows that the Church is clearly conscious of being able to decide what is the essential rite of ordination at a particular time. At the same time, Pius XII makes it quite clear by the technical wording of his decision that this is a jurisdictional act of the Church's economy, leaving undecided whether this decision is an application of dogmatic and revealed truth or not.[28]

Personally, with many other theologians, I think that no 'substantial' rite was ever laid down by Christ Himself, so that all the later decisions of the Church were acts of ecclesial economy and government. In making these decisions, the Church will normally be guided by the oldest traditions of the Church and by the actual needs of the people. Pius XII wanted to return to former traditions out of prudence, because their antiquity might be an indication that they were instituted by Christ. What the Church needed, as he indicated himself, was to avoid any further discussion and doubt about the validity of ordination.

The same ought to be said about the Letter 'Apostolicae curae' of Leo XIII on the validity of Anglican Orders, published on 13 September, 1896.[29] I don't want to discuss here the Anglican point of view in this matter, for, as I said at the beginning of my paper, our ecumenical purpose should be first of all the critical analysis of Roman positions and doctrines. As happens so often, the decision of

---

[26] D-S n. 2301; *The Teaching of the Catholic Church*, n. 644b.

[27] F. X. HÜRTH, 'Constitutio Apostolica "Sacramentum Ordinis"', Commentarius', *Periodica de re morali*, 37, (1948), 9–44, esp. Appendix, ibid., 45–6.

[28] 'We *declare* with certain knowledge (whenever the rite might have been instituted by Christ), and, as far as it may be necessary (whenever this would not be the case) we *determine* and *ordain* . . .' (the italics are ours), *The Teaching of the Catholic Church*, n. 644b. See on those distinctions F. X. HÜRTH quoted in note 27.

[29] D-S nn. 3315–19.

Pope Leo XIII has been exalted into a definition of faith, as if the Pope had declared that Anglican Orders were irrevocably void and invalid in the eyes of the Church and of God as well.

The nature of this pontifical decision, however, is prudential and tutioristic. It could be paraphrased in this way: the Consultors of the Holy Office unanimously concluded that on the basis of the current theology, especially that of P. Gasparri and A. Lehmküll, there were serious doubts about the validity of Anglican Ordination. The tutioristic attitude of the Church in those matters therefore obliged the Consultors to consider these Ordinations as invalid. To add greater authority to the decision of his Congregation the Pope himself 'motu proprio' endorsed its decision officially. This confirmation by the Pope did not change the nature of the act itself. There is no valid reason to regard it as a definition 'ex cathedra', as some still do. Therefore this decision cannot be regarded as irrevocable, and is still open for re-consideration.

I want finally to stress a third point. Catholics usually think that ordination in their own Church is above suspicion. This is a naïve illusion. We know now, simply to enumerate a few important facts, that the abbot Cassian was ordained by a priest in Egypt;[30] and that under Charlemagne, Willehad, the first bishop of Bremen in Germany, and Ludger, the first bishop of Munster, both ordained other priests in Germany before their episcopal ordination, and this under the politico religious jurisdiction of the emperor himself.[31] At the beginning of this century three papal bulls were discovered granting to some abbots, who were not bishops, the privilege of ordaining other priests and deacons.[32] Vasquez mentions that the same privilege was granted to Franciscan and Benedictine missionaries in India, but the texts of these Bulls have not yet been found.[33] There are similar instances in the first centuries of the Church, though

---

[30] Cassianus, *Collationes* IV, 1: CSEL XIII, 2, 97–8.

[31] *Monumenta Germaniae Historiae*, ed. by G. M. PERTZ, *Scriptorum*, II, 1829, 380, 12, 381, 48 and 383, 8–20, and 408, 53; 410, 35 and 411, 8 and 21. See EDWIN HATCH, *The Organisation of the Early Christian Churches*, London, 1882, 2nd ed., 110, note 52, and *Essays on the Early History of the Church and the Ministry*, London, 1918, 402, note 1.

[32] D-S nn. 1145–6, 1290 and 1435.

[33] Vasquez, *Disputatio in III Thomae*, III, Lyons, 1620, Comp. with *In III Thomae*, disp. 243, c. 4 where he gives his own theological interpretation.

these are not as well established as the former. The most important among them is that there is a serious probability that for three centuries a college of 12 presbyters of Alexandria in Egypt appointed and ordained one of their order to fill the episcopal seat.[34]

To imagine that all these ordinations were invalid, simply because they do not conform to the regulations of Canon Law and the common doctrine of theologians is too easy an escape. But if they were not necessarily invalid, we would have to apply more flexible norms to judge the invalidity of ordinations as such.

These historical facts also prove that even in the Catholic Church the validity of ordinations can present us with thorny problems. St Thomas, who, besides being a saint and a scholar, possessed sound common sense, reckoned with the possibility of invalid ordinations when he wrote: 'We may piously believe that regarding the ultimate effects of the sacraments, our High Priest (Jesus Christ) may make up for any deficiency, and that He would not permit this (namely the invalidity of an ordination because of a non-existent baptism) to remain unknown in such a way as that the Church would suffer from it.'[35]

The first conclusion which presents itself is that we have to avoid considering the validity of ordinations as a separate, isolated fact in itself, to be evaluated on its own limited merits, and not as a constitutive part of the whole Church. The validity of ordination cannot be used efficiently as an isolated criterion when discussing the problem of intercommunion. It belongs intrinsically to the nature of the Church itself, which ordained men for the service of God in faithfulness to Christ's mission. It is therefore a matter of

[34] E. W. BROOKS, 'The Ordination of the Early Bishops in Alexandria', *Journal of Theol. Studies*, 2, (1910), 612–13; W. TELFER, 'Episcopal Succession in Egypt', *Journal of Eccl. History*, 3, (1952), 1–13; JAMES H. MOHLER, *The Origin and Evolution of the Priesthood*, Staten Island, 1969, 66–8. Something similar might have existed in the Church of Lyons: E. MOLLAND, 'Irenaeus of Lugdunum and the Apostolic Succession', *Journal of Eccles. History*, 1, (1950) 12ff. There is also a decree from the Council of Ancyra (314–19) which forbids the chorbishops (probably a kind of pastors for the villages around the episcopal cities) to ordain other priests without the permission of their bishop: see SOHLER, op. cit., 74–6.

[35] *Summa theologica*, Suppl. q. 35 a. 3 ad 2. This 'Ecclesia supplet' was currently accepted in case of an absolution by an unvalidly ordained priest, or even, in case of necessity, for an absolution given by a layman: Thomas, *In IV Sent*. qu. 17 1, 3, 1, 3 quia 2 c. et ad 1., and Albertus Magnus, *In IV Sent.*, dist. 17 E art 58 and 59.

ecclesiology, before being a matter of decision as to whether the essential rites were observed or not.[36]

5. *The Conclusion*

The first conclusion of our analysis is that the criteria we have examined are important, but that they cannot be easily applied to any concrete situation as a kind of juridical rule. They have to be weighed in their mutual cohesion, and specially within the complex reality of the Church's life, history and faith. For they belong structurally to the kernel of the Church, her substantial core, the living communion of all her members under the guidance of the Holy Spirit as expressed in the many visible relations which support and structure that communion.

A second conclusion touches the authority of the guidelines issued by the Secretariat for Christian Unity. In this connexion it will suffice to quote a definite statement by Cardinal William van Rossum, cardinal from 1911, Prefect of the Congregation for the Propagation of the Faith from 1918, who died in Maastricht in 1932. He was one of the most influential collaborators of Benedict XVI and Pius XI.

In the *Introduction* to his theological work on the essence of the sacrament of Order, he made the following declaration: 'I want to specify that I am not going to use in my study the decrees of the Holy Roman Congregations. Not that I think that I don't owe to those decrees my most profound respect, submission and obedience. It is, however, evident to everybody that the decrees of the Holy Congregations in this matter only refer to practical solutions of particular cases, and are therefore not doctrinal decisions. It is the tradition of the Holy Congregations in practical and doubtful cases to respect the freedom of opinion of different authors, to follow a tutioristic view (that is, the safer opinion), and therefore, if there is to be found, according to particular authors, the probability that defects may affect the administration of the sacrament, to lay down that the sacrament should be repeated "sub condicione". Therefore

---

[36] KARL LEHMANN, 'Das dogmatische Problem der theologischen Ansatzer zum Verständnis des Amtspriestertums', in: *Existenzproblemen des Priesters*, ed. by F. HENRICH (Münchener Akademie-Schriften, 50), München, 1970, 121–75. See also *Schreiben der Bischöfe des deutschsprachichen Raumes über das priesterliche Amt*, Eine biblisch-dogmatische Handreichung, Trier, 1970, esp. 29–65.

it is permissible, and even preferable, in any investigation of the sacramental rite of ordination, to take no account of these practical decisions.'[37]

The position of Cardinal van Rossum is plain. The Church, having to pronounce on a practical problem as important as that of sacramental dispensation, is 'morally obliged'[38] to choose the 'safer' solution. This is what is called in theology 'sacramental tutiorism'. Such judgements are of a prudential nature – that is, the ecclesiastical authority has to weigh the pros and cons with a definite preference for the 'safer' answer. The actual arguments are furnished by theologians and other specialists in the field, by the consultors of the Roman congregations, and by any committee appointed for a particular case.

It is to be expected that in a time of crisis and tension like the present the Church's helm will be influenced more by curial theologians than by what are sometimes called today 'peripheral authors'. It is also clear that the word 'safe' is in itself a very ambiguous term. Something can look safe now, and eventually show itself very much the reverse. A decision may look safe for the future, especially in a period of rapid evolution, but cause disturbances in the present. But there is no doubt about the nature of the method itself, or basically about its wisdom. This is the tradition of the Roman Congregations, and the better informed of the bishops know it, and act accordingly.

I think that the decisions about intercommunion taken by Vatican II are of the same nature. Cardinal van Rossum, when he referred to the decisions of the Roman Congregations, was not questioning their authority as such, but the nature of the decision itself as a practical act, and he inferred rightly that no immediate dogmatic conclusion could be based on it.

In the same way, the purpose of our critical analysis so far has not been to question the authority of either the Council or the Secretariat to make rules about intercommunion. Our intention was to examine the very nature of those decisions. As I have said before, Roman Catholics are often strongly inclined to over-emphasise the

---

[37] CARD. WILLIAM VAN ROSSUM, *De essentia Sacramenti Ordinis*, Freiburg, 1914, 8. It is my translation.

[38] About the 'moral obligation' in sacramental matters, see D-S 2101.

doctrinal weight of what comes from Rome, or for that matter from their own local bishops. There is a substantial difference as far as obedience is concerned, if we think that we have to do with final decisions, or if we know that we are simply being asked to implement regulations inspired by the religious and pastoral problems of the day. The latter are still open for local experiment or adaptation in a Church which has accepted, at least in principle, a certain degree of pluralism, in as much as many decisions were entrusted by the Second Vatican Council to the local episcopal conferences in communion with Rome. Finally, it has to be acknowledged that the conclusions of the Secretariat were influenced by the need to put on the brake in a situation which in some countries might have got out of hand. This is exactly why one insists upon the 'tutiorist' character of these decisions. It seemed to the central, competent authorities 'safer' to keep the movement towards intercommunion within bounds. In some countries this curial and episcopal tutiorism had another reason, the desire to avoid causing confusion and scandal among the less well-informed members of the Church. This is naturally something to which bishops would have given attention. On the other hand tutiorism becomes a *dangerous*, not a *safe*, attitude, when it seems likely to doom the Church to total immobility.

III. *Some More Positive Reflections on Intercommunion*

The mention of the extreme pressures sometimes exerted to bring about greater freedom for intercommunion serves as a good introduction to our third and final section, on positive views of intercommunion.

We are confronted with a serious situation in most of the Churches. The younger generation looks at our discussion with indifference, if not with scorn. The tension of the famous 'generation gap' is to be felt in many other situations and in the secular world as well. A deep dissatisfaction with, and animosity against, the older generation, the wise men, the learned and prudent men, the men who have compromised with the Establishment, with capitalism, with wealth and with power structures, is virulent also in religious matters. But there is more than that. There is a kind of ecumenical impatience. Younger people despise the continual appeal to the need for a prudent and slow evolution toward unity. They simply don't believe it. It is as well to be aware of this, for they are the future. We belong already to the past. We cannot honestly contend that this impatience is entirely wrong. We cannot be sure without further discernment of the spirits whether the Spirit of God is not working among the young. If the Spirit is inspiring them, then we should listen to the prophetic voices of protest. It would not be the first time that Churchmen in authority have been too slow to see the signs of the times, the divine '*kairos*'; that theologians have forgotten the living will of God in playing pompously with clever confessional distinctions. Even those organisations which all over the world are taking so much trouble to foster the Ecumenical Movement may fear that growing unity may endanger their comfortable civil service mentality and work. It is pleasant to print floods of reports, surveys and conclusions, to travel all over the world and to meet many people, and to enjoy talking about religion, about peace and unity, about God and happiness. One easily forgets that the ecumenical movement is a suicidal movement. Victory means death.

The 'discernment of the spirits' however, is not an easy task. In the meantime those in authority in the Churches, as well as theologians and religious sociologists, and those who share this noble and difficult endeavour to restore unity in the name of Christ – if they want to keep some influence and authority for the good cause, have to save their credibility. There is a deep credibility gap between the official representatives of Ecumenism and other groups in the Church, especially the younger ones. That is the reason why I sincerely deplore the fact that the official ecumenical guidelines of the Roman Catholic Church, and of other Churches too, sometimes lack credibility.

To remain within the scope of this paper, that is, to stick to the critical analysis of what is happening in my own Church, I must first of all mention the definitions which are given of the 'extra-ordinary circumstances' in which some forms of Intercommunion may be allowed. The *Directory* mentions the peril of death, emprison-ment and persecution. These belong to a preconciliar casuistry, very common in handbooks of Canon Law and morality, and do not cover the more deeply distressing religious situations which can occur at the present day.

The reason for this peculiar approach to the problem lies in an impoverished theological view of worship and of the Eucharist. The decree on Ecumenism says: 'Such worship depends chiefly on two principles: it should signify the unity of the Church; it should provide a sharing in the means of grace. The fact that it should signify unity generally rules out common worship. Yet the gaining of a needed grace sometimes commends it.'[39]

This kind of approach manifests an individualistic conception of the sacraments as 'means of grace' for me, which, especially in relation to the Eucharist, is disappointing indeed. This official attitude is the more calamitous in that the younger generation is suffering from precisely the same evil, the 'privatisation' of the sacraments and of worship. They accept the obligation to attend the celebration of the sacraments only insofar as they feel like it. The official criterion changes the perspective only slightly; instead of a personal feeling it proposes as motive a personal gain of grace. Not that one would dream of despising the grace of God, but modern theology has developed far enough to give a richer, a more biblical and patristic, a more ecclesial view of the sacraments and of the Eucharist in particular. That is what I called our lack of credibility. We are still living in the past. The grounds put forward for greater restraint in the matter do not convince.

The official approach to the problem of intercommunion also contains a typical juridicalism which does not appeal to the modern mind in general, and still less to younger people. The Secretariat accepts in principle, and also in practice, the possibility that 'dispensations' may be granted on particular occasions, as happened in Assisi in 1966. I doubt if this kind of canonical 'dispensation' can have a deep ecumenical impact.

The disturbing proof that the Roman Catholic Church may at long last have misunderstood the ecumenical concern of many Christians lies perhaps in the fact that the Eastern Churches, which as a whole were well treated by the Vatican Council and the Secretariat, remain aloof and irresponsive to the way in which 'economy' is practised by Rome. There are of course many reasons for this lack of response, and the motives involved are by no means all theological or ecclesiastical, but this only illustrates the complexity of the

---

[39] *Unitatis Redintegratio*, n. 8; Abbott, p. 352.

decisions which have to be taken. However, it is only fair to point out that the principle that no step towards intercommunion should be taken without the agreement of the other Churches concerned is explicitly mentioned in the Decree on Ecumenism.

One doubts whether an individualistic and juridical approach to the problems of intercommunion will foster a real ecumenical rapprochement. The best defence of this approach is that when guidelines and regulations of this kind have to be issued for the Catholic Church throughout the world, they have to remain on an abstract level, because the situation differs in practice from country to country. The real concern of both the *Directory* and the later *Declaration* seems to have been to put on the brake, rather than to promote prudent evolution towards a better understanding of what intercommunion is about.

Let us now look at the problems of common worship in the celebration of the Eucharist. One immediately faces the crucial question. Some forms of common participation in the other sacraments have been allowed, as in the case of mixed marriages. In more and more countries the Christian Churches have acknowledged one another's Baptism. There is no doubt that we are encouraged to pray together. We now meet one another more frequently and with the full approval of our Churches in many international and national ecumenical organisations. We work together in many extra-ecclesial activities.

The Eucharist remains the painful, crucial issue. In the face of the 'ecumenical impatience' of so many there are still forms of rapprochement which we have either neglected altogether or not tried sufficiently. At the Faith and Order meeting at Louvain in August 1971, there was a strong feeling that the members of divided Churches ought to make much greater contact in fields of human activity which have nothing at all to do with church relations. We are still foreigners to one another. Mutual support and acquaintance in secular society would help to remove the unhealthy feeling of estrangement which clouds our contact in the ecclesiastical sphere. In these things life comes before theory and doctrine.

Nevertheless we cannot simply avoid the crucial problem of the Eucharist, the Sacrament of Our Lord's unity and love.

I would like to enumerate some important aspects of the Eucharist which have been re-discovered by modern theology. I warn you, not all of them are necessarily in favour of Intercommunion. The problem is complex. This is another reason why I personally understand the perplexity of the Secretariat for Christian Unity in meeting them adequately in a document provided for the whole world.

First, there is a real difference here, I think, between the Eastern and the Roman Catholic Churches on one side, and the Churches which originated from the Reformation on the other. As in so many other problems the Anglican Communion seems to occupy a place somewhere in between. I think this is a question of intellectual honesty. For the first group of Churches the Eucharist is theologically if not always in practice, the living centre of their faith. For the latter there may still remain some fear of an exaggerated sacramentalism.

Secondly, for the Eastern Churches and the Roman Church the Eucharist belongs to the sacraments of our Christian initiation. There was no doubt about this in the past, when catechumens received them for the first time during the night of Easter or of Pentecost. Nowadays for many members of the Roman Church at least this statement has no special meaning.

Thirdly, the Eucharist belongs to the mystery of our Christian initiation in a way which is different from that of Baptism and Confirmation. Baptism and Confirmation are administered once and for all. They are therefore called constitutive sacraments, since by and through their reception one is constituted a full member of the Church of God. The Eucharist, however, has to be repeated, and belongs to the community much more than to any particular member of the Church. Every sacrament has to be considered as a corporate celebration of the whole Church, but the Eucharist is the sacrament of the Church's communion as such and of its unity.

Vatican II is doubtless referring to a very old tradition, when it declares in the text quoted above, that the Eucharist, as a sacrament 'signifies the unity of the Church'. Among many other proofs of this I need only mention the common conviction of exegetes that Paul conceived his notion of the Church as a body in explicit connection with the one Body of Christ: every member of this Church was a partaker in the Eucharist. The splendid work of Fr H. De Lubac on the notion of the Body of Christ in the Middle Ages proves the same for later times.[40]

If the Eucharist is the sacrament of the Church as one body, because it is the sacrament of the living Body and Blood of Christ, the visibility among us of the Risen Lord for this Body, then the sacrament of the Eucharist is the central sacrament. According to the best theologians of the Middle Ages all other sacraments are ordained towards the Eucharist as towards their fullness and accomplishment.

This is not to be understood in a static manner. The Eucharist is the central sacrament not only because it is the sacrament of the Risen Lord, but also because it is the sacrament and the visibility, the guarantee and the promise of the coming Lord. We celebrate the Eucharist continuously all over the world in remembrance of His death and resurrection, but we also do it in the faithful expectation of His eschatological Kingdom, 'until He comes'.

Therefore if we confess that the Eucharist 'signifies the unity of the Church', we do this in a dynamic way. There is indeed already a degree of unity among us, based on Baptism and Confirmation, fed and sustained by the Word of God in the Scriptures, activated by our living communion with one another and with the past. But this unity is neither perfected nor accomplished nor fulfilled on earth. We look forward in the very celebration of the Eucharist to the accomplishment of our sinful and broken unity in the fullness of the Kingdom. This is no mere speculative view, but a very realistic awareness of our human condition in the flesh of sin. We Roman Catholics for instance cannot contend that we are already perfectly united in Christ in the fullness of faith and charity. Like other Christians we have to grow toward final unity in Christ and His Spirit.[41]

[40] I Cor. 10:17. See L. CERFAUX, La théologie de l'Eglise suivant Saint Paul (Unam sanctam, 54), Paris, 1965[2], 223–40, and HENRI DE LUBAC, Corpus Mysticum, Eucharistie et l'Eglise au Moyen Age, Paris, 1949[2].

[41] B. COOKE, 'Eucharist: Source or Expression of Community?', Worship, 40, (1966), 339–48, 'The Eucharist: Celebrating the Presence of the Lord', Concilium 10/4 (December 1968). M. HURLEY, 'The Sacrament of Unity: Intercommunion and some Forgotten Truths', The Way, 9, (1969), 107–17, stresses the 'penitential' aspect of the Eucharist, and refers further to JOHN QUINN, 'The Lord's Supper and Forgiveness of Sin', Worship, 42, (1968), 281–91, and J. M. TILLARD, O.P., 'L'Eucharistie, purification de l'Eglise pérégrinante', Nouvelle Revue Théologique, 84, (1962), 449–74 and 579–97.

If the Eucharist signifies the unity of the Church it signifies it in an ambivalent way. In celebrating the Eucharist we are resting as it were between a unity which is already there, and a unity which is still to come, which we hope to receive from God through Christ and His Spirit. It is here that I, as a theologian, would locate any consideration about the efficacy of the Eucharist as a means of grace. The primary fruit of the Eucharist is our growing unity, and within this unity we receive grace, because God's living and loving presence is realised in and through the community. Grace is not a thing in itself, and that is the reason why I was so unhappy with the formulation of the Second Vatican Council. Grace means nothing other than the living presence of God in our life. But God reaches us, each one of us, through and in the community, through and in our togetherness, through and in our standing together before God and celebrating His salvation.

The Eucharist is the sacrament of the Pilgrim Church, the sacrament of the Exodus. We should partake it, spiritually at least, as the Jews did before leaving Egypt. 'In this manner you shall eat it: your loins girded, your sandals on your feet, your staff in your hand; you shall eat it in haste' (Exod. 12:11).

We could express the same idea through other biblical images. In the Bible God's salvation is being realised wherever God is assembling His people, His heritage, the people of His choice. Christ died, said St John 'to gather into one the children of God who are scattered abroad', (John 11:52). In the Eucharist God gathers His people again around his Living Son through the power of His Spirit.

There is another reason why the Eucharist must be considered as fostering a growing unity. The Eucharist is the sacrament of the unity of our life in the world. In every Eucharist we are reminded of our secular responsibilities in this world. The Eucharist also has deep ethical implications. One of the most moving books of Teilhard de Chardin is the little work he wrote when he was unable in China to celebrate the Eucharist: 'La Messe sur le monde'. In the Eucharist we celebrate the fact that we are assembled as God's people, not for our own sakes, but for the salvation of the world. The Eucharist is not an intramural devotion, a sectarian piety, nor is it primarily 'a means to get some more grace'.

Finally, I want to stress another aspect of the sacraments which has a special significance in the celebration of the Eucharist. During the patristic and medieval periods it was a common view that the sacraments are a living and concrete expression of the faith of the Church. According to St Thomas the faith of the Church constituted a sacrament, in such a way that without this faith any sacrament would be meaningless and void. This idea was lost after Trent. The faith of the Church has therefore a proper and constitutive role to play in every celebration of the Eucharist. In this light we are able to see why the criteria we have analysed in our second section remain so ambiguous and uncertain, when taken separately. They can only be understood when seen within the reality of the living historical community. The Church is no platonic idea, up in the air, between earth and heaven. The Church is us, and in a very concrete way. The Eucharist is the place where this Church is built up continuously, repaired, restored, purified, and gathered for the salvation of the world.

If we want to apply these principles to the problem of Inter-communion, we see that there exists an analogy between the situation within the Church itself and the ecumenical situation. In the latter there is also an initial unity: a common Baptism, a common possession of the Word of God in the Scriptures, a common tradition of faith and before anything else the living Presence of God in the Lord and through His Spirit. This unity is not perfect. The Church strives towards its accomplishment and plenitude, as a gift of God. Whenever the participants take the Eucharist sincerely as it was instituted by Christ, and remain sincerely conscious of the scandal and the pains of their divisions, one may see an argument in favour of Intercommunion. The Eucharist is celebrated on that particular occasion as *the* sacrament of our lost unity, as the confession of our faith that only the Risen Lord can restore.

There are, however, in the celebration of the Eucharist, serious reasons which militate against too hasty an application of this view. According to the oldest traditions some visible unity of life and communion seems to be a necessary prerequisite for intercommunion. Some form of permanent communion should be established first. The ideal example seems to me the situation of a mixed marriage, where both husband and wife, though sincerely belonging to different

Churches, strive to surmount their confessional differences in the small community which God has blessed in their marriage. In some countries bishops have permitted some conditional form of Inter-communion. The Dutch bishops, for instance, formulate their conditions in this manner: 'that the non-catholic party was baptised, that he feels able to accept the faith of the Catholic Church, as expressed in her celebration of the Eucharist, and that he is permitted access to the Lord's Supper in his own Church.'[42]

Are there other circumstances? I would support such circum-stances as may exist within an ecumenical group working together for a certain time. Even in this case I would not think it advisable that Intercommunion should be practised regularly, lest the member of the group forget the seriousness of their confessional differences. We have to avoid any danger of relativism.

Inspired by the Report of the Archbishops' Commission for Inter-communion of the Church of England, *Intercommunion Today*,[43] M. Hurley suggests a form of ecumenical concelebration, a 'joint celebration' of the Eucharist by members of different Churches on particular occasions, and under special conditions intended to avoid any misunderstanding or scandal among the less informed and educated members of the same Churches. I would think that in order to foster a feeling of mutual honesty and loyalty, that a special adapted ritual might be established for that kind of occasion. The form of the prayers, the selection of the readings should emphasise and illustrate the fact that this Eucharist is being celebrated as a penitential rite for our divisions, and as a solemn prayer 'though Christ our Lord', that this celebration may foster our common unity.

There are probably other cases where Intercommunion might be justified: in the Third World, for example, in situations of persecu-tion or of national crisis. The important point is that such a cele-bration should be prepared with care, with full mutual openness and sincerity, with concern for our weaker brothers and sisters who might misunderstand our coming together in the celebration of the Lord's Supper. At no moment should the sad reality of our divisions

---

[42] W. L. BOELENS, 'Erwägungen zur Interkommunion', *Der Seelsorger*, 37, (1968) 235–42, see 242.

[43] *Intercommunion Today*, London, 1968, see M. HURLEY, 'The Sacrament of Unity', v.s., footnote 41, p. 28.

be slightened or cheapened. We should never allow any emotional depreciation of the seriousness of our differences in faith. This manifests in the end our sincere respect for the others' consciences, since, if we are divided, we remain so because we are convinced in conscience that we ought to remain so. Nobody can be allowed out of impatience or emotional aversion for 'dogmatic' fidelity to belittle the religious convictions of our brethren in Christ from other denominations.

Another important point here is about publicity. Publicity cannot be avoided today, when the communications media are eager to highlight any movement in the direction of intercommunion. At the Faith and Order meeting in Louvain, in August 1971, a Catholic journalist published an article in which he openly challenged Cardinal Suenens as to what he intended to do when he celebrated the Eucharist in the Church where Faith and Order was meeting. Inevitably, the Cardinal was obliged to issue a public statement in which he asked the members of the conference not to receive Holy Communion on that occasion. I have no idea as to whether he had thought of permitting intercommunion without drawing public attention to the fact, but the sensation created by the newspaper article made any form of intercommunion impossible.

The reason for this is that the ordinary members of the Church would probably not be able to understand such an act of inter-communion. Pastoral decisions depend strictly on the attitude of the faithful in the country, city or group concerned: it is necessary both to avoid scandalising the faithful, and to uphold the Eucharist as the expression of the Church's unity and faith. There is always more chance of pastoral economy and flexibility where people are better educated and well-informed. But theologians who specialise in ecumenical work and thought easily forget that real unity can only be brought about and established by the ordinary members of the Churches. They in their turn have to be prepared for it. Only when we have a well educated priesthood and laity can we expect the bishops to become less rigid and severe.

BIOGRAPHICAL NOTE

CANON M. F. WILES *has been Regius Professor of Divinity in the University of Oxford since 1970. Before that he was Professor of Christian Doctrine at King's College, London from 1967. His books include* The Christian Fathers (*1966*), The Divine Apostle (*1967*) *and* The Making of Christian Doctrine (*1967*).

2 Sacramental Unity in the Early Church

PROFESSOR MAURICE WILES

I

THE PROBLEM OF INTERCOMMUNION IS A CONTEMPORARY problem which cannot be solved by parallels and precedents from the days of the early church, for there are none. But the particular problem of intercommunion is part of a wider issue – the relation of communion worship to the unity of the church. This was not the most prominent issue in the early church's thought about the eucharist, but it was an important part of it. Standard works on the development of eucharistic doctrine tend to stress the ways in which the understanding of it as heavenly food and as the Christian sacrifice took shape in the life and consciousness of the church. It seems therefore that there may be some value in a study which seeks to isolate, so far as that can legitimately be done, early thought about the eucharist in relation to the unity of the church.

The unity of the church in the thought of the New Testament is something both local and universal. The two were not necessarily or theoretically in conflict, though tension could easily arise between them as the relationship between the Jerusalem and Gentile churches bears witness. Action which made for unity within a local Gentile church might be a source of rupture between that church as a whole and the churches of Judaea. Both kinds of unity mattered to St Paul. Divisions within the church of Corinth or within the church as a whole were equally abhorrent to him. I do not think that one ought to say that one is more important than the other for him. But it is worth noticing that what I have described as a division within the church as a whole would more naturally be described by Paul as division between the churches.[1] There was certainly for him a single people of God but when speaking of 'the church' his direct reference is normally to the single congregation. Too much should not be made of this which is primarily a linguistic point, but it ought not to be overlooked altogether in an age when it is sometimes implied that it is a little improper to use the word 'Church' except of the church universal.

But however they be described both kinds of division were dangers known to Paul and both were to him false divisions of essential unities. Furthermore in both cases Paul sought to overcome the difficulty not merely by exhortation and reminder of the existing unity but by sacramental expression of it. The importance which he attached to the collection for the poor saints at Jerusalem (an issue which was sometimes a source of strain and embarrassment to him in his relationship with the churches of his own foundation) was the fact that it gave tangible expression to the mutual interdependence of the church. The Jerusalem church might have its doubts about the full validity of the uncircumcised Gentile churches, but that was no justification for the Gentile churches to go it on their own. Rather it enhanced the importance of their provision for the practical needs of the Jerusalem church, not as a form of spiritual blackmail but as a voluntarily chosen and clearly visible expression of the church's real unity in Christ.[2] Mutual Responsibility and Interdependence within the Anglican communion was intended to be not a matter of mere financial convenience but also a sacrament of unity.

No mention is made in this wider context of the eucharist as a sacrament of unity. It is with regard to divisions within the local

---

[1] Cf. J. Y. CAMPBELL, The Origin and Meaning of the Christian Use of the Word 'Ecclesia', J.T.S. xlix, (1948), 138–40 (reprinted in Three New Testament Studies (Brill, 1965), pp. 50–2).

[2] Cf. K. F. NICKLE, The Collection (S.C.M., 1966). O. CULLMAN, Catholics and Protestants (Lutterworth, 1960), pp. 34–41.

community that the eucharist is affirmed to fulfil this role. Indeed it is only at that level that it can properly be said to fulfil the role sacramentally at all. It is only the members of the local congregations who can be said in the literal meaning of the words 'to partake of the one loaf'. The fact that other congregations in other parts of the world practise the same sacramental rite may be an important expression of unity, but it is only in a secondary sense a sacramental expression of unity. The expression is only sacramental in a primary sense for those who actually 'partake of the one loaf'. It is in this context and in this sense that Paul emphasises so strongly the unitive significance of sacramental participation in the one loaf of communion worship. What is true here of Paul is true, I believe also, of the patristic age in general. This is not to claim that the unity of the church universal was denied or regarded as of little importance; that I believe would be false. But it is to claim that the role of the eucharist as a sacramental expression of unity belonged far more to the context of local church unity than to that of the unity of the worldwide church

II

Essentially the same picture with the same balance between emphasis on the local and the universal emerges from the writings of Ignatius as from the writings of Paul. Ignatius is well known as the first writer to speak explicitly of the 'catholic' or 'universal' church. The concept is a real and important one for him, but it is not the direct or central concern in his writing. His primary insistence is on the need for the unity of the local church as a bulwark against the vagaries of heresy.

This local unity finds its focal expression in the person of the bishop. This is more than a mere matter of expediency. The single figure of the bishop is for Ignatius a kind of sacramental expression of the unity of God. The true Christian penitent returns 'to the unity of God and the council of the bishop' (*Philadelphians* 8), and it is clear enough that in Ignatius's view it would be impossible to do the former without the latter. The bishop is therefore a focus of unity for church life in all its aspects. 'Let no man do aught of the things pertaining to the church apart from the bishop' (*Smyrnaeans* 8).

But within 'the things pertaining to the church' which are to be held together by their unfailing relation to the person of the bishop, the eucharist clearly holds a very special place. The sentence just quoted from the letter to the Smyrnaeans is followed by the words: 'Let that be held a valid eucharist which is under the bishop or one to whom he shall have committed it.' The condemnation of any eucharist not under the bishop or his delegate does not appear to be related to any special authority which has been transmitted to the bishop in succession but solely to him as the sacramental expression of the unity of God and therefore of the church.

The point is made more emphatically with relation to the eucharist in *Philadelphians* 4: 'Be careful therefore to observe one eucharist (for there is one flesh of our Lord Jesus Christ and one cup into union in his blood; there is one altar, as there is one bishop, together with the presbytery and the deacons my fellow-servants) that whatsoever you do, you may do it after God.' The oneness of the eucharist follows both from the oneness of the Christ whose flesh it is and from the oneness of the bishop (himself expressing the oneness of God) apart from whom it may not validly be celebrated.

Now one of the characteristics of the heretics, whom Ignatius sees as a threat to the church, was their abstention from the eucharist. It does not seem that they were abstaining for primarily schismatic reasons in order to have their own eucharist apart from the bishop, but rather that for docetic reasons they were unwilling to practise a sacramental eucharist at all. 'They abstain from eucharist and prayer, because they allow not that the eucharist is the flesh of our Saviour Jesus Christ, which flesh suffered for our sins, and which the Father of his goodness raised up' (*Smyrnaeans* 6). These men are clearly church members (otherwise one could not speak of their 'abstaining' from the eucharist) who deliberately do not attend the church's eucharist for reasons of doctrinal conviction of a spiritualistic or docetic kind. With this rejection of the material aspect of Christian worship went also, according to Ignatius, a failure in the material aspect of Christian love in practical care for the widow, the orphan and the afflicted. In Ignatius's view this kind of failure is utterly incompatible with any semblance of true Christianity, however much the heretics may continue to name the name of Christ. Those who cut themselves off from association with the church's eucharist are to be cut off by the members of the church from any kind of association whatever. 'It is therefore meet that you should abstain from such, and not speak of them either privately or in public' (*Smyrnaeans* 7).

Thus the bishop is the essential focus of the unity of the local church. That local unity also finds expression of an almost equally important kind in the eucharist. Yet the unity of the one eucharist is in some measure derivative from the unity of the bishop apart from whom it cannot validly exist. But there does not appear to be for Ignatius any comparable focus or sacramental expression of the wider unity of the universal church. It is widely accepted that the fact that Ignatius does not mention any bishop in his address to the Church of Rome is evidence that there was no single bishop of that church at that time. Yet there is certainly no suggestion that Ignatius regards it for that reason as any less a true part of the church universal. The wider unity of the church could exist validly 'apart from the bishop', without, that is to say, there needing to be a bishop in every place to give expression to it. Ignatius does not seem to look for any other expression of the wider church unity than the person of Christ himself. His oft-quoted reference to the 'catholic' church comes in that very section of the letter to the Smyrnaeans (8) where he asserts the invalidity of any eucharist – or other church activity – done apart from the bishop. He writes: 'Wheresoever the bishop shall appear, there let the people be; even as where Jesus may be, there is the universal church.' The sacramental expression of unity is for him a matter of the local church. This is clearly true of its primary representation in the person of the bishop. It seems also to be true of the secondary, but still very important, representation of it in the one eucharist. This, too, as the sacramental character of the one loaf would lead us to expect, is essentially expressive of the unity of the congregation assembled to share it together.

III

So far I have been drawing a firm line of distinction between the unity of the local church and the unity of the church universal. But the two concepts cannot be kept at arm's length from one another. In two ways in particular the interrelation of the two came to the fore in the course of the second century. In the first place the local church cannot be easily and without question identified with the single congregation gathered around the one loaf. In a small provincial town with comparatively few Christians the identification is obvious enough. But in the larger cities with growing numbers it is not so straightforward. Numbers might become too large for the regular gathering of all Christians together in one place, while the city might still be the only obvious unity in terms of which it would be natural to conceive the local church. So there would arise a local church with more than one eucharistic gathering. In the second place Christians of a particular tradition and nationality who had moved to some other place would feel a sense of belongingness to the church of their origin and upbringing as well as to the church of their new home. Both these problems were particularly acute in Rome, the largest city of the empire, and also one with a highly cosmopolitan population drawn from all quarters of the known world. It is within the context of these problems that the so-called 'quartodeciman controversy' of the second century is to be understood.

The substance of the controversy can be told quite briefly. There were living in Rome in the second century a substantial number of Christians of Asiatic origin. The tradition of the Church in Asia was to observe the Christian paschal celebration on the day of the Jewish Passover, Nisan 14, whereas the Roman Church observed it on the Sunday following. There is no evidence that this divergence of custom was felt to be an embarrassment in the middle of the second century as long as the two divergent customs were practised in Asia and Rome respectively. But when the Asiatic Christians insisted on following their local custom in Rome, this was felt in Rome to be a threat to the proper unity of the church there. Nevertheless it was agreed between Anicetus of Rome and Polycarp of Smyrna that the difference of custom should continue, and the two practices existed for a time side by side within the church at Rome. But towards the end of the century Pope Victor made a further and more determined attempt to secure conformity within the church under his authority. We have not the evidence to assess Victor's motives with any confidence. It is possible that he was motivated by an autocratic love of power or by an administrative desire for tidiness. But it is by no means certain that his motives were purely of this order. It may well be that he had a real problem on his hands. Both Marcion and Valentinus had developed their heretical ideas and practices with separatist groups in Rome. An Asiatic group refusing to conform on an issue which, whether justly or not, could well appear suspect on grounds of Judaising, might well seem – indeed might easily have been – a danger to the well-being of the Roman church. Certainly from whatever motives Victor treated the matter as one of urgency. When the churches of Asia, through their spokesman Polycrates, continued to support the right of the Asiatics in Rome to continue there their own apostolic tradition, Victor tried to have the Asiatic churches as a whole treated as excommunicate by all the other churches of the known world. Victor's threats did not receive full support from the other churches to whom he appealed, even where they may themselves have followed and approved the same pattern of Paschal observance as the church of Rome. The exact course of the dispute is not recorded, but certainly in the long run the Asiatic churches did come to accept the Roman practice.[3]

If this interpretation of the controversy be correct, we have a case in which the need to deal with unity at a local level led on inevitably to consideration of unity at a universal level. Conformity of practice was first insisted on at the local level, but it could not effectively be secured there without a similar conformity of practice in the world-wide church as a whole. The immediate irritant, which gave rise to the wider problem, was the existence of an Asiatic group within the church at Rome holding its own eucharists and in particular holding its most solemn eucharist of the year on a different occasion from other congregations.

This Asiatic group may possibly have been the first distinct group with its own eucharistic life in Rome, but the facts of the case at least suggest the possibility that there were a number of other similarly separate congregations. The likelihood of this is strongly supported by certain words of Irenaeus. Irenaeus objected to Victor's attempted coercion of the Asiatics and in the course of a letter to Victor in which he recalls the earlier practice of tolerance in the days of Anicetus and Polycarp, he writes: 'None were ever cast

[3] See G. LA PIANA, 'The Roman Church at the End of the Second Century' (Harvard Theological Review, XVIII, 1925, pp. 201–78); S. L. GREENSLADE, Schism in the Early Church (S.C.M., 1953), pp. 25–6, 99–101.

out because of this course of action (i.e. differing date of paschal observance) but those very elders before thee, though they did not observe it, would send the eucharist to members of those communities who observed it.' (Eusebius, *H.E.* v, 24, 15.)

The implication of these words of Irenaeus are of particular importance for our present concern. We have seen how the one loaf was expressive of the unity of the congregation which shared it. But the situation soon arose where in a city like Rome the members of the church could not all share in the single eucharistic gathering. Was it possible to give sacramental expression to the unity of the local Christian community where there had to be a number of separate eucharistic celebrations? We know from Justin Martyr that it was customary to express the unity of Christians unable to be present at the eucharistic gathering because of sickness or some similar cause with the church community by sending to them a portion of the consecrated loaf (1 Apology 67). The words of Irenaeus (though not unequivocally explicit) suggest that it was customary to do the same in order to express sacramentally the unity of the separated congregations. We have clear evidence of a practice of this kind in the fourth century. Both Miltiades (311–14) and Siricius (384–99) are recorded as having sent a portion of the consecrated bread, called the 'fermentum', to other churches in the city where the eucharist was being celebrated by presbyters under their jurisdiction.[4] The main emphasis in those records is laid on the act as symbolising the authority of the Pope over his presbyters. Their authority to celebrate the eucharist was not something which existed independently of their relationship to their bishop. But the original emphasis may well have been more upon the unity of the congregations as Irenaeus words would suggest. Indeed there is really little difference between the two emphases. The complex of ideas – one church, one bishop, one eucharist – belongs closely together as we have seen already in the writings of Ignatius.

Thus the 'fermentum' provided a sacramental means of expression of the unity of the local church, even in the extended sense of that term by which it must be understood to include a number of distinct congregations. How widespread the practice was we have no means of telling. But references to what appears to be a virtually

---

[4] See L. DUCHESNE, *Liber Pontificalis* (1886), I, xxxiii (p. 169 n. 4) and I, XL (p. 216 n. 2).

identical custom are to be found in some of the canons of the Eastern Church, showing that it was more than a purely Roman custom. The 32nd canon of the Council of Laodicea (mid fourth century: date uncertain), for example, forbids the reception of 'eulogiae' from heretical groups on the ground that they are 'alogiae' (follies) rather than 'eulogiae'.[5] The exact status of the 'eulogiae' here mentioned is a matter of dispute. They may have been a form of blessed bread sent as a gift and not the sacrament itself (see Lampe, *Greek Patristic Lexicon*, p. 570). But it seems more likely that the bread sent was originally the eucharistic element itself and that the 'eulogiae' of which this canon speaks could still have been in that form. Certainly the practice was a serious expression of communion, which could not rightly be enjoyed with congregations opposed to the church's faith.

Thus there was a way in which the eucharist could provide a sacramental expression of unity beyond the single congregation. It was certainly practised in Rome between the second and fourth centuries, and probably more widely. But there were obvious practical limitations which restricted the extent to which this further expression of sacramental unity could be carried. In particular growing reverence for the consecrated elements themselves made the sending of them on journeys of some distance seem a risky and un-desirable custom, and clearly restricted the range of this particular method of expressing a wider sacramental unity. We have evidence of this restriction both from Rome and from the East.

Innocent I (401–17) describes the practice at Rome in his day in a letter to Decentius of Eugubium who had consulted him on a number of practical questions. One of those questions concerned 'the fermentum, which we send to all city churches (per titulos) on the Lord's day'. On this subject Innocent says that 'the presbyters of churches situated inside the city, who are unable to join with us on that day because of the people committed to their care, receive at the hand of acolytes a fermentum which has been prepared by us, so that they may not reckon themselves cut off from communion with us on that day of all days. But I don't think this ought to be done for out-lying parishes (per parochias), as the sacrament ought not to be carried too far; nor therefore do we send it to the presbyters who are

---

[5] Ed. F. LAUCHERT, *Die Kanones der wichtigsten Altkirchlichen Concilien* (1896), p. 75.

situated in the more scattered cemetries, and the presbyters there have the right and permission of doing the rite themselves'.[6] In similar vein the 14th Canon of Laodicea decrees that 'the sacred elements (τὰ ἄγια) are not to be sent as a 'eulogia' to other παροικίας at the Easter festival'.[7] Exactly what is envisaged by these two passages – especially the very condensed 14th Canon of Laodicea – is open to debate. Is it right to translate τὰ ἄγια as 'the sacred elements' or could the phrase refer to some other blessed bread of less than fully sacramental character? Does the forbidding of the practice at Easter imply that it was permissible at other times? Or was it, more probably, only practised at Easter and therefore in fact being forbidden altogether? Does παροικία here mean a diocese (as is generally assumed, e.g. Lampe, *Patristic Greek Lexicon*, p. 1042) and therefore imply that the practice could continue between churches within a diocese? Or does παροικία mean a parish, a congregation and the Canon therefore imply the total abolition of the practice?[8] However these questions are to be answered – and the scanty evidence precludes our answering them with any confidence – there is little doubt about the general tenor either of Innocent's letter or of the 14th Canoni The early practice of expressing a wider sacramental unity through a sharing of the one loaf beyond the single congregation is in process of severe restriction. It may never have been very widespread, but motives of reverence for the elements seem to have ensured that any survival beyond the early centuries would have to be in a less strictly sacramental form, not using for this purpose bread that was actually a part of the consecrated eucharist.

[6] P.L. XX 556–7.
[7] Ed. F. LAUCHERT, op. cit., p. 72.
[8] The precise meaning of the term παροικία at this stage of its development is very difficult to determine. We have already seen in Innocent's letter an example of its use to mean 'parts of a diocese outside the main city' and there is an exact parallel in Basil, Ep. 240 (P.G. XXXII 897 B). P. DE LABRIOLLE examines the whole question in an article entitled *Paroecia* (Recherches de Science Religieuse XVIII (1928), pp. 60–72) and shows that even in official documents the words παροικία and διοίκησις are not used with precise and distinct meanings in the fourth century. It seems to me probable that the Canon here under consideration is intended to restrict the practice of sending the sacrament to other churches more drastically than is generally assumed. The idea that the practice ever existed between different dioceses seems to depend chiefly on a misreading of areneaus's letter to Victor, which understands the practice there referred to, to involve I sending of the sacrament from Rome to churches in Asia.

IV

In the last section we saw how the problem of the church's unity grew in complexity with the increasing size and number of Christian congregations and with the increasing mobility of Christians. In particular we looked at one sacramental means of expressing that wider unity, which can be traced in that early period but which was not destined to be a lasting or large-scale solution to the problem. And certainly the fourth century saw the problem growing very greatly and very rapidly in extent. With the increasingly favourable attitude of the Empire to the Church congregations grew in number and Christians were able to travel more freely and more extensively. Moreover the Arian controversy in the early years of the century was a more world-wide phenomenon than any earlier comparable dispute within the church. Rival congregations were to be found in many centres, each out of communion with the other but each having a network of Christian groups in other places with whom they were in a state of mutual recognition and fellowship.

In such a situation a Christian was forced to choose where his allegiance lay. The barriers were seen as absolute barriers. To enter into communion fellowship with members of a congregation not in communion with your own implied cutting yourself off from your own fellowship. The second Canon of the Council of Antioch (A.D. 341) illustrates how seriously both any breach of communion fellowship and any fellowship with those out of communion were regarded. The Canon declares: 'All those who come to the Church of God and hear the sacred Scriptures, but do not join with the people in prayer or who in any irregular way (κατά τινα ἀταξίαν) turn away from the partaking of the eucharist shall be excommunicated until such time as they have done penance and shown by their deeds their change of mind, and can at their own urgent entreaty obtain pardon. And it is unlawful to associate with those who are excommunicated, or to assemble even in private houses for prayer with those who do not pray with the church, or to receive those who will not join with one church into another. If a bishop, presbyter, deacon or any other ecclesiastic is found to be associating with those who are excommunicate, he himself shall also be excommunicated as disturbing the order of the church.'[9] Two closely related convictions find expression in this canon. In the first place communion fellowship is so basic to church membership that any improper abstention from it leads to formal excommunication. And secondly communion fellowship is so profound a sharing with the whole body of the church that it must mean all that or it is a blasphemy. No kind of religious association – let alone communion fellowship – is permissible with one who is not himself in communion with the whole church body of which one is a member. One could not conceivably have true communion fellowship with two different people or two different groups of people who were consciously and deliberately out of communion with one another.

The way in which this problem was experienced in practice is well illustrated by the story of Apollinarius's expulsion from the church of Laodicea. Sozomen, who records the incident, sees it as the real cause of the Apollinarian heresy; it is very doubtful if it was as crucial in that respect as Sozomen makes out, but that does nothing to destroy the significance of the incident for our present purpose. While returning from exile to Alexandria, Athanasius passed through the city of Laodicea. He was unwilling to communicate with George, the bishop of Laodicea, who was a supporter of the Eusebian party. He did, however, enter into close relations with Apollinarius. For this Apollinarius was excommunicated by George; he had committed the crime of communicating with one who would not communicate with the church, of which he was a member, in the person of its bishop. Apollinarius, according to our records, was not himself unwilling to be in communion with George; indeed he did his utmost to persuade George to receive him back into communion, but George remained inexorable. It was this incident, in Sozomen's judgement, that was the really decisive cause of the Apollinarian schism.[10]

Thus there was no sanctioned intercommunion between members of the rival Christian groups, which were characteristic of the schism in Antioch and similar centres in the fourth century. Holding the views that they did about each other's faith, there could not have been such intercommunion – if communion fellowship had any

[9] Ed. F. LAUCHERT, op. cit., pp. 43-4. The authenticity of the ascription of these canons to the Dedication Council of Antioch is doubtful; they may very probably belong in fact to a council much nearer to the time of Nicaea (cf. W. TELFER, *Paul of Constantinople*, Harvard Theological Review, XLIII, 1950, pp. 55-6).

[10] Sozomen, *H.E.* vi, 25.

reality or substance about it. They did not regard one another as deviants from the true faith in some particular points of interpretation. They were rivals, each seeing the other as having abandoned the foundation of true faith, as having failed to maintain on the one hand the unity and transcendence of God and on the other the full divinity of Christ. Communion fellowship, coexisting with such an evaluation of each other's faith, was not possible.

We probably approach nearest to the kind of disunity between Christian denominations which we know today in certain phases of the Donatist schism. Even so it is not very near. They too saw one another as incompatible rivals in a way vastly different from the ecumenical attitudes of the present day. But there were times of comparatively peaceful coexistence. By the fifth century the schism had been in existence for three generations and men had never experienced Christianity in Africa without it. A Donatist husband and Catholic wife could admit that they worshipped the same God and that there was something wrong in the fact that they did not worship him together. There is a note of genuine ecumenical concern in the words of Augustine when he writes: 'Husbands and wives find unity in their marriage bed and disunity at the altar of Christ . . . slaves and masters divide the God they have in common, who himself took the form of a slave, that by his slavery he might make all men free.'[11] Here at least is a recognition of the problem, a feeling of the pain and the wrongfulness of division. But despite such measure of recognition as Augustine could ascribe to Donatist Christians – even to the extent of acknowledging the formal validity of their sacramental ministry – there could have been for him no question of intercommunion. Communion fellowship was expressive of the love and unity which belonged essentially to the body of Christ, and despite all the complexities and qualifications of Augustine's far-ranging thought, that body was for him coterminous with the one visible, catholic church.

V

It would be wrong to draw any conclusions for our contemporary situation from this historical sketch. As we said at the outset, our

[11] Augustine, Ep. 33, 5.

situation is vastly different. Our evaluation of the truly Christian status of those with whom we disagree even on major issues is wholly different from the attitude of early catholic Christians to those from whom they were separated on issues of doctrine or church order. But these reflections do seem to me to underline a fact which is obvious but too often overlooked. The eucharist is, among other things, a sacrament of *unity*; but it is only a *sacrament* of unity within a local setting. The unity of the church is more than a local issue but it is to its local expression that the unitary and unifying aspects of the eucharist are directly and primarily related. To put the main emphasis in considering issues of intercommunion on its appropriateness in the light of the situation of the local church is not to despise or to deny the wider nature of the church's unity; but it is to be true to the nature of the eucharist as a sacrament of unity.

REFLECTIONS ON DISCUSSION

The main thrust of the discussion was to raise the question of what our attitude ought to be to this early tradition in general. Is the insistence upon the whole complex – one Lord, one faith, one Church, one eucharist – a theological insight of profound importance to be applauded and to be preserved? Or is it part of a defensive and exclusive outlook in which both Church and eucharist are robbed of their eschatological dimension and made to serve the needs of our present and partial sociological groupings? It would be easy to see why Ignatius in the particular situation in which his letters were written should have thought and taught in the way he did, but should his vision then be as much a model for later Christian practice as it has been? If we accept that there are eucharistic overtones in the accounts of Jesus's feedings of the multitudes and eating with publicans and sinners, might that not properly point us in the direction of a fully open practice of communion?

The fundamental issue is one that relates not only to the eucharist but to Christianity as a whole. Is it possible to do justice to the affirmations of faith without at the same time implying an element of exclusiveness? Is not any positive faith necessarily divisive in relation to those who reject that faith? Yet this inevitable element of over-againstness can be expressed in very different ways. Changing conceptions in, especially Roman Catholic, missionary policy which would stress the idea of a sacramental presence within a predominantly non-Christian environment were cited in evidence. The element of difference between Christians or between Christianity and other religions cannot and should not be disguised or denied. But a more open practice of eucharistic communion, in which the sacrament is less precisely related to existing ecclesiastical structures and in which participation is offered to any who are ready to identify themselves with what is there being proclaimed and done, ought not to be regarded as necessarily involving a form of indifferentism for which the positive affirmations of Christian faith are undervalued.

BIOGRAPHICAL NOTE

NICHOLAS LASH *is Fellow and Dean of St Edmund's House, Cambridge. Born in 1934, educated at Downside and Oscott, he is a priest of the Northampton diocese. After several years in parish work, he moved to Cambridge, where he obtained his Ph.D. for a study of the methodology of Newman's* Essay on Development. *Member of the editorial board of the 'Dogma' section of* Concilium. *Author of* His Presence in the World *(London 1968), and* Change in Focus *(London 1973); he has edited and contributed to a number of collections, including the ninth Downside Symposium,* The Christian Priesthood *(London 1970).*

3 Credal Affirmation as a Criterion of Church Membership

NICHOLAS LASH

1. Introduction

ACCORDING TO THE STATEMENT ON INTERCOMMUNION issued, in 1968, by the Roman Catholic Ecumenical Commission for England and Wales, 'To receive holy Communion together is normally an expression of *unity in faith*. . . . But our tragic position at present is that we are divided in faith.'[1] The Statement went on implicitly to acknowledge a point made by the Anglican report, *Intercommunion Today*, which said: 'All discussion of intercommunion presupposes that a certain, if incomplete, unity of faith . . . already exists between the parties concerned.'[2]

What, then, do we understand by 'unity in faith'? What is meant by 'incomplete', 'substantial'[3] or 'full' unity in faith? How is unity in faith to be discerned or achieved?

[1] *Intercommunion: The Position of the Roman Catholic Church* (London 1968), p. 14.
[2] *Intercommunion Today: Being the Report of the Archbishops' Commission on Intercommunion* (London 1968), p. 92.
[3] 'An important stage in progress towards organic unity is a substantial consensus on the purpose and meaning of the Eucharist' (Anglican/Roman Catholic International

The problem is twofold: it concerns the nature of Christian faith, and the criteria by which such faith (and hence sharing, or unity in faith) may be assessed. Traditionally, one function of the Creed has been to express the faith of the Church and, by so doing, to indicate its limits. Hence the title of this paper: credal affirmation as a criterion of Church membership.

Although this paper is written from a Roman Catholic standpoint, the issues with which it is concerned may also be of interest to those who, traditionally, are suspicious of any attempt too closely to link Christian faith with the acceptance of creeds and formulas. There are few Christian groups which do not assume that *some* explicit expression of faith – in acknowledgement, for example, of the Lordship of Christ, or of the authority of Scripture – is a criterion of belonging to the Church, the worshipping community.

In the first section, I shall examine one form of the distinction between 'faith' and 'beliefs', in order to suggest some ecclesiological implications of this distinction. In the second section, I shall comment on two questions concerning the concepts of 'creed' and 'dogma'. Firstly, what sort of language are we using for what purpose in using the Creed? Secondly, is that agreement in belief, which is held to be necessary before we can celebrate the Eucharist together, restricted to the articles of the Creed, or must it also embrace other aspects of Christian doctrine? Finally, I shall briefly examine the notion of agreement and disagreement as a problem which has become increasingly acute, due to a heightened awareness of the implications of historical discontinuity and cultural pluralism.

2. *Faith and Beliefs*

To use a creed is to make a confession of faith. It may therefore be helpful to explore the distinction between 'faith' and 'beliefs'. This distinction is not unknown in English philosophy, but that is not the angle from which I wish to approach it. Initially, I shall draw on an

---

Commission, *Agreed Statement on Eucharistic Doctrine*, 1971). The Introduction to the *Agreed Statement* said that: 'Our intention was to reach a consensus at the level of faith'. The use of the term 'substantial' has, I think, widely been construed in the following manner: '. . . the agreement is described as substantial, i.e., it is not complete and full' (ANDREW RYDER, 'The Anglican/Roman Catholic Statement on the Eucharist: Comment and Discussion', *Clergy Review*, LVII (1972), p. 169).

essay of Raymond Panikkar's, entitled 'Faith, a Constitutive Dimension of Man'.[4] After connecting certain features of Panikkar's study with passages in which, in his recent book on *Method in Theology*, Bernard Lonergan makes a similar distinction,[5] I shall suggest some ecclesiological implications of the distinction.

Panikkar's starting-point is that of a theological anthropology: 'If the creature is simply *relation* to God, . . . man . . . is that unique being whose natural rapport with the foundation [of his being] becomes the ontological link which constitutes him as man.'[6] He describes faith as 'existential openness toward transcendence'.[7] The adjectives 'ontological' and 'existential' indicate the constitutive, pre-thematic nature of faith as distinct from the various conceptual or linguistic forms of belief, or unbelief, in which faith finds expression. Panikkar appeals to that tradition of discourse, Eastern, Greek and Christian, which is indicated, for example, by the maxim: *Crede ut intelligas*. To speak of faith in this way, I might add, is to indicate the ontological ground of that 'fiduciary' attitude to language which John Coulson has ascribed to Coleridge, Newman and the later Wittgenstein,[8] and which can also be recognised in the concerns of Kierkegaard, Blondel, contemporary existentialism and much Marxist writing. One could also draw attention to certain features held in common by Panikkar's concept of faith, Tillich's 'ultimate concern', and the perspective from within which Bonhoeffer wrote: 'living unreservedly in life's duties, problems, successes and failures. . . . That, I think, is faith . . . that is how one becomes a man and a Christian'.[9]

[4] R. PANIKKAR, 'Faith, a Constitutive Dimension of Man', *Journal of Ecumenical Studies*, VIII (1971), pp. 223–54.

[5] BERNARD LONERGAN, *Method in Theology* (London 1972), pp. 115 24.

[6] PANIKKAR, p. 227.

[7] PANIKKAR, p. 244.

[8] See JOHN COULSON, *Newman and the Common Tradition: A Study in the Language of Church and Society* (Oxford 1970).

[9] Letter of 21st July 1944, quoted from HEINZ ZAHRNT, *The Question of God*, trans. R. A. WILSON (London, 1969), p. 160. Wilson's translation captures Bonhoeffer's sense more accurately than the Fontana edition of Dietrich Bonhoeffer, *Letter and Papers from Prison* (London 1959), p. 125. Bonhoeffer's formulation is strikingly similar to that by means of which Rahner sometimes expresses his view of the saving faith of the 'anonymous Christian': cf. e.g., 'Anonymous Christians', *Theological Investigations*, vol. VI, trans. Karl-H. and Boniface Kruger (London 1969), p. 394.

At one level, therefore, Panikkar is out to combat that rationalism which characterises much theological reflection on the nature of faith: 'To speak about faith is to translate faith into belief – but the translation is not the original.'[10] Philosophy since Descartes has characteristically assumed that 'Faith is what separates men while reason is what unites them.'[11] Panikkar wishes to reverse this: faith, as existential openness, as an ontological determination of the specifically human, unites men. It is at the level of beliefs, the level of thematisation and linguistic expression, that men are profoundly divided.

There are, according to Panikkar, three prevalent conceptions of faith, two of which he rejects as inadequate. 'The first conception, founded on the primacy of Truth, leads to the identification of faith with *orthodoxy*, i.e., with correct doctrine properly formulated. The second insists on the moral character of the religious act, on the supremacy of the Good, and consequently leads to the identification of faith with *orthopoiesis*. . . .'[12] As opposed to these two interpretations, which do not seem false but only unilateral, we wish to offer a concept of faith as *orthopraxis*.'[13] 'Through faith, man acts as an artist, expressing himself through his *poietic* capacity.'[14] But human faith is not simply action that constitutes man's world; it is also action that transforms, perfects, the agent. Man is saved by faith.

To ward off possible objections, two further points need to be made. In the first place, Panikkar's conception of faith as constitutive of human nature does not threaten its gratuitousness. In common with Karl Rahner, and the majority of contemporary theologians, he is concerned with man as he is, in the concrete, not with some metaphysical concept of 'pure nature'. In the second place, to affirm that faith is constitutive of human nature is not to deny that *un*faith,

---

[10] PANIKKAR, p. 224.   [11] PANIKKAR, p. 229.

[12] Later, Panikkar comments: 'negative moral deportment could be an obstacle to a real life of faith, but an irreproachable ethical life is not equivalent to a life of faith' (p. 237). This asymmetry is similar to that which characterises the proposition: God is love.

[13] PANIKKAR, p. 232.   [14] PANIKKAR, p. 237.

faithlessness, is an available option: 'Just as error is possible in the doctrinal order and mistakes are possible in human conduct, so pseudo-praxis is possible: it would be any action that does not build man up.'[15] Moreover, his analysis illuminates 'the traditional idea that loss of faith is, in a certain sense, *contra naturam*'.[16]

From Panikkar, therefore, I wish to borrow the distinction between 'faith' and 'beliefs', and to notice that, on such an analysis, faith may be ascribed to many who would hesitate to thematise or conceptualise their faith in theistic or Christian beliefs: 'Man today is usually declared unbelieving because he refuses to objectivise his faith.'[17]

According to Bernard Lonergan, 'Faith is the knowledge born of religious love'.[18] Knowledge, not understanding. Faith is that dark knowledge which is the exception to the otherwise invariant structure of human cognition, in which the recognition of value is preceded not merely by conscious experience, but also by understanding and rational judgement. Or, to put it another way, faith is the 'major exception' to the Latin tag: '*Nihil amatum nisi praecognitum*'.[19] Man loved by God is 'in love. But who it is we love, is neither given nor as yet understood'.[20] Faith is the knowledge born of religious love; the structure is Johannine: 'this is the love I mean: not our love for God, but God's love for us'.[21]

Thus, although the interpretation is more explicitly theological than Panikkar's, the phenomenological description is strikingly similar. The grace of God poured into a man's heart awakens in him 'an apprehension of transcendent value'.[22] He knows himself loved, even though, if he attempts to thematise, to conceptualise, to name, the source of that love, he may name it wrongly or decide that it has no name. This faith, this dark knowledge born of religious love, seeks expression in language. Men feel impelled to give an account of the hope that is in them. Such linguistic expressions of faith are, for

[15] PANIKKAR, p. 239.
[17] PANIKKAR, p. 231.
[19] LONERGAN, *Method*, p. 122.
[21] 1 Jn. 4, 10 (Jerusalem Bible).
[16] PANIKKAR, p. 227, n. 15.
[18] LONERGAN, *Method*, p. 115.
[20] Ibid.
[22] LONERGAN, *Method*, p. 115.

Lonergan as for Panikkar, 'beliefs'. The grace of God poured into a man's heart gives rise to faith, and faith sccks expression in beliefs.[23]

I drew attention to Panikkar's claim that it is faith, as constitutive, which unites men, and beliefs – as exercises of the human reason – that divide them. Lonergan's analysis points in the same direction. Faith is one, for God is one, and his love is one. But beliefs are many, because many different men struggle differently to understand and to give expression to their faith. In Christian tradition, the articulation of faith in beliefs occurs, centrally, in the celebration of the liturgy and the confession of the Creed. In Creed and liturgy, the Christian community has a vocabulary of symbols in the use of which it expresses its memory, its understanding, and its hope. We shall consider the nature of credal statements in the next section. For the moment, I want to suggest the ecclesiological consequences of the distinction that has been drawn between faith and beliefs.

The faith of which we are speaking is *saving* faith. 'Faith', says Panikkar, 'is absolutely necessary for salvation . . . Christian theology . . . cannot escape the alternative: either only those who have Christian faith are saved, or salvific faith can also be found among so-called "non-believers".'[24] For centuries, a theology generated in the supposedly Christian culture of medieval Europe regarded Christian belief as the norm, and the problem of the 'salvation of the non-believer' as a question on the theological fringe. Today, we have to reverse the emphasis of our curiosity. Explicit Christian belief is the exception. Unless we maintain that most men are damned, the faith of the non-believer represents the 'ordinary' way of salvation.[25] To put it another way: if faith is man's response to God's revelation, then the man without faith is the man to whom God has not revealed himself, or who has refused to

---

[23] Lonergan insists that his form of the distinction between 'faith' and 'beliefs' is traditional in content, even if unfamiliar in terminology: 'for in acknowledging religious beliefs we are acknowledging what was also termed faith, and in acknowledging a faith that grounds belief we are acknowledging what would have been termed the *lumen gratiae* or *lumen fidei* or infused wisdom' (*Method*, p. 123).

[24] PANIKKAR, pp. 240–1.

[25] Cf. HEINZ ROBERT SCHLETTE, *Towards a Theology of Religions*, trans. W. J. O'Hara (London 1965), p. 81.

respond to that revelation. If men are saved by faith, and if God wills all men to be saved, can we say with assurance that there is any man to whom God does not reveal himself? In terms of our distinction between faith and beliefs, we can say that all men are called to saving faith; not all men are called to express that faith in Christian belief.

What has this to do with the problem of membership of the Church? Suppose we ask the question: is 'the Church' the community of *faith*, or the community of *belief*? If the former, shall we not have to say that 'the Church' embraces, in some sense, all men in so far as their praxis is not pseudo-praxis; in so far as they remain, in Panikkar's phrase, existentially open toward transcendence?

We can, I think, throw a little light on this problem by reminding ourselves that our notion of 'the Church' must always be determined by our notion of God's reign and kingdom. There was, for a long time, a tendency – especially in Roman Catholic theology – to equate Church and Kingdom. The weakness of this equation consisted in the fact that the future Kingdom was identified with that present determinable, confessing, worshipping community which we usually call the Church. (Hence the development of restrictive views on the availability of salvation: *extra ecclesiam nulla salus*.) Recently, there has been a tendency rather sharply to separate the two concepts: the term 'Church' is reserved for the sociologically and historically discernible group of Christian believers, and the term 'Kingdom' for the ultimate outcome of human history. This seems dangerously to relax the eschatological tension. I would prefer to suggest that it was not the equation of Church and Kingdom that was unsound, so much as the manner in which it was made. Therefore, instead of saying: Where the confessing, celebrating Church is, there is the Kingdom; I suggest that we say: Where the Kingdom (incipiently) is, there is the Church.

In other words, the Church is the form of the presence in history of the future Kingdom. But the forms of that presence are manifold (neglect of this has led to the history of theology being littered with inadequate, univocal definitions of the Church). If the Church is the manifold presence, in history, of the mystery of man's ultimate 'end' (both '*telos*' and outcome), then it is clear why we cannot absolutely identify the Church with any particular human grouping, or circumscribe it in any single descriptive definition.[26]

Wherever 'salvation' is present in, is already realised in, history – there, in some sense, the Kingdom begins to be. Therefore, wherever 'salvation' is present in history, there, in some sense, is the Church. Therefore, wherever saving faith is present in history, there, in some sense, is the Church.

The distinction between 'faith' and 'beliefs' thus implies that there is a dimension of the Kingdom's presence, a dimension of the Church, considerably wider than that minority who share Christian beliefs.

It could be objected that this line of thought would imply that the Church is largely invisible. No: faith, as I have described it, faith as existential openness, faith as praxis, is not invisible. Man's response in love, trust, courage and commitment, man's 'life in the Spirit', is visible in all the myriad activities men undertake, individually and corporately, motivated and animated by that love. Love is not invisible. But love, in general, does not disclose itself as having that absolute, unrestricted goal which Christian belief declares it to have. Love, as such, is ambivalent. Existential openness, as unthematic, is ambivalent. Sharing bread and wine, for example, is not an invisible activity, but it is ambivalent. It could be the rich eating while the poor starve outside.

If faith as a constitutive dimension of man is to have, and to be shown to have, that unrestricted goal which Christian belief declares it to have, then the meaning of the faith, born of God's love, that saves *all* men, needs to be made explicit, to be openly declared, by *some* men.

The Church is both the community of faith and the community of beliefs. To speak of the community of faith as the Church is to speak of that form of the Kingdom's presence which is coextensive with all in human history that is not refusal, inauthenticity, sin. To speak of the community of beliefs as the Church is to speak of that form of the Kingdom's presence which is the 'sign amongst the nations', the

---

[26] The thrust of this section of the paper could, I believe, be shown to be in harmony with the architecture of the first two chapters of the Constitution *Lumen Gentium* of Vatican II. Notice the handling of the biblical imagery of the Kingdom in Chapter 1, and the pattern of argument in Chapter 2, especially arts. 13–16.

explicit symbol of mankind's future in God and, as such, the prophetic critic of mankind's refusal to respond to that vocation.[27]

It is tempting to conceive of these two aspects as concentric circles. But, although they overlap, the circles are not concentric: the believer who is faithless – who does not 'possess the Spirit of Christ',[28] is as real a phenomenon as the non-believer who lives by faith.[29]

So far as the theme of this paper is concerned, I suggest that the following two general conclusions can be drawn from this brief analysis of the distinction between faith and beliefs.

In the first place, discussion of the problem of unity and disunity in faith may not be restricted to an examination of agreement and disagreement at the level of belief. It must also take into account unity and disunity in style of life and activity.[30] But, if 'doctrinal formulations cannot by themselves be any longer regarded as a sufficient test' of unity in faith,[31] neither may ethical comportment be regarded as a sufficient test. In Panikkar's terminology, neither 'orthodoxy' alone nor 'orthopoiesis' alone, but rather their integration in 'orthopraxis', is the context in which agreement is to be sought.

In the second place, if faith is, in the concrete, a constitutive dimension of man, man thus constituted is a project, a process, a task, not a fully achieved and perfected reality. That man should become what, by God's Word, he is declared to be, and what, by

---

[27] The distinction I am recommending is similar to that which Rahner draws between 'the sanctified world' and 'the Church': cf. *Theological Investigations*, VI, p. 19.

[28] Cf. *Lumen Gentium*, art. 14.

[29] Or, as F. D. MAURICE put it, in a characteristically suggestive and imprecise manner: 'The world is the Church without God; the Church is the world restored to its relation with God. . . . Deprive the Church of its centre, and you make it into a world', *Theological Essays*, introd. E. F. Carpenter (London 1957), p. 277.

[30] Is it not significant that individuals have been excommunicated as frequently for misguided conduct as for erroneous beliefs? And surely the Reformation protest was as much against certain prevailing religious customs as it was against the beliefs that were thought to inform those customs? In more recent times, Anglican and Protestant objections to 'Romanism' and 'infallibility' have, as Newman said, been partly aimed at 'the difference which at first sight presents itself between [the Catholic Church's] formal teaching and its popular and political [i.e., organisational] manifestations' (*The Via Media of the Anglican Church* ([3]London, 1877), I, xxxvii).

[31] JOHN COVENTRY, 'The Intercommunion Debate', *American Ecclesiastical Review*, CLXII (1970), p. 118.

God's Spirit, he is enabled to be, is the substance of our human and Christian hope. 'Complete agreement' at the level of *belief* is, as I shall suggest later in this paper, an impossibility. More fundamentally, the concept of 'complete' or 'full' unity in *faith* should be discarded as hopelessly confused. God's gift is already and always one. Man's self-constituting acceptance of that gift is the project of human history, the achievement of which is eschatological.[32] So far as the symbolic, liturgical expression of faith in the language of creed and rite is concerned, our search is not for 'full' unity, but for sufficient unity in belief and practice to enable the Church as the community of belief effectively to symbolise the goal of the community of faith.

3. Creed and Dogma

Catholics, Anglicans, Lutherans, Calvinists, Orthodox (leaving on one side the problem of the *Filioque*) and others, all use the same Creed. Yet we say that our disagreements at the level of belief are sufficiently profound to prevent us from celebrating together that central symbolic expression of Christian belief, the Eucharist. This is the paradox with which this section is concerned, and in the light of which we shall reflect briefly on two questions. Firstly: What is the 'logical type' of the Creed? What sort of language are we using for what purpose in using the Creed? Secondly, in our search for sufficient agreement in beliefs, is our area of concern restricted to the Creed, or are we also bound to seek agreement concerning those beliefs which have been authoritatively proposed by the Roman Catholic Church in modern times, beliefs expressed in certain canons of Trent and Vatican I, and in the two 'marian dogmas'?

3.1. The Language of the Creed

The fundamental use of the Christian Creed is as an element in an act of worship. In a certain sense, we can say that the Church as the community of belief is created by the confession of the Creed, for it is in the act of confession that faith achieves expression in Christian

---

[32] 'La remise en honneur de l'idée de praxis est d'abord le résultat du renouveau de l'eschatologie elle-même' (C. DUMONT, 'De Trois Dimensions Retrouvées en Théologie: Eschatologie – Orthopraxie – Herméneutique', *Nouvelle Revue Théologique*, XCII (1970), p. 572).

belief. The earliest form of the Creed was that of baptismal interrogation, eliciting the neophyte's confession of faith. The great eucharistic prayers, articulating the meaning of the believing community's central act of self-expression, are explicitly doxological in form, and Trinitarian in structure.

Thus, whatever other types of discourse are necessarily employed in giving expression to that exceedingly complex reality which is Christian religious assent, the fundamental use of the language of belief is doxological, worshipful.[33] As de Lubac puts it: 'je peux dire: *Credo in Deum* parce que j'ai dit tout d'abord: *Credo in Te, Deus meus* . . . le langage *objectif* du *Credo*, pour être légitime, doit être le manifestation du langage *existentiel* de l'acte dont il témoigne'.[34]

'We still suffer from the deep impact in our theological tradition of three centuries of rationalism.'[35] This distortion is often strikingly evident in the way in which Catholics handle ecumenical problems concerning the extent of our 'unity in faith' with other Christians. Thus it is that the specific concerns of this paper account for the emphasis laid on the doxological component of the language of belief. Nevertheless, I wholeheartedly endorse Rahner's comment that 'le concept de doxologie (tel que, par exemple, le défend E. Schlink) ne peut pas être l'*unique* facteur structurel sur lequel

---

[33] 'Das Dogma ist gedachte Liturgie, die Liturgie gebetetes Dogma' (WALTER KASPER, 'Geschichtlichkeit der Dogmen?', *Stimmen der Zeit*, CLXXIX (1967), p. 407). The phrase occurs in a section entitled: 'Das Dogma als Doxologie'. Kasper is one of many theologians who have followed Edmund Schlink in laying stress on the importance of the doxological element in dogmatic discourse: cf. EDMUND SCHLINK, 'The Structure of Dogmatic Statements as an Ecumenical Problem', trans. G. Overlach and D. B. Simmonds, *The Coming Christ and the Coming Church* (Edinburgh 1967), pp. 16–84; G. DEJAIFVE, 'Diversité et Unité de la Révélation,' *Nouvelle Revue Théologique*, LXXXIX (1967), p. 24; A. DULLES, 'Dogma as an Ecumenical Problem', *Theological Studies*, XXIX (1968), pp. 397–416; G. A. LINDBECK, 'The Problem of Doctrinal Development and Contemporary Protestant Theology', *Concilium*, I, 3 (1967), p. 71; WOLFHART PANNENBERG, 'Analogy and Doxology', *Basic Questions in Theology*, trans. George H. Kehm (London 1970), I, 211–38; KARL RAHNER and KARL LEHMANN, 'Kérygme et Dogme', *Mysterium Salutis, I/3, L'Eglise et la Transmission de la Révélation* (Paris 1969), p. 199 (reference is to the French edition because the English version omits, without warning, a substantial amount of both text and notes: *Kerygma and Dogma* (New York 1969); THOMAS F. TORRANCE, *Theological Science* (London 1969), p. 160.

[34] HENRI DE LUBAC, *La Foi Chrétienne: Essai sur le Structure du Symbole des Apôtres* (Paris 1969), p. 313.

[35] PIET F. FRANSEN, 'Unity and Confessional Statements: Historical and Theological Inquiry of R.C. Traditional Conceptions', *Bijdragen*, XXIII (1972), p. 4.

reposerait la confession de foi au Christ'.[36] The fact of the matter is that dogmatic statements are irreducibly complex.[37]

It should by now be evident, therefore, that to insist on the primacy of the doxological element in credal and dogmatic discourse is not to reduce the use of the Creed to a 'declaration of attitude'.[38] It *is* such a declaration, but it is more than this. Christian praise and adoration are grounded in the Church's memory[39] and express its hope. But the faith which thus achieves doxological expression as memory and hope is, nevertheless, an existential attitude, a policy of action. We can, indeed, say, with Le Roy, that 'A dogma . . . [is] the formula of a rule of practical conduct',[40] provided that we remember that neither orthopoiesis alone, nor orthodoxy alone, adequately characterise faith.

The interdependence of praise, memory and hope is structurally more explicit in the eucharistic prayers than in the Creed itself.[41] One of the reasons for this is that the Creed, as we have received it, serves not only the function of the primitive baptismal confession, but also that of the *regula fidei*. As Newman said, the Creed consists of 'heads and memoranda of the Church's teaching'.[42]

---

[36] RAHNER, 'Kérygme et Dogme', p. 242 (my stress).

[37] If reductionism is to be avoided in the assessment of the 'logical type' of dogmatic statements, it is equally to be avoided in the assessment of the senses in which they may be said to be *true:* cf. NICHOLAS LASH, 'Development of Doctrine: Smokescreen or Explanation?', *New Blackfriars*, LII (1971), pp. 101–8; DONALD MACKINNON, 'Subjective and Objective Conceptions of Atonement', *Prospect for Theology*, ed. F. G. Healey (Welwyn 1966), p. 173.

[38] E. LE ROY, *What is a Dogma?* (Chicago 1918), p. 63.

[39] My use of this phrase is general and non-technical. It does not imply – as it often does in current theology – the adoption of the somewhat problematic hermeneutical stance recommended by Knox: Cf. JOHN KNOX, *The Church and the Reality of Christ* (London 1963), pp. 38–60.

[40] LE ROY, op. cit., p. 68.

[41] 'Certes les Symboles ne s'introduisent que fort tard dans la célébration sous une forme spécifique. Mais bien avant cela, l'anaphore eucharistique elle-même est une profession de foi, très proche des formules baptismales' (J.-P. JOSSUA, 'Signification des Confessions de Foi', *Istina* (1972), pp. 50–1).

[42] J. H. NEWMAN, 'The Brothers Controversy: Apostolical Tradition', *British Critic*, XX (1836), p. 187. Hanson surely oversimplifies the matter when he roundly asserts that 'the rule of faith . . . was not a creed . . . [but] was simply an account, divided into subjects, of the content of the preaching and teaching of the Church contemporary with the writer' (R. P. C. HANSON, *Tradition in the Early Church* (London 1962), p. 93). For a trenchant criticism of Hanson's study, see MAURICE BÉVENOT, '*Traditiones* in the Council of Trent', *Heythrop Journal*, IV (1963), p. 346.

Historically, the shift in emphasis from the Creed as doxology to the Creed as *regula fidei*, as doctrinal formulation, is illustrated by the fact that, unlike 'the Niceno-Constantinopolitan Creed, that of Chalcedon was not incorporated in the liturgy'.[43]

'In contrast to Walter Kasper, who emphasises the doxological function', Schoonenberg insists 'that the polemical orientation of dogma is essential . . . dogma's primary function . . . is to fence off the ways in which Scripture may not be interpreted'.[44] So far as the Creed is concerned, I would prefer to say that, as it expands under the pressure of doctrinal controversy, the doxological function is not usurped by, but is rather overlaid by, the regulative function.[45] Nevertheless, the importance of Schoonenberg's observation consists in his recognition of the fact that, *as* regulative, 'a dogma has a negative meaning. It excludes . . . certain errors instead of positively determining the truth'.[46] At Nicea, for example, this exclusion was achieved by using the metaphor *homoousios* to assert a second-order proposition 'to the effect that the Son is consubstantial with the Father, if and only if what is true of the Father also is true of the Son, except that only the Father is the Father'.[47] Thus, the expansion of the Creed, as *regula fidei*, was not a matter of using Hellenic concepts to tell us something which we did not know before, but of employing Hellenic techniques of reflection in order formally to regulate, with greater precision, the use of language concerning the Christian mystery.[48] This regulation 'leaves the believer free to conceive the

---

[43] WALTER KASPER, 'The Relationship Between Gospel and Dogma: An Historical Approach', *Concilium*, I, 3 (1967), p. 74.

[44] P. SCHOONENBERG, 'Historicity and the Interpretation of Dogma', *Theology Digest*, XVIII (1970), pp. 133, 136.

[45] It was not until long after the 'growth' of the Creed had ceased that, in the Middle Ages, its doxological character was almost completely lost sight of until the Reformation: see Concilium General Secretariat, eds., 'The Creed in the Melting-Pot', *Concilium*, I, 6 (1970), p. 137.

[46] LE ROY, op. cit., p. 57.

[47] BERNARD LONERGAN, 'The Dehellenisation of Dogma', *Theological Studies*, XXVIII (1967), p. 345. Cf. *Method*, p. 307.

[48] As Newman remarked of the introduction of the term 'person' into Trinitarian doctrine: 'We knew, e.g. before we used it, that the Son was God yet was not the Father but differing in sonship from Him; the word Person tells us nothing in addition to this. It is only the symbol of the mystery; the symbol, that is, of our ignorance', *The Philosophical Notebook of John Henry Newman, Vol. II: The Text*, ed. Edward Sillem and revised A. J. Boekraad (Louvain 1970), p. 105.

Father in scriptural, patristic, medieval, or modern terms'.[49] In other words, disagreement concerning the most appropriate way of conceiving of God or Christ is not necessarily disagreement concerning the meaning of the Creed.

The negative, polemical thrust of a credal or dogmatic statement reminds us of the fundamental inadequacy of all human discourse concerning God. Creed, and dogma are no exception to the rule that any theological statement 'directs its hearer beyond himself into the mystery of God'.[50] The fact that the *via negativa* is at the heart of all good theology should make us hesitate before excommunicating those who, while sharing with us the use of the basic statements of Christian belief in confessing the Creed, differ from us in their subsequent interpretation and explication of those basic statements.

We began this section by asking what sort of language we are using for what purpose in using the Creed. The complexity both of Christian religious assent, and of doctrinal history, make it impossible to provide any single, simple answer to this question. Fundamentally, the confession of the Creed is an act of worship: it is spoken to God before it is spoken about him. It is an act of worship in which are expressed the Church's memory and its hope. To confess the Creed as true is to affirm the validity of that memory and the soundness of that hope.[51] The language of the Creed also includes a regulative component, and thus serves as a criterion of membership of the community of belief. But our consciousness of the inevitable inadequacy of any linguistic expression of the mystery of faith should make us hesitate before deciding that anyone who is willing to share our memory, our hope, and our task of witness – a willingness expressed in his use of the Creed – is sufficiently divided from us in belief as to inhibit us from sharing together in the celebration of the Eucharist.

---

[49] LONERGAN, 'The Dehellenisation of Dogma', p. 345.

[50] KARL RAHNER, 'What is a Dogmatic Statement?', *Theological Investigations*, vol. V, trans. Karl-H. Kruger (London 1966), p. 58.

[51] Although questions of fundamental theology, concerning the extent to which the fruits of exegetical and historical enquiry form the warrants of our claim that the memory is valid and the hope well-founded, are of considerable importance, they do not come within the scope of this paper.

3.2. *Additions to the Creed?*

The second question to be raised in this section concerns the extent to which, before celebrating the Eucharist together, we are bound to reach agreement concerning those further beliefs, not explicitly expressed in the Creed, which Roman Catholic theology declares to have been defined as '*de fide*'.

'One thing alone', said Newman, 'has to be impressed on us by Scripture, the Catholic idea, and in it [all the propositions of Catholic doctrine] are included. To object, then, to the number of propositions, upon which an anathema is placed, is altogether to mistake their use; for their multiplication is not intended to enforce many things, but to express one'.[52] The problem of the unity of Creed and of dogma is at least as complex as the problem of the unity of the New Testament. It is sufficient for my purpose, however, to draw attention to the fact that increasing awareness of the difficulties that attend the claim that Bible, Creed and dogma are intended to 'express one thing', has not led theologians to abandon the search for 'the essence of Christianity' or the 'outer clarity' of Scripture.[53] Even if we wish to claim that the whole of the Bible is divinely inspired, we are not content to regard the Scriptures as an agglomeration of divinely authenticated 'atomic' truths. Similarly, even if we wish to claim that all dogmatic statements are protected from fundamental error, we are not content to regard the 'teaching of the Church' as an agglomeration of divinely authenticated interpretative responses of Christian belief.

In other words, is not an acceptance of the authority of Scripture, as a whole, or of the subordinate authority of the entire class of dogmatic statements, compatible with the recognition that 'it can all be said' in a smaller compass? And if it can 'all be said' in the compass, for example, of the Creed, why should we suppose that it is either necessary or desirable to 'expand' the Creed further, or to add to it, or to ascribe to recent dogmatic definitions a normative status which

---

[52] J. H. NEWMAN, *Fifteen Sermons Preached Before the University of Oxford* (³London 1871), p. 336.
[53] Cf. e.g., s. w. SYKES, 'The Essence of Christianity', *Religious Studies*, VII (1971), pp. 291–305; WOLFHART PANNENBERG, 'Redemptive Event and History', trans. Shirley C. Gurthie, Jr.., *Basic Questions in Theology* (London 1970), I, 15–80.

is, in practice, equivalent to that which we ascribe to the Creed?
(I have in mind here, for example, the practice – when converts are
admitted into the Roman Catholic Church – of inviting them to
subscribe to an extended version of the Creed, which includes a
summary of the teaching of Trent and of Vatican I.)

To insist upon the unity of the Creed is to urge that its parts can
only be understood in the light of the whole: 'Loin d'être une liste
quelconque, une collection, une série, un catalogue, il est un tout
fortement constitué.'[54] This unity was threatened when, in the early
Middle Ages, the history of the Creed was forgotten, and it came to
be regarded as a collection of 'twelve articles . . . composed by the
Apostles themselves, one article each'.[55] From one point of view,
therefore, Schillebeeckx is correct in saying that it was 'lack of
knowledge of history, and above all of the pre-history of the
apostolic *symbolum*, [which] led theologians of the Middle Ages to
regard the *symbolum* as the all-embracing *articulus* (or "joint") of
faith, around which the totality of dogma turned'.[56] But, from another point of view, that judgement is too harsh. Was it not a sound
theological instinct which thus led medieval theologians to distinguish the 'articles of faith' from other doctrinal statements according
to the centrality of their content in the Christian mystery as a whole?
Right up to the time of Trent, the content of '*fides*' was very broadly
and empirically conceived, as 'embracing everything that the
Church universally imposes in the order of salvation: doctrine,
liturgical and sacramental practice and canon law'.[57] Thus, at this
period, 'The formula "articuli fidei et Ecclesiae sacramenta" is
. . . expressing the very core of the larger reality, called "fides et
mores".'[58] Subsequently, however, the criterion according to which
a doctrinal statement was classified as an 'article of faith' came to be,
not the centrality of its content in the Christian mystery as a whole,
but rather the degree of solemnity, authority or certainty with which
it had been proposed for belief by the appropriate authority.

---

[54] DE LUBAC, *La Foi Chrétienne*, p. 57.
[55] Concilium General Secretariat, eds., 'The Creed in the Melting Pot', *Concilium*, I,
6 (1970), p. 136.
[56] E. SCHILLEBEECKX, *Revelation and Theology*, trans. N. D. Smith (London 1967),
p. 231.
[57] FRANSEN, 'Unity and Confessional Statements', p. 18.
[58] FRANSEN, art. cit., p. 21.

This shift towards doctrinal positivism did not simply blot out the older system of classification (nobody, presumably, believes that the doctrine of papal primacy, as defined at Vatican I, is as fundamental to Christian belief as the doctrine of the divinity of Christ), but it did give rise to a situation in which the qualification *'de fide'* is attended by not a little ambiguity.

It has sometimes been suggested that the dogmas of, for example, papal infallibility or the assumption of our Lady, are obstacles to Christian unity because these doctrines are a matter 'of faith', and not simply 'of theology'. Therefore, Roman Catholics cannot 'abandon' them, and other Christians – even if they are prepared to recognise them, when suitably 'explained', as expressing theological opinions not contrary to Holy Scripture – are unlikely to agree that their acceptance is a necessary condition of orthodox Christian belief. Therefore Christians remain divided 'in faith', and therefore eucharistic communion remains a distant and apparently unattainable goal. I suggest, however, that a return to ancient usage where the qualification *de fide* is concerned (a return hinted at in Vatican II's recognition of a 'hierarchy of truths'[59]), would enable us to acknowledge that disagreement concerning these doctrines does not constitute so grave a divergence in belief as to justify the maintenance of 'separate tables'.

When Newman was arguing his way into the Roman Catholic Church he maintained that it is illogical to recognise the legitimacy of that 'development' which resulted in the Trinitarian and Christological statements of the great Creeds, while refusing to accept the Tridentine Profession of Faith, the Creed of Pius IV: 'That the hypothesis, here to be adopted, accounts not only for the Athanasian Creed, but for the Creed of Pope Pius, is no fault of those who adopt it.'[60] In other words, the latter 'Creed' is presented as the legitimate successor and expansion of the former. Thirty years later, seven years after the Vatican Council, we find that he has shifted his position rather closer to that which I have been recommending: 'The Apostles' Creed is rudimental; the so-called Creed of Pope Pius is controversial, and in this point of view is parallel to the

[59] See *Decree on Ecumenism*, art 11.
[60] J. H. NEWMAN, *An Essay on the Development of Christian Doctrine* ([3]London 1878), p. 31.

Thirty-nine Articles, which no one would call a creed. We may call it Pope Pius's Creed improperly, as we call the Hymn *Quicunque* the Athanasian "Creed", because it contains what is necessary for salvation, but there can be but one rudimental and catechetical formula, and that is the Creed, Apostolic or Nicene.'[61]

To end this section, a brief comment is in order concerning the absence from the Creed of any mention of the Eucharist itself. Not only has this puzzled many people,[62] but it surely renders even more fragile my suggestion that agreement in the use of the Creed is sufficient evidence of shared belief to justify sharing in eucharistic communion? Before the Eucharist is an 'object' of faith it is the *context* in which faith finds expression in the symbols of Christian belief. *What* is affirmed, 'objectively', in the celebration of the Eucharist is, so it seems to me, sufficiently indicated in the 'language' of the rite itself – the gestures of eucharistic celebration and the words of the eucharistic prayer that declares the significance of the action performed.

4. One Form of Sound Words?

The relationship between the Creed and modern dogmatic definitions is not unaffected by the copernican shift that has taken place in our conception of theological method and doctrinal history. So long as the basic model of doctrinal process was assumed to be that of unidirectional, deductive explication or 'unfolding' of the implicit content of divinely revealed premises, it was comparatively easy to maintain that the Church could continue to reach conclusions which were as indisputable, and hence as permanently normative, as the premises from which they were derived (however mysterious the divinely authenticated 'logic' of that derivation!).

Today, the situation is very different: 'theology was a deductive, and it has become largely an empirical science. . . . Where before the step from premises to conclusions was brief, simple, and certain, today the steps from data to interpretation are long, arduous, and, at

---

61 J. H. NEWMAN, *The Via Media of the Anglican Church* ([3]London 1877), I, 230.

62 Not that it need have done so. So far as the Apostles' Creed is concerned, its baptismal origin accounts for the fact that 'It only includes those main truths, a confession of which was required of catechumens' (SCHILLEBEECKX, *Revelation and Theology*, p. 231). The other 'great Creeds' were already complete before the first serious outbreaks of eucharistic controversy in the Church.

best, probable'.[63] Today, the *fides quaerens intellectum* again uses the techniques of the '*quaestio*' rather than the '*thesis*'.[64]

The statements of the New Testament continue to constitute a uniquely privileged field of data for theological reflection; they no longer serve as premises for theological 'proof'. Similarly, once we accept that the statements of the Creed are fundamentally religious or doxological, then, although these statements continue to exercise a privileged, regulative function in theological enquiry, 'they cannot be directly employed as premises for drawing out logical consequences.'[65]

The history of doctrine is today 'understood less as a continual process of "development", that is as a progress achieved through a gradual unfolding of what was already implicit, and more as a series of formulations of the one content of faith diversifying and finding expression in different cultural contexts'.[66]

The problem of establishing the criteria according to which statements made in different cultural contexts may be shown to agree or disagree with each other is currently central to debates in theological hermeneutics, in the history and philosophy of science, in sociology and anthropology.[67] It is not possible, here, to enter

---

[63] BERNARD LONERGAN, 'Theology in its New Context', *Theology of Renewal, Vol. I: Renewal of Religious Thought*, ed. L. K. Shook (New York 1968), pp. 37–8.

[64] 'The essence of faith seems to me to lay in the question rather than in the answer, in the inquisitive attitude, the desire, rather than in the concrete response one gives to it' (PANIKKAR, 'Faith', p. 248). Similarly: 'I regard . . . Christian truth as an interpretation whose truth-value is primarily found in the questions it asks and secondarily in the answers it gives' (GEORGE VASS, 'On the Historical Structure of Christian Truth, II', *Heythrop Journal*, IX (1968), pp. 279–80).

[65] W. PANNENBERG, 'What is a Dogmatic Statement?', *Basic Questions in Theology*, trans. George H. Kehm (London 1970), I, 203. The key word is 'directly'. The religious statements of the Creed undoubtedly entail factual propositions. But it is dangerous to assume that the entailed propositions are 'obvious'. The indicative form of credal statements must not blind us to the need, in each case, to undertake a rigorous and delicate programme of historical interpretation. For a current illustration of this problem, see RAYMOND E. BROWN, 'The Virginal Conception of Jesus', *Theological Studies*, XXXIII (1972), pp. 3–34.

[66] YVES CONGAR, 'Church History as a Branch of Theology', *Concilium*, VII, 6 (1970), p. 87.

[67] The debates in the history and philosophy of science are magisterially surveyed in: ERNAN MCMULLIN, 'The History and Philosophy of Science: A Taxonomy', *Minnesota Studies in the Philosophy of Science, Vol. V, Historical and Philosophical Perspectives of Science*, ed. Roger H. Stuewer (Minneapolis 1970), pp. 12–67; cf. IMRE LAKATOS and ALAN MUSGRAVE, eds., *Criticism and the Growth of Knowledge* (Cambridge 1970). For

into these debates, but the mere reminder of their existence may serve to introduce one final aspect of the problem with which this paper is concerned: namely, the extent to which agreement in belief may only be held to have been reached in so far as a common verbal formula has been agreed upon by means of which that belief is to be expressed.

In the previous section, a case was outlined for the thesis that agreement to use the Creed may, so far as the intellectual component of faith is concerned, be sufficient evidence of shared belief to justify the celebration together of the Eucharist. But what do we mean by 'the Creed'? Do we mean the Apostles' Creed, the Nicene Creed, the Tridentine Profession of Faith, or some platonically conceived reality of which each of these formulas is a particular instance?

We have already seen something of the complexity, from the point of view of 'logical type', of the language of the Creed. It has been argued that, however necessary it may be not to lose sight of the fact that the propositions of the Creed embody straightforward factual claims, more complex affirmations of eschatological hope, and second-order prescriptions regulating the limits of Christian discourse, nevertheless their fundamental thrust is religious or doxological. So far as this fundamental level is concerned, it can be argued that the Apostles' Creed 'says just as much' as the Nicene Creed. In other words, in so far as the Creed is an attempt poetically, or symbolically, to give verbal expression to the *entire* Christian mystery, the Apostles' and Nicene Creeds may be regarded as substantially identical, as expressing the same faith. My desire so to argue is not born of any lust for imprecision, but is rather the fruit of my conviction that, in religious discourse as much as anywhere else, we need continually to bear in mind Aristotle's dictum that 'It is a mark of the educated man and a proof of his culture that in every subject he looks for only so much precision [*akribeia*] as its nature permits.'[68]

---

sociology and anthropology, see: BRYAN R. WILSON, ed., *Rationality* (Oxford 1970); PETER WINCH, *The Idea of a Social Science and its Relation to Philosophy* (London 1958).

---

[68] *The Ethics of Aristotle*, trans. J. A. K. Thompson (London, Penguin Classics 1955), pp. 27–8 (Bk. I, Ch. 3). No one who has had the privilege of working for several years with Donald MacKinnon can fail to have had impressed upon him the importance of this dictum.

Moreover, there are sound historical grounds for rejecting the notion that agreement in belief necessarily entails the use of one and the same set of words to express that belief. 'At least until the conversion of Constantine . . . the recitation of identical credal formulas was not considered essential to Christian fellowship.'[69] We should not overlook the significance of the fact that, at the Council of Florence, the Greeks were permitted to retain their Creed, in which the '*Filioque*' did not feature: 'Although verbally [the two creeds] seemed contradictory . . . they were seen as expressing different aspects of the same divine mystery. Thus the Council of Florence implicitly rejected the equation "one faith = one dogma".'[70] Finally, it has recently been argued[71] that it would be arbitrary to restrict to theological, as distinct from dogmatic statements, the implications of Vatican II's recognition that 'The apostolic heritage . . . has had a different development in various places as a result of variety of character and living conditions.'[72]

Today, we are more conscious than any previous generation could have been of the discontinuities in human history, and of the implications for doctrinal unity of cultural and linguistic pluralism. Problems of hermeneutic, problems of discerning agreement and disagreement between groups of human beings operating in different cultural contexts, have both a diachronic and a synchronic dimension. Diachronically, we want to know whether we believe the same things, in some significant sense, as earlier generations of Christians believed. Synchronically, we want to know whether some other group, that is our partner in ecumenical discussion, believes the same things as we do — even though its form of words, style of life and worship, are *prima facie* very different from our own.

To repeat the words that some earlier generation of Christians employed, in their different social, linguistic and cultural context, is no guarantee that the common element in the two belief systems outweighs their differences. Similarly, even if, in the ecumenical dialogue, two groups of Christians agreed to use terminologically

[69] AVERY DULLES, 'Dogma as an Ecumenical Problem', *Theological Studies*, XXIX (1968), p. 408.
[70] DULLES, 'Dogma', p. 409.
[71] DEJAIFVE, art. cit. (above, note 30).
[72] *Decree on Ecumenism*, art. 14.

identical credal formulas, this would be no guarantee that the common element in the two belief systems outweighed the differences. This is an intra-denominational as well as an inter-denominational problem.[73] How do we know that the Catholics of Peru share the same beliefs as the Catholics of Ireland, Spain or Japan? On the basis of what criteria are Archbishop Helder Camara and Major Patrick Wall held to share a common system of beliefs?

One thing is certain. Agreement and disagreement are not patent of quasi-mathematical demonstration. There is always a penumbra of uncertainty surrounding any agreement that we judge to have been reached. And the search for agreement has no end. People change, situations change, meanings change. Agreement is constantly sought for, more or less successfully achieved, only to be sought for again. 'Full', complete, final agreement in beliefs is, as I suggested in the opening section of this paper, an illusory goal. And the attainment of an illusory goal cannot be the necessary precondition of eucharistic fellowship. Within the Roman Catholic Church, the maintenance of eucharistic fellowship is acknowledged, in practice, as being compatible with considerable divergence in social, cultural and political goals and values, in forms of liturgical expression, theology and belief.[74] We are, I suggest, distressingly inconsistent in applying different standards, where our own internal relations as Roman Catholics are concerned, from those which we invoke in order to justify our present discipline in regard to intercommunion.

If 'complete agreement' in belief is an illusion, what attainable goals are there, sufficient to justify and, indeed, to demand, the common celebration of the Eucharist? I suggest that we might look for a solution in the concept of 'mutual recognition'. In the early centuries, the Churches sought to *recognise*, in each other's beliefs, order, and style of life, the face of Christ as they had come to know him in their own memory, experience, worship and witness. Concern for mutual recognition implies a twofold discipline. We not only have to listen to, attend to, show respect for, the life and language of another

---

[73] For an important survey of the problems with which this paragraph is concerned, see: KARL RAHNER, 'Pluralism in Theology and the Unity of the Church's Profession of Faith', *Concilium*, VI, 5 (1969), pp. 49–58; cf. Panikkar's discussion of 'orthodoxy' in 'Faith', pp. 233–6.

[74] See CHARLES DAVIS, 'Unity and Christian Truth', *Eastern Churches Quarterly*, XVI (1964), pp. 101–16.

group; we also have constantly to be examining our own memory, our own belief, our own experience and celebration, in order less inadequately to hear, and so more obediently to verify in our midst, the presence of the risen Christ.

5. *Conclusion*

The existing discipline of the Roman Catholic Church in regard to intercommunion rests upon a particular set of assumptions concerning the nature of the Church and of the language in which the faith of the Church is expressed. This paper will have served its purpose if it has shown the urgency of the need critically to re-examine some of these assumptions.

I have argued that there are grounds for suggesting that Christians who use what they mutually recognise to be the same Creed are not sufficiently divided in belief as to justify the maintenance of 'separate tables'.

In our search for 'sufficient agreement' in belief, we should be seeking to recognise, in the *praxis* of other Christian communities, the presence of Christ. The Lord goes before his people. We are continually present to him, but his presence to us can only be verified to the extent that we are prepared continually to undergo a profound *metanoia* of language, understanding, structure and activity. It would be curious if the dramatic shifts that we have experienced, in recent years, in ecclesiological consciousness, in our conception of religious truth and the manner in which it is discerned, sustained and celebrated in history, did not call for correspondingly radical changes in our eucharistic discipline.

INTRODUCTION

John Coventry's Note was not prepared for the Burwalls meetings. It was added to the Symposium because some felt that other Roman Catholic contributions to the book, with the exception, perhaps, of Professor Fransen's, had not given a specific reference to the kind of proposition which Father Coventry sets out in his opening paragraph: 'An Anglican–Roman agreement on eucharistic doctrine does not bring Roman Catholics any nearer to receiving communion from Anglicans, if their orders are invalid.' Father Coventry's Note should be read sympathetically, as a skilful attempt to report briefly what has been and is being argued more substantially elsewhere. For a quite different, because radical Protestant, approach, to the Anglican–Roman Catholic agreement on eucharistic doctrine, the reader should look at Dr Kent's essay, 'Old-Fashioned Diplomacy', in Part Three.

BIOGRAPHICAL NOTE

JOHN COVENTRY *is a lecturer in Christian Doctrine at Heythrop College (University of London). He was born in 1915, became a Jesuit in 1932, read Greats at Oxford, and is a member of the Roman Catholic national Ecumenical Commission, of which he was the first secretary.*

Note on the Mutual Recognition of Ministry

JOHN COVENTRY S.J.

MANY READING THESE PAPERS MAY BE LIABLE TO FEEL
that the whole discussion of intercommunion remains up in the air
until the question of ministry is settled. A Roman Catholic might
well argue: 'If the Communion Service of other Christians is not a
true Eucharist, or more specifically if Our Lord is not present,
because they lack a true ministry, then the question of our receiving
their Eucharist – the question of intercommunion in its accepted
sense of *mutual* admission to Communion – simply does not arise.
An Anglican-Roman agreement on eucharistic doctrine does not
bring Roman Catholics any nearer to receiving Communion from
Anglicans, if their orders are invalid.'

A previous Downside Symposium considered the nature of the
Christian Ministry[1] but could not include the question of validity,
which is complex enough to need a symposium to itself. Hence the
editors of the present volume have decided to include this summary
note. Its purpose is to give very brief indications of contemporary
theological views (with some indication where the arguments leading
to them have been given scholarly treatment), that are leading to the
review of traditional catholic (not simply Roman Catholic) positions.

[1] *The Christian Priesthood*, ed. N. Lash and J. Rhymer (London 1970).

The author of this Note wishes to make clear that it does not, as it stands, give his own full views, nor pretend in the available space to give substantial arguments or conclusions about the points raised. But it would be a mistake to give the impression that only catholic theologians are being led to modify previous positions. Protestant thinkers too are reconsidering various questions: the centrality of the Eucharist to the worship, indeed to the nature, of the Church; the value of episcopacy as a sign of apostolic succession and as a bond of unity; the sacramental nature of ministry as making Christ's priesthood visible and effective in particular ways within the Christian community; ordination as conferring special gifts of the Spirit for the exercise of ministries, etc. Thus it can be seen that a convergence is taking place. This Note deals only with part of one side of this convergence. In doing so it does not purport to set forth unanswerable arguments that simply have to be accepted, but only to indicate the chief grounds on which reconsideration is taking place.[2] These, then, are as follows.

(1) Contemporary New Testament scholarship indicates that in the Church of the first two or three generations, while 'office' in the local Church was a common feature, the manner of its organisation and exercise was varied; it does not seem that a uniform organisation of ministries in the local Churches was considered important. There is not sufficient evidence to establish the view that transmission of authority or powers from the original Twelve was thought necessary. There is no evidence about who could or could not preside at the Eucharist. Hence it remains a possible view that authority to appoint ministers, including the celebrant at the Eucharist, was thought to reside in the believing community and to be passed on simply by the continuance of the community in the apostolic faith. The term 'apostle' is variously used: from the meaning of the word (a missionary), and from the available evidence, it is clear that the primary function of an apostle was not to preside over a local Church but to preach the Gospel in fresh fields and to found new local Churches.

[2] The literature on the subject is vast and scattered. Convenient sources for further reading are: *Eucharist and Ministry*, vol. IV of the series 'Lutherans and Catholics in Dialogue', US Catholic Conference, 1312 Massachusetts Avenue, Washington, a summary of which is given in *One in Christ*, vol. VII (1971), no. 4, pp. 371-78; *Concilium*, vol. IV, no. 8 (April 1972), entitled 'Mutual Recognition of Ecclesial Ministries?'

(2) The ordering of local Churches under one bishop seems to have owed a lot to the city-state pattern of the eastern provinces of the Roman Empire, and became universal only late in the second century. The Church of Rome may not have adopted mon-episcopacy till the second century. The pattern of ordination to eucharistic ministry only by bishops in the succession of apostolic office took a matter of centuries to become fixed.

This historical picture gives rise to theological questions. Granted that, once established, a mon-episcopal structure is seen to have theological values, and can be said to have become universal under the guidance of the Spirit, does it follow that the Church must always thereafter retain this structure? Can we say that thereafter the Holy Spirit only acts through ministries that are conferred and authenticated by bishops in historical succession?

(3) Episcopal succession seems first to have been thought of as the succession of a bishop to an apostolic see, not of one bishop to an other; hence the episcopal local Church, rather than the bishop, claimed apostolic succession. It is generally recognised that apostolic succession cannot simply be a matter of episcopal pedigree. True apostolic succession is succession in the apostolic faith, life, mission, teaching, witness and service. Episcopacy within such a succession is a sign of true apostolicity; it can only be an effective sign in so far as the reality is there; it cannot by itself and in isolation guarantee true apostolicity.

(4) The idea of a 'character' imprinted by some sacraments originated in the context of baptismal controversy, and its purpose was to assert that baptism cannot be repeated. It was only later that what was originally a metaphor (drawn from the brand-mark or the seal in wax) came to be given metaphysical significance, mistakenly as some think, in terms of some interior ontological 'entity' conferred on or permanently modifying the soul. Originally there was only thought of one character, that of baptism, but the idea later spread to confirmation, and still later to ordination.

When Trent spoke of the sacraments of baptism, confirmation and order as imprinting 'a certain spiritual and indelible sign in the soul, because of which they cannot be repeated' (DS. 1609), the Council used the language then current in the Latin Church. Its intention, however, was simply to reaffirm the unrepeatability of these sacraments, not to canonise and define the idea of the transference of some entity to the soul. Scholastic theologians at the time varied between regarding the character as an ontological reality, as a relation, or as a legal relation, and these hesitations are reflected in the phrase *signum quoddam spirituale et indelebile*. Some modern theologians consider that the traditional idea of character is amply covered by the past historical event of these sacraments, as definitive events in the life and experience of recipients and community, which can no more be erased from history than vows of marriage or religion. And they point out that Trent does not strictly say that a priest cannot cease to be a priest, but only that he cannot be reordained.

(5) Emphasis on 'the character' of the priesthood is thought to have created imbalances, notably a concentration on the person of the minister rather than on the nature and purpose of ministry, and on transmission of powers rather than on the gift of the Spirit. Eastern Orthodox theologians wish to reject any idea of some 'thing' being transmitted in ordination, or any idea of efficient causality. The community, they argue, does not first exist and then ordain by a process involving such causality, because ministry is from the outset constitutive of the community. To ordain is to give to the ordinand new personal relationships within the community of the Spirit by prayer to the Spirit to give him the grace needed for the charge entrusted to him.

It is clear that these perspectives question the relevance of much argument that has taken place about the 'validity' of orders.

(6) Jerome maintained that it is only by ecclesiastical law, not by the institution of Christ, that the right of ordination is reserved to bishops. Melancthon and Calvin appealed to this view, arguing that presbyteral ordination might be against existing law, but was not therefore invalid in the sense of ineffective. The argument is supported by some well-attested pre-Reformation cases of ordinations by abbots and priests that were accepted by the Church. Protestant theologians have in general urged that it was never the desire of the Reformers to reject episcopacy or episcopal ordination, but that they were forced into it by being forced out. Methodists have maintained the same with regard to the Church of England. In both cases it is urged that the demands of preaching the true Gospel and the needs of Christian people override current positive law.

(7) Trent declared Lutheran ministers who were not ordained by bishops to be 'not legitimate' (*illegitimos*). It is argued that this means that they were 'illicitly' not 'invalidly' ordained; that Trent was fully aware of the opinion of Jerome and did not wish to rule decisively against it. Indeed, an argument can be constructed from the official *relatio* of the Commission on *Lumen Gentium* (n. 21) that Vatican II also expressly avoided settling the question whether only bishops can ordain priests.[3]

(8) From these considerations it can be seen that the particular question raised by the Bull *Apostolicae Curae* is not whether Anglican bishops are true bishops, but one of application on a wider scene, viz. whether an ordination can confer a true eucharistic ministry, when the ordaining minister positively excludes the idea of sacrificial priesthood. Fr Fransen's paper in this volume has noted the prudential and juridical nature of Leo XIII's decision in this case. The theological argument against Anglican orders is that the framers and users of the Edwardine ordinal wished positively to exclude the idea that the Mass was a sacrifice, and hence the intention of ordaining to a sacrificial priesthood; that their obvious and in itself sufficient intention of ordaining Christian ministers was cancelled out by their intention not to ordain sacrificing priests, and so their ordinations did not transmit priestly power; hence, finally, whatever the intentions of Anglican ordainers in a later age, the power of transmitting the Church's priesthood was in fact lost. To arrive at theological certainty of the nullity of Anglican orders on these grounds one would have to be certain:

(a) Of the doctrine of conflicting intentions at the centre of the argument, which has never been more than a theological opinion.

---

[3] 'Episcopal consecration together with the office of sanctifying, also confers the offices of teaching and governing. . . . For from tradition, which is expressed especially in liturgical rites and in the practice of the Church both of the East and of the West, it is clear that by means of the imposition of hands and the words of (episcopal) consecration, the grace of the Holy Spirit is so conferred, and the sacred character so impressed, that bishops in an eminent and visible way undertake Christ's own role as Teacher, Shepherd and High Priest, and that they act in His person. Therefore it devolves on the bishops to admit newly elected members into the episcopal body by means of the sacrament of orders.' (*Lumen Gentium*, n. 21.)

(*b*) That ordination transmits powers by a process of continuing causality, such that a break in transmission renders subsequent ordinations ineffective (and would all Roman Catholic orders be above suspicion on such a theory?).

(*c*) That a Christian community's capacity to celebrate a true Eucharist depends on the presence of a minister to whom such powers have been duly transmitted, something which cannot be established for New Testament times.

(9) If arguments for presbyteral ordination were accepted, it would not appear necessary to have any form of conditional ordination for the recognition of such orders. Recognition itself would suffice, perhaps celebrated in some service of reconciliation.

(10) The use of the term 'valid' has differed in Christian tradition: in saying Donatist baptism was valid, Augustine affirmed that it was unrepeatable but denied that it gave the Spirit or remitted original sin. The wide use of the term in recent catholic theology has been much bound up with the ideas of indelible character (of baptism and priesthood) and of the transmission of powers (for ordaining, for forgiving sin, for the consecration of the eucharistic elements). But, as the presence of the character or of the powers is not open to any empirical test, a judgement of validity (i.e. that the sacrament is a true and effective sacrament and not a mere sign) has necessarily been based on assessment of whether the approved conditions, including where relevant those for the transmission of powers, have been fulfilled.

The wide variety of usage (e.g. for convalidation of a marriage) has led some thinkers to argue: either, that 'valid' has in fact become a legal term meaning 'having a full claim to recognition by the Church as a true and effective sacrament'; or that it means 'de facto recognised or guaranteed by the Church as a true sacrament'. Part of what a sacrament means to the recipient is that it carries the Church's assurance that God is here acting: I can be sure that Our Lord becomes truly present, that my sins are forgiven. A true sacrament is an acknowledged act of Christ's Church.

One can go on to argue that in recognising orders the Church is guaranteeing their effectiveness, but that in witholding recognition she cannot guarantee their ineffectiveness, as language like 'absolutely null and utterly void' would lead one to suppose. In witholding recognition she leaves one in doubt. To guarantee ineffectiveness would be to limit the action of the Spirit to the approved action of the Church. But this is untenable. The Church can be, and is, a sure sign of the Spirit's action; she cannot by her pronouncements become a sure sign of the Spirit's non-action.

If this is accepted, then the meaning of 'valid' is seen to coincide with 'is in fact recognised by the Church', whether one is considering orders or any other sacrament. At the moment the Catholic Church does not recognise Anglican Orders. What matters to the Roman Catholic is *that* the Church should recognise them, not any process (e.g. of conditional ordination) leading up to such recognition. Some, urging that the Church is herself the basic and inclusive sacrament, argue that all the Church needs to do is to give her recognition.

(11) The recognition by Vatican II of the ecclesial reality of other communions is seen to have effects for ministry. Apart from the Orthodox, it is not clear to which communions the full name 'Church' should be attached. (Pope Paul's concluding remarks in his canonisation speech, addressed to the Anglican Communion, when he said that he looked forward to the day when he could embrace his Sister Church, are ambiguous.) The phrase 'ecclesial reality' is not precise, and suggests that some communions have more of the fullness of the Church, more of what is constitutive of the Church, than others.

Vatican II argued that a communion that has catholic elements is to that extent a Church. A number of theologians, impressed by their concrete experience of the life of other communions, wish to turn the argument round and to assert that, in so far as a communion can be seen to be 'Church', it must also have a ministry; but the ministry does not by itself constitute the Church, and it would not be legitimate to call a communion a Church solely on the grounds that its ministry was recognised. It would not be at all acceptable to Anglicans, for instance, if the day came when Rome recognised Anglican orders and went on to say, '*therefore* you are a Church'. Anglicans would surely reply, 'No: it is because we are a Church that we have a true ministry, and that you should recognise it.'

Yet the fullness of ministry is one of the elements constitutive of the Church. So the considerations of this paragraph would suggest that recognition of ministry cannot be considered apart, but is one of the elements in a process of total recognition of a Church. This is a point of view with which the Orthodox would appear to concur.

(12) Finally, in asserting that bishops have the fullness of the priesthood,[4] Vatican II has brought out into the open the idea that the sacrament of order need not necessarily be either wholly present or wholly absent; it can be conferred and participated in more or less. The idea was always there to bring out in so far as in catholic theology the three Major Orders were considered to be a sharing more or less in the fullness of the Church's ministry. However, now the Council has by implication asserted that a *priest* has not got the fullness of the priesthood.

This raises the question whether the ministry of other communions need be thought of as either all that goes to the fullness of the Church's ministry, or as null and void. It stands to reason that there can be no more or less in the consecration of eucharistic elements. Yet, if the ministry of a Church is a sign of the fullness of Christian life in that communion (i.e. of true apostolic succession), then it would be possible for any communion to regard the ministry of another communion as in some respects deficient (e.g. non-episcopal, lacking in some aspects of sacramental life such as penance, not preaching the fullness of Christian truth, historically a sign of schism, etc.), without thereby being able to conclude that that other ministry was not a true eucharistic ministry. And it is with conditions for sharing in the Eucharist, rather than with the total conditions for union, that this volume is concerned.

---

[4] 'This sacred synod teaches that by episcopal consecration is conferred the fullness of the sacrament of orders, that fullness which in the Church's liturgical practice and in the language of the holy Fathers of the Church is undoubtedly called the high priesthood, the apex of the sacred ministry.' (*Lumen Gentium*, n. 21.)

INTRODUCTION

Archbishop Dwyer's agenda was produced at an early stage in the discussions and is included here because this list of questions suggests something of what was in the mind of the Theology Commission in considering the problems of intercommunion.

BIOGRAPHICAL NOTE

GEORGE PATRICK DWYER *has been the Roman Catholic Archbishop of Birmingham since 1965. Prior to this he had been Bishop of Leeds for eight years.*

A Suggested Agenda for Symposium on Intercommunion

ARCHBISHOP DWYER

The Eucharist as Sign of Unity

As the Eucharist is the sign of unity, joint sharing in it by Christians will vary according to the degree of unity that exists between them.

At one extreme Ukrainian and Roman Catholics, who are united in Faith, Worship and in obedience to one Authority, have total sharing without restriction and even concelebration subject to administrative permission.

At the other extreme there can be no sharing at all between Christians and the unbaptised since the sign would be void of meaning.

Between these extremes the degree of sharing (in Roman Catholic and others' practice) varies according to the degree of unity which exists.

What Kind of Unity is Needed as Basis?

The authorities of any Christian Church have to consider:

what kind of unity is required to justify sharing in the Eucharist?
what canonical limitations may be necessary even so, to safeguard other values, e.g. the specific witness of a particular Church?

The questions at issue would seem to be therefore theological and canonical.

Theological Questions

Is unity based on Christian baptism sufficient in itself to justify unlimited intercommunion (a) reception of Holy Communion? (b) concelebration?

Or is unity of Faith also required to make the sign real? If so, to what extent?

Is unity of Faith in the real objective presence of Christ in the Blessed Sacrament necessary and sufficient in itself theologically to justify unlimited intercommunion?

Is anything further necessary to justify, theologically, concelebration, e.g. common belief in the sacrificial nature of the Eucharist?

Is the distinction between the Eucharist as a sign of unity and as a means of grace theological or merely canonical (i.e. disciplinary)? Roman Catholic practice (Ecumenical Directory, part one, n. 55) distinguishes between the Eucharist (a) as a sign of unity: absence of full unity (Faith: Worship: Authority) prohibits in itself common sharing; (b) as a means of grace: this justifies *granting* Holy Communion exceptionally in case of necessity (which necessity itself varies, e.g. much less stringent in regard to Eastern Orthodox than to Reformed Churches. Moreover, a Roman Catholic may not *receive* Holy Communion even in case of necessity except from a minister who is regarded as validly ordained).

Canonical Question

Even if it were shown that there is a theological basis for total unlimited intercommunion and even concelebration, are some canonical (i.e. merely disciplinary) limitations necessary or advisable to avoid misleading the people regarding the witness which different churches regard as specific and essential to themselves? For example, the Presbyterian would feel bound in conscience to make clear that his church and faith are not the same as the Roman Catholic and vice versa.

Method

Elements for a solution would need to be sought in Scripture and in theological considerations but not least in the history of the Church.

24 March 1971

PART TWO

INTRODUCTION

IN THIS SECOND PART THE CONTRIBUTORS WIDEN THE area of the discussion, setting the issue of intercommunion in the context of membership. There may be a steadily increasing tendency for Churches to accept one another's baptism as valid, but there is no agreement as to the conditions of baptism, and still less agreement about the kind of teaching which should precede confirmation, or even about the age at which confirmation should ideally take place. John Austin Baker underlines the scandal of the fact that at initiation the Churches require of the new entrant a more rigorous commitment to belief than will apparently ever be demanded of him thereafter. Hence the relevance of the Jewish parallel (quite apart from the considerations which Robert Murray raises in his contribution to Part Three). Rabbi Jacobs says that in Judaism the dividing line runs between practise and belief; it is not easy to speak of a 'Jewish theology' as such, nor is there a Jewish priesthood. There is a sense in which a Jewish atheist remains a Jew. From the point of view of the Christian Church, that is, what is often seen as necessary to survival does not seem so vital to the Jewish tradition, a tradition as tenacious of life as Christianity itself.

Eric Sharpe's paper looks at the same question of emphasis in terms of India. He draws attention to the section of liberal Christian opinion in India which has held that 'formal' membership of the Church is always unnecessary (cf. the comments of J. A. Baker on the 'open Church'), and doubly so in a country like India. He quotes from William Miller of Madras who thought that insistence on baptism had greatly harmed the cause of Christianity in India. Sharpe makes his point partly in historical terms, discussing the relationship of Christianity to caste; our other historical example comes from the nineteenth century, in Hamish Swanston's description of the background and developments of the affair of the Revisers' Communion in 1870. This is a historian's paper, offering the appropriate instance, gently delineating what resistance to change really means in the present by exhibiting it at its most blunt and block-headed in the past. In effect, Dean Stanley said, men who are willing to communicate together for the love of Christ should do so and not wait for the consent of the Puseys of this world, which will never be obtained by the methods of rational persuasion. One may say, more-over, that the roots of the present ecumenical situation lie in this Victorian period, when the impatience with division and the free-dom to contradict it remained the privilege of an élite: by the late twentieth century – for the Revisers Communion took place more than a century ago, which is no credit to any of us – this impatience has spread (as Father Fransen, for instance, has emphasised in his opening paper). The remaining contributions to this section, by David Clark and Robert Towler, try to throw further light on the sociological nature of this impatience, David Clark by distinguishing the very different ideas of membership which coexist in modern urban society; Robert Towler by taking the ecumenical impulse itself, and asking how far ecumenical enthusiasm grows from religious idealism and how far from the prompting of social causation of a much more material kind. Towler's paper, like David Clarke's, is easily misunderstood in ecclesiastical circles, and perhaps was in the course of the Symposium itself: sociology does not appeal to theologians. Nevertheless, if the question of intercommunion is to be solved, Church leaders must examine seriously what were long ago called the social sources of denominationalism, because the twen-tieth century Church is no longer in a position to impose what may seem to be a theologically valid answer if the theologically valid ignores what is socially possible. This is also one of the conclusions which may be drawn from Sharpe's essay on Christianity in India. Robert Towler's essay also makes a contribution to the important debate on the nature of social causation, a subject which sociologists have neglected far too confidently in the past, and his criticisms of what Professor Bryan Wilson and Dr Robert Currie have written about the ecumenical movement is very valuable.

BIOGRAPHICAL NOTE

HAMISH SWANSTON, a Roman Catholic priest who did his doctoral research on Anglican theology in the nineteenth century, and at present lecturing at the University of Kent at Canterbury, is Professor in the theology department of Boston College, Massachusetts. He is the author of a number of books including *Community Witness* (London and New York, 1967), *The Kings and the Covenant* (London and New York, 1968), and an introduction to sacramental theology, *Jesus Now*, (London, 1970) published in two paperback volumes.

4 The Revisers' Communion

HAMISH SWANSTON

WEDNESDAY, 22 JUNE 1870, WAS APPOSITION DAY AT
St Paul's School and the company was entertained to a programme of
Speeches, or, as non-Paulines might ignorantly suppose, 'dramatic
recitations', extracted from the *Archarnians* (245–440), *Richard III*
and *The Rivals*, though the piece from the *Antigone* (725–890) had to
be omitted 'owing to the lateness of the hour and the intense heat of
the weather'. After these exertions to the Mercers'-hall that evening
went the Bishop of Llandaff, who replied to the toast of 'Church and
State', and the Bishop of Ripon, who replied to 'the House of
Lords'.[1]

Bishop Ollivant of Llandaff had arranged his day rather better
than had Bishop Ellicott of Gloucester and Bristol who 'at the last
moment' had to ask his brother of Ely to supply his place at the
Distribution of Prizes at King's College School, where, with the
Bishop of Madras, he listened to selections from *Le Grondeur*,
Henry IV, Part I and the inevitable *Archarnians* (659–885).[2]

The Bishop of Llandaff was not simply more expert in the
management of an engagement book than the Bishop of Gloucester
and Bristol, he was more careful in his devotions. At 11.30 that
morning he had taken the precaution of kneeling between perfectly

---

[1] Cf. *Times* report, 23 June 1870. [2] Cf. *Times* report, 23 June 1870.

orthodox members of the New Testament Company at the tomb of King Edward VI for the Revisers' Communion.[3]

Not only was the English weather more certain in 1870 than it seems today (though Dean Stanley's obituary sermon for Charles Dickens on the Sunday before had been generally inaudible on account of his summer cold) but life went at a more efficient pace. 'How rapidly things move now', puffed Westcott to Hort.[4]

The proposal that the Church of England should give a lead in the revision of the Authorised translation of the Bible had been placed before a startled Convocation by Bishop Samuel Wilberforce of Winchester on 10 February 1870, only four months before the first working session of the New Testament Company. Dr Pusey had written immediately to the Bishop in protest at his proposal. 'There is', he warned, 'a fashion in criticism' which was just now 'a fashion in being liberal, not insisting overmuch on orthodox interpretation', and so all kinds of strange new phrases would be substituted for the good old translations to the confusion of honest men. Englishmen have been brought up to believe that the Bible is their religion, and 'if their confidence in the Bible is shaken, so will be their Christianity'.[5] Despite this saintly disapproval the Convocation of Canterbury appointed a Committee which met on 24 March to draw up a scheme of revision. The fifth of the Committee's resolutions achieved some later notoriety for it empowered the Companies of Revisers for the Old and New Testaments to enlist the assistance of scholars who did not belong to the Church of England.

Invitations were sent out to various eminent folk, and the Committee seems to have made a great effort to enlist the best available men, though it is odd that whilst Kennedy, the Professor of Greek at Cambridge, was invited, Jowett, the Professor at Oxford, though the author of what is still one of the most useful commentaries on the major Pauline Epistles, was not. Dr Pusey declined the Bishop of Gloucester and Bristol's invitation, 'on the ground', he told Liddon,

---

[3] Ollivant was invited to the Westminster Communion because he was Chairman of the Old Testament Company. There was no stir after his Company's Communion for to that service only the orthodox came.

[4] Westcott to Hort, 29 May 1870, A. WESTCOTT, *Life and Letters of B. F. Westcott*, 1903, I, 390.

[5] Pusey to Wilberforce, 12 February 1870, LIDDON'S *Life of E. B. Pusey*, IV (J. O. Johnston and W. C. E. Newbolt), 1897, p. 230.

'that on the verge of seventy one must make one's choice of what one would still do on earth for God, and that I hope I am doing good by my Commentary, whereas I anticipated no good from Revision'.[6]

From the first, however, the Revision was understood in quite different ways by those who supported it. Wilberforce's proposal was said to have been made in an effort to distract men from the internal difficulties of the English Church. Stanley's promotion of the idea was on account of its possibilities for the enlarging of the Church among all sorts of Englishmen. While both were content to follow the lead of the late Dean Alford in making the demand for revision and in supporting 'attempts at more friendly communion in all matters with Protestant Nonconformists', Wilberforce with, as Stanley put it, 'the mutability natural to the character of that prelate',[7] soon lost his zeal for the project, and he became mightily disturbed when Stanley got out of hand and invited Unitarian and Roman Catholic divines to have a part in the Revision. John Newman, however, 'courteously refused, on the ground of his not having paid any special attention to the subject'.[8]

That sort of layman who delights in being consulted got vastly excited about it all. Gladstone, for example, noted with pride in a letter to Shaftesbury that 'in 1870 the Pope and his myrmidons, when they are apparently bold enough for most things, yet have not attempted either this or the handling of the Greek text'.[9]

Once the Company had been selected for the New Testament revision other business was as expeditiously arranged, including the celebration of a Communion before the first session. The idea of such a service was first bruited by Westcott in a letter to Dean Stanley only a fortnight before the event. Stanley told the Lower House of Convocation on 17 February 1871, that he had 'had misgivings about holding the service' but he had conferred with the Bishop of

---

[6] Pusey to Liddon, 30 May 1870, *Pusey*, IV, 230. It was not, therefore, 'the presence of the Unitarian at holy communion' which 'prevented the revisers having among their members Dr Pusey' as Professor Owen Chadwick has suggested, cf. *The Victorian Church*, Part 2, p. 46 (1970).

[7] STANLEY, 'The Revised Version of the New Testament', posthumous article in *Times*, 20 July 1881.

[8] Ibid.

[9] Gladstone to Shaftesbury, R. G. WILBERFORCE, *Life of Bishop Wilberforce*, 1882, III, 349.

Gloucester and Bristol, the acting chairman of the company 'and it was with his consent'[10] and on the suggestion of the Cambridge scholars that invitations were issued to the service. Stanley insisted that since the Communion was to ask a blessing on the work of the Revision all the Company should be invited. Westcott reported this to Lightfoot:

> Stanley heartily accepted the proposal of Holy Communion if the *notice* is sent to all. To this I see no objection. He will celebrate, and with him all the responsibility rests. We at least (and, I think, *Scotch* Presbyterians) can have no scruple in availing ourselves of the offered service. You think so too, I hope.[11]

It was typical of Westcott that he should emphasise that Stanley was to take all responsibility for the Communion, that he should speak of a notice rather than an invitation being sent to the Company, and that the established Scots should somehow appear to him more his sort of Christian than other Presbyterians. Westcott's son remarked later that he did not suppose that his father had contemplated 'that one who could not join in the Nicene Creed would desire to communicate',[12] and I think he judged his father rightly. But famously, one such unorthodox person did communicate. Dr Vance Smith, the learned Unitarian minister of St Saviour Gate Chapel in York, knelt next to the unfortunate Bishop of Gloucester and Bristol.

The effect of the Communion service on those who attended seems to have been hugeous. Hort wrote next day to his wife:

> It was one of the great services of one's life, as you may imagine; very quiet, but singularly impressive . . . Stanley alone officiated. We all knelt in a single row round the grave of Edward VI, almost upon it.[13]

and two weeks later he was as enthusiastic in his description of the day to a friend:

---

[10] *Chronicles of Convocation*, Canterbury Province, 1871, at date cited.
[11] Westcott to Lightfoot, 17 June 1870, *Life of Westcott*, I, 391.
[12] *Life of Westcott*, I, 392.
[13] Hort to his wife, 23 June 1870, A. F. HORT, *Life and Letters of Fenton Anthony Hort*, 1896, II, 135.

The Communion in Henry VII's Chapel was one of those few great services which seem to mark a point in one's life. There was nothing to disturb its perfect quietness and solemnity; everything was kept out except the place, the occasion, the communicants, and the service itself; and these combined together into a marvellous whole. The two sessions of work which followed carried on, rather than disturbed, the impression.[14]

and a further two weeks later, when the agitation was beginning to sound forcefully against the Communion he wrote to John Ellerton:

. . . what one goes back to again and again is that marvellous Communion in Henry VII's Chapel, for which we have to thank first Westcott and then Stanley. Its quiet solemnity with all the combinations of accompaniments is never to be forgotten. It is, one can hardly doubt, the beginning of a new period in Church history. So far the angry objectors have reason for their astonishment. But it is strange that they should not ask themselves what other alternatives were preferable, and what is really lost to any great interest by the union, for once, of all English Christians around the altar of the Church. . . .[15]

And Westcott in a letter to Hort that summer remarked:

I don't think that that wonderful Communion will be lost.[16]

Stanley, on the Bishop of Gloucester and Bristol's suggestion, inserted a description of the Communion in the *Times*, 27 June 1870, which after listing the various Christian bodies represented in the Company speculated rather prematurely:

. . . it is surely not without a hopeful significance that neither on the side of the Church nor of Nonconformity was there any 'religious difficulty' raised as to joint participation on such an occasion in the most venerable and sacred ordinance of the Christian religion.

[14] 7 July 1870, ibid., II, 136.
[15] 19 July and 10 August 1870, ibid., II, 139.
[16] 7 July 1870, *Life of Westcott*, I, 393.

and, he went on to say of the Henry VII Chapel:

> it may be doubted whether it has ever been the scene of an event
> so fraught, if rightly considered, with possibilities of kindly
> intercourse between jarring factions, and pacific solution of par-
> ring problems as that which happened, silent and unobserved, on
> the 22nd June.

Such possibilities were not realised. Westcott's son was able to say of
the huge row which followed this announcement of what had
happened that 'this unhappy controversy is fortunately by this time
ancient history and may well be forgotten',[17] but though the conflict
which then arose among Anglicans does not make so much noise in
the histories of nineteenth century church matters as the squabbles
about Tract XC, or Gorham or even Voisey, I think it rivalled in
claim upon our present interest only by that great debate engen-
dered at the publication of *Essays and Reviews*.

In the higgledy-piggledy summer of 1870 the Oberammergau
Christus was called up for military service, Pio Nono saw the years
of Peter and was declared infallible, 'Women's Rights' received
three derisory cheers at an Oxford Convocation, Professor Tyndall
at the Liverpool meeting of the British Association spoke of the
'Scientific uses of the Imagination', the conservationists were
worried about what the Commissioner of Works was doing in the
New Forest, the House of Commons debated an Education Bill
designed to prescribe in the new Rate-Supported Schools such
religious training 'as shall render it unnecessary for the child of any
Christian parents to claim the protection of a Conscience Clause',
the Court of Arches allowed the Puseyesque doctrines of the Revd
W. J. Bennett to be within the pale of Anglican eucharistic teaching,
there were riots in Cork and a 'Peace Demonstration' in London,
and Charles Wood wrote to the Archbishop of Canterbury voicing
the Christian Union's complaint of the complicity of the episcopate
in the Westminster Scandal.

While rejoicing that a Socinian should have recited the Nicene
Creed at the Abbey Service, Wood felt it 'a dishonour to Our Lord
and Saviour of the gravest and most emphatic character' that 'the
most sacred privilege of Church Communion should be conceded to

17 Ibid., I, 392.

persons who deny the Church's characteristic doctrines'.[18] He trusted that Tait would assure the world that the Abbey authorities could in no degree claim the approval or sanction of His Grace.

Wood's letter was concerned with orthodox doctrine and the significance of a man's membership of the Church. He objected specifically to the admission of a Socinian *as a Socinian*. But he confused his doctrinal objection by a reference to discipline, and it was rather with this accidental reference than with the substantial objection that the Archbishop concerned himself.

On 2 July Tait replied to Wood, noting first that his letter opened up 'a very difficult and important question, viz. how far the Clergy of the National Established Church of England are bound to admit all persons who present themselves to take part in the Church's services unless some legal disqualification can be proved'. Though he seems to be taking his stand upon English Law the Archbishop's letter goes on to show that he was thinking of the Laws of the Church:

The Rubrics prefixed to the Service for Holy Communion state at considerable length who are to be repelled from the Holy Table and I doubt whether in the terms of these rubrics you would find any exclusion such as you seem to contemplate, while the ninth Canon, speaking of persons who "separate themselves from the Communion of Saints" . . . "accounting Christians who are conformable to the doctrines, government, rules and ceremonies of the Church of England to be profane and unmeet for them to join with in Christian profession" seems not to apply to the case of those who voluntarily come forward and express a desire to join in the Church's worship. The eleventh Canon, if it should be considered as bearing on such cases in the present state of the Law would have a far wider application than your letter indicates.

The legal realities having been made clear, the Archbishop went on to talk of the proper modes of complaint and administration:

I have no hesitation in telling you that I was in no way consulted

---

[18] Wood to Tait, 29 June 1870, *Tait Papers*: Official Letters, Canterbury, R-W, 168, Lambeth Palace Library (subsequently referred to as *Tait Papers*); published with Tait's reply, *Times*, 9 July 1870. I am grateful to the Archbishop of Canterbury and the Trustees of Lambeth Palace Library for permission to publish extracts from the Tait Papers.

by the Ordinary of Westminster Abbey on the subject to which you allude. Your letter, therefore, would perhaps have been more fitly addressed to him than to me.[19]

And coming at last from behind these useful stalking horses Tait allows himself the freedom of opinion so far as to join with Wood in rejoicing at the participation in the communion of persons 'of whom this could scarcely have been expected', he notes that he would scarcely have thought it right to repel 'as you seem to desire' anyone who wished to join in the service, and especially one who 'had been thought fit to take part in the great religious work of revising the present version of the Holy Scriptures'.

Wood had most evidently not been interested in effecting an individual refusal of communion but in obtaining a general condemnation of invitations to the unorthodox being issued by Anglican authorities. The Archbishop, having first made it appear that Wood was disappointed that an unseemly commotion had not been made at King Edward's grave, transferred the discussion of participation from communion to revision:

> I myself trust that fellowship in this work may draw together many who have hitherto been kept asunder, and I shall not be surprised if Unitarians, as well as others, are greatly benefited by being associated in this attempt faithfully to interpret the written Word of God, undertaken as the Service to which you allude shows it to be, in a spirit of earnest prayer for Divine guidance.[20]

The Archbishop's letter was thus a clever piece of work which put the Christian Union in a false position and removed the debate from the sensitive area of eucharistic theology to the generally agreed ground of scriptural translation. It was evident that no sane man would ally himself with those who opposed the participation of a Unitarian in the scholarly activity of revision. At least it was so evident at the beginning of the debate.

Though Tait declined a doctrinal discussion with Wood the need for such discussion remained, and it was appropriate that such an exploration of theological matters should have been attempted when Convocation met early in July.

[19] Tait to Wood, 2 July 1870, *Tait Papers.*
[20] Ibid.

On 5 July in response to the Bishop of Rochester's presenting the Christian Union petition drawing their Lordships' attention to 'an ostentatious abandonment of the last shreds of ancient discipline' and 'a scandal . . . fraught with possibilities of disaster', the bishops addressed themselves to the Westminster Communion.[21]

Confronted by such a petition the Bishop of Gloucester and Bristol denounced the manner and denied the fact, designating the petition as 'fundamentally uncharitable' and 'in many respects utterly mistaken'. He then offered his own quite different account of what had gone on, acknowledging that 'those who knelt reverently round the tomb of Edward VI did not trouble themselves to ask Pharisaical questions about who might be kneeling beside them', and asserting that 'the Church of England did not require a man to ask who was about to receive with him'. Here the Bishop made an important contribution to the debate. His affirmation that to question a communicant about his belief would mar the whole principle of communion was made an instrument in the interpretation of the law. He brought the arguments of law and doctrine together and made it impossible for the bishops to seek a refuge in the one without attending to the other.

The Bishop of Ely, who had helped Gloucester out of his diary-muddle that fateful day, came again to his support. Sensing perhaps that the Unitarian was not the only unwelcome communicant, he declared that if any Non-conformist presented himself at Communion while he was administering he should certainly not object to him, because he had not yet learnt that Non-conformists were not Christians. This charitable intervention led the bishops from the important questions of whether Non-Conformists, and Unitarians, and indeed all other Englishmen, churchmen, sectarians, and quiet atheists, were properly to be counted members of the liturgical community of the National Church.

The House was recalled to its dogmatic duty on the late arrival of Bishop Wilberforce who had been at the marrying of Lady C. Nelson. He was horrified to discover that the Bishops of Gloucester, Ely and Salisbury were all unrepentant, that even Bath and Wells

---

[21] The account of the debates in Convocation which follows is extracted from *Chronicles of Convocation*, Canterbury Province, 1870, and from the more emotive reports of the proceedings in the *Times* for the date following.

'was thoroughly unsound', and that the rest of the Bishops thought they had justified themselves once they had shown 'that they had no part in sending the invitation' and that they had 'had no means of right of inquiry who were admitted by the authorities of the Abbey to the Communion'.[22] Wilberforce, however bizarre his concept or the Christian Church, was at least aware enough of realities to appreciate that there was something more to discuss than who was responsible for the arrangements of the Westminster service. No other Bishop at this time seems to have had any clear idea as to what he thought had happened when an Anglican invited a Unitarian to share in the Communion and the Unitarian accepted the invitation.

In the Lower House a memorial on the matter was dismissed without a hearing and on the next day, 6 July, the general tone of the debate was to favour the Westminster proceedings. Archdeacon Groome of Suffolk was so little caring for the objectors that he gave notice of a resolution that 'His Grace the President be requested to convey the thanks of the Lower House of Convocation to the Very Rev. the Dean of Westminster for granting the use of the King Henry VII Chapel for religious service to the committee appointed for the revision of the authorised translation of the Bible.'[23] Stanley, when the resolution came up next day, amid those chuckles and applauses that customarily accompanied his interventions, asked that the vote of thanks not be put for 'he was quite satisfied with what he had done' and he wanted no other approval than the approval of his own conscience.[24]

It became quite clear later that Stanley's charming waver had been, as he admitted to Sandford, an instrument of policy by which he prevented the Lower House debating the propriety of the Communion.[25]

From the muddle of the Upper House and the diplomacy of the Lower House debates it can only be inferred that there was not among the clergy at this time overmuch concern for the theological significance of the Communion.

Nor were the gentlemen of the religious press greatly interested in

[22] Wilberforce to Liddon, 16 July 1870, *Wilberforce*, IV, 352.
[23] *Chronicles of Convocation* at date cited.
[24] Ibid.
[25] Stanley to Sandford, 28 July 1870, *Tait Papers*.

nice theological argument. Neither so careful of law as the Bishop of Gloucester and Bristol, nor so generous of mind as the Bishop of Ely, they made a deal of sacristy noise. The *Church Herald* of 6 July warned its readers that the Communion 'may be taken as a deliberate embodiment of insult and defiance to the whole of Catholic Christendom, and to the ancient faith of the Christian world . . . a Presbyterian, Baptist, Independent – these are bad enough; but a Socinian!'. And the *Church Times*, ambitious perhaps to be thought the ecclesiastical thunderer, declared no less sensationally: 'The invitation of the Dean of Westminster to the heretics and schismatics . . . to participate in the Holy Sacrament of the Altar is the deepest insult that has ever been offered to the Church of England', Stanley had 'cast pearls before swine and given that which is most holy to the dogs'. All argument was foreclosed with the sentence: 'There can be no possible defence for such an act of desecration as the administration of the Holy Communion to Presbyterians, Baptists and Unitarians.' The popular religious clamour was thus neatly directed against those who were represented as attacking the honour of the Anglican Church. This was evidently supposed a more popular cause than the Christian Union's concern for the honour of Christ.

The first debate in Convocation and in the country had thus been concluded without any public recognition of the peculiarly theological issues that divided men in their responses to the Westminster Communion.

On 8 July, Wood wrote again to the Archbishop. He and his friends had not, he said, expressed an opinion 'on the fact that Bishops and Priests should have communicated with those who are, I suppose, whatever excuse may be made for them, in a state of schism', or on the duty of repelling men from the Altar, 'believing as we do that the responsibility of communicating is everywhere thrown upon the communicant himself', still less were they protesting about violations of canons or rubrics. 'The point which chiefly distresses us and to which we did call Your Grace's attention is that persons rejecting the claims of the Church, including a Socinian, should be *invited* to receive Communion at his hands by a Clergyman of the Church of England.'[26] The Christian Union

[26] Wood to Tait, 8 July 1870, *Tait Papers*.

wanted simply that the Archbishop contradict the statements spread abroad that the Church approved such an invitation.

To Wood's effort to keep the discussion within doctrinal terms Tait replied tersely that he had nothing to 'communicate in this matter than is already set forth in my letter of the 2nd'.[27] And if Wood had been a decent sensitive chap there the correspondence would have ceased. But he wrote again on 9 July. He received a reply from Archdeacon Sandford telling him not to bother His Grace again. Sandford rehearsed Tait's arguments again, making the objectors seem anxious for a brawl at each parish communion, obscuring the question of the invitation, and praising the Unitarian's sincerity, and he added as his own opinion that once the Westminster Service had been decided upon the Dean 'had no other course open to him than to issue a general note to all who were to be engaged in the work of revision'.[28]

Tait had earlier suggested that the Communion was entirely within the law. On 11 July, *The Times* published a letter from Vance Smith claiming that 'every Englishman is, *ipso facto*, legally a member of the Church of England' having 'the right to present himself at Communion if he should wish to do so', and that no 'minister of that Church has the right to exclude him (not being excommunicate) on any ground whatever, except that of practical and notorious immorality'. Many English Christians did not, he said, avail themselves of their right not because they acknowledged some legal bar to their communicating but because they esteemed the Anglican services not 'truly conformed to New Testament models'. Vance Smith made it quite plain that he had only taken his rightful place at the Communion after the most pressing invitation of the Dean.

After the publication of this letter Wood wrote again to Sandford:

Has it really come to this – that a Unitarian should be able to write to *The Times* – saying that he understood himself to be invited to receive Holy Communion in Westminster Abbey – that he went – refusing to say the Nicene Creed – considering the Holy Communion nothing but a memorial and the service in the prayer

---

[27] Tait to Wood, 9 July 1870, *Tait Papers*.
[28] Sandford to Wood, 11 July 1870, *Tait Papers*.

book unscriptural – and that still the Bishops should make no sign.[29]

At the first discussion in the Upper House the Bishop of Salisbury had said plainly that there had been no invitation to the Communion, and Sandford had made the same point. Now Vance Smith had asserted a distinct invitation. Wood told Sandford:

> I do not think it could be said before with truth that no invitation had been sent to the Unitarian, since his letter there can be no doubt how the matter presented itself to his mind – Is it too much to ask – that the Archbishop – or someone in authority on his behalf – should say that they disapprove of such an invitation – and disallow the Holy Communion being given to those who are not validly baptised and desirous of being confirmed.[30]

Obviously the invitation threw responsibility on the representative of the Church. The whole design of the official account was called in question.

Sandford had relied on the assurance of Ellicott of Gloucester and Bristol that 'no distinct formal invitation whatever' was issued to anyone, but the Archdeacon had the sense to realise that the adjectives might conceal the sending of some sort of invitation. He wrote at once to Stanley to check this.

Stanley had other news to offer Sandford than the simple reassurance he required. He told Sandford that the Bishop of Winchester himself had 'given his full assent' to the Unitarian's participation in the work, and that Vance Smith had in fact been baptised in the Church of England 'and for all that I know, might have been confirmed', and he added 'as to his opinions, it would be a very strange theory which should compel me to refuse the Communion to Sir Isaac Newton, Milton and Channing'. But Stanley confirmed that he had sent a distinct invitation to each of the Non-Conformists and the Unitarian.[31]

At the news of Vance Smith's baptism Sandford wrote happily to Wood and in his excitement glossed the invitation as a simple

[29] Wood to Sandford, 15 July 1870, *Tait Papers*.
[30] Ibid.
[31] Stanley to Sandford, 18 July 1870, *Tait Papers*.

advertisement of the service.[32] Wood's reply was a reiteration of his complaint that the doctrinal aspect of the affair was being ignored and he asked 'as a mere layman' to be granted five minutes of the Archbishop's time.[33] He may have gained his audience and been appeased, at any rate he does not appear again in Tait's correspondence on this matter. His place is taken by the memorialist T. T. Carter who had gathered a sample 1,529 or 1,530 signatures 'from his acquaintances' to protest the Church's silence on the Westminster scandal.[34]

Vance Smith, learning of this new petition, wrote to Tait in just the terms he needed to keep the petitioners at bay.[35] Vance Smith declared that he did not deny 'the divinity of our Lord' as he found it declared in the New Testament. And he refused to allow Carter and his acquaintances to be the arbiters of orthodoxy:

> It is, indeed, probable that I differ from the Memorialists, as they from me, in regard to what the New Testament declares on several important points, but for this I am in no way answerable to them.

He had attended the Communion 'in no other spirit than that of a reverent and earnest desire to join in a sacred rite of our religion – one which I considered to be especially becoming in the particular circumstances under which it was celebrated'. He presented a theological challenge to the protesters by assuming a definition of the Church made in terms of those who celebrate 'in remembrance and in confession of our common Head', and not in terms of any particular interpretation of the work of Christ. He proffered indeed a higher doctrine of the Communion than that which Wood and Carter had presented:

> Some persons, it is true, regard the Communion rite as especially expressive of faith in the doctrines of the particular Church in which it happens to be administered. I do not so regard it; nor do I think that any person, or any body of persons, has authority to so

---

[32] Sandford to Wood, 21 July 1870 (rough draft), *Tait Papers*.
[33] Wood to Sandford, 1 August 1870, *Tait Papers*.
[34] Carter to Tait, 11 August 1870, *Tait Papers*.
[35] Smith to Tait, 4 August 1870, *Tait Papers*.

lower the character of the Service and make it, as it were, the mere symbol of their own special form of Christian belief. The Communion is for me raised above this kind of sectarianism, and is distinctively expressive, not of faith in any humanly defined doctrines whatever, but of Faith in Christ and of discipleship and allegiance to Him.

Vance Smith characterised the tactics of the memorialists as 'unworthy of the nineteenth century and suitable only to the darkest times of papal usurpation'.

The Archbishop communicated his thanks for this forearming against Nicene rattlers, remarking that Vance Smith's confession of faith would greatly assist him in making any 'answers that I may be called upon to give to various memorials which I hear are to be addressed to me'.[36]

So when Carter's memorial arrived Tait was ready for it. The Archbishop blandly ignored all the evidence for a distinct invitation being sent, merely remarking with a seeming simplicity that must have annoyed the High Churchmen that 'had he not previously refused to act such a notice would I presume have been sent to the Eminent Roman Catholic Divine who was also requested to serve on the Committee'. But, having reviewed the legal arguments he presented before, Tait went on to elaborate an interpretation of the law which would offer a way into new relations with other Churches:

While I hail any approaches that are made to it by the Ancient Churches of the East, and by the great Lutheran and reformed Churches of the Continent of Europe, and while I lament that the Roman Church by the fault of their leaders are becoming further removed at a time when all the rest of Christendom is drawing closer together, I rejoice heartily that so many of our countrymen at home, usually separated from us, have been able devoutly to join with us in this holy rite, as the inauguration of the solemn work which they have in hand. I hope that we may see in this Holy Communion an omen of a time not far distant when our unhappy divisions may disappear, and, as we serve one Saviour and profess to believe one gospel, we may all unite more closely in

[36] Tait to Smith, 6 August 1870, *Tait Papers.*

the discharge of the great duties which our Lord has laid on us of preparing the World for his Second Coming.[37]

When Carter, in a further letter,[38] pressed the claims of present discipline instead of acknowledging the eschatological hope Tait had expressed he received a curt note in reply.[39] And Tait was sharper still in reply when the Archbishop of Capetown wrote on behalf of the Church of South Africa of 'the dishonour to our Lord and the compromise of our whole Communion'.[40]

A reading of these letters in the Tait archives at Lambeth Palace suggests that the official representatives of the Church began by thinking they could deal with a theological question by purely legal instruments, and that the pressures of the High Church memorialists and Vance Smith's account of the Eucharist forced the Archbishop to consider carefully what he meant when he spoke of the Church. Tait's sense of Christ at last allowed him to offer a theologically more generous account of the Church than those who had opened the doctrinal debate. He moved through the course of his replies from a reliance on the twenty-seventh Canon as a criterion of communion and on gentlemanly courtesy as a criterion for intercommunion, through talk of sincerity and abomination, to the facing of questions of orthodoxy and ecumenism, to a realisation then of his office as a call to Christian responsibility in England, and at last to a sense of the eschatological value of the Christian mission.

At the start of the summer's correspondence Tait might have defended his attitudes in conformity with the old 'healing practice' of communion for eighteenth-century Non-Conformists, at the end he was able to resist every objector not by recourse to legal or dogmatic instruments of argument but by an appeal to the realities of faith. The controversy shows a man in the making. He may indeed have come to a proper enough understanding of the nature of the Church to lead Anglicans into a new sense of their identity and vocation among the Churches in England.

Certainly not a few Anglicans were ready to be shown a way into

---

[37] Tait to Carter, 11 August 1870, *Tait Papers*.

[38] Carter to Tait, 15 August 1870, *Tait Papers*, published in *Times*, 23 August 1870.

[39] Tait to Carter, 18 August 1870, *Tait Papers*.

[40] Capetown to Canterbury, 27 September, Canterbury to Capetown, 1 October 1870, *Tait Papers*.

closer relation with other Christians. A number of signs were given that summer of a rising ecumenical hope. The evening before the Revisers' Communion High Church young clergymen, some gentlemen of the laity, and a large number of ladies of whom, as *The Times* correspondent said, 'it would be no libel to say that they were "mature",' met to hear Mr Ambrose Phillipps De L'Isle speak on 'the reunion of the three great branches of the Christian Church',[41] and on the day of the Communion itself Anglicans of a different temper heard Mr T. Salt read a paper on 'the future position of the Church of England' in which he urged his hearers to work that the Church might become 'an institution of larger sympathies' recalling those Dissenters who had been estranged by persecution and apathy.[42]

Tait was, however, too sick a man to provide the proper leadership for such hopes. He summoned energy enough to signify his approval of the Revisers by making a visit to the New Testament Company the first engagement of his convalescence,[43] but he had to delegate his presidency of Canterbury Convocation to the unimaginative Bishop of London, who had no sense at all of the demand for a renewal of Anglican self-understanding as the Church of Englishmen. And it was precisely on this matter that *The Times* voiced the general disappointment at the proceedings of the Upper House. Commenting on the episcopate's fuss over the Vatican Council's ignoring of their orders, *The Times* said that 'Bishops seem to be inveterate legitimists' with 'a lingering feeling that Roman prelates are "the real thing".' They should be concentrating their attention not upon 'the effete Church of Rome' but upon 'the living and active bodies of Nonconformist Christians in their own country, . . . and by a singular coincidence, at the very moment when they are thus making advances towards members of the Roman Communion some of them are found to express regret at the recent admission of Nonconformists to the administration of the Sacrament in Westminster Abbey'.[44]

The Bishops at the reconvening of Convocation, 14 February

[41] Cf. *Times*, 22 June 1870.
[42] Cf. *Times*, 23 June 1870.
[43] Tait spent an hour with the Company, 13 July 1870.
[44] Cf. *Times*, editorial, 12 July 1870.

1871, were not, however, disposed to reconsider their theological attitudes towards others. They were more concerned to recover their reputation with certain noisy sections of their own people. The debates of this session disappoint any expectation of leadership in Christian understanding. The same old sentences recur, and this time they are accompanied by undignified squeals disclaiming responsibility for past actions.[45]

The Bishop of Winchester was anxious to undo the effects of his own fifth resolution of the previous March. It had never, he complained, occurred to him that it could be used to cover an invitation to a Unitarian. He was all the more urgent because he found that all religious men agreed with him in demanding that none but the orthodox should have a seat at the Revision. 'For the honour of truth itself his removal from the company is necessary.'

Everyone looked at poor Ollivant of Llandaff whose vote had obtained the election of the offending sectary. He scampered for cover, declaring that he was often too deaf to realise what was going on, and had been 'somewhat surprised' when the Bishop of Gloucester and Bristol had informed him that he had voted for this gentleman. On this introduction of his name Ellicott thought he might have a chance to get out from under his earlier defence of the Communion. If Ollivant had voted under a misapprehension then of course Vance Smith must be removed. He was not to get off so lightly. The Bishop of Ely remembered that it was Ellicott who had proposed the Unitarian's name at the selection meeting. Ellicott at once denied the allegation and remarked that there was absolutely no doubt at all that the Bishop of Ely had voted for Vance Smith's inclusion in the company. At this unfortunate reference the Bishop of Ely shifted a little and grumbled that no one could have foreseen what would happen in Henry VII's Chapel.

Though not equally enthusiastic for Wilberforce's present motion the Bishops of Lincoln, Norwich, Salisbury and Exeter agreed to vote for Vance Smith's exclusion. Only the Bishop of Peterborough ventured the inconsiderate question how a man's being a Unitarian could disqualify him as a translator. 'If he were an honest man the fact of his being a Unitarian would not prevent him giving an honest

---

[45] The account of this debate is extracted from *Chronicle of Convocation*, Canterbury Province, at the dates cited.

opinion. If he were not an honest man he had no business there at all.' Rescinding the resolution would, he said, simply make the bishops look ridiculous.

At this the bishops decided it was time they went home to their lodgings.

In the Lower House the Dean of Westminster had prevented Dr Jelf and Chancellor Massingberd obtaining a conservative vote and the debate was adjourned there too.

Next day the Bishops found themselves again caught up in the Revision affair. Rochester was still worried about 'the injured honour of their Lord' which cried for 'reparation'. Bangor thought they would really have to start the whole selection of revisers again. St Asaph scurried back and forth declaring that the House must keep faith with Vance Smith, and then again they ought not to break faith with the great Head of the Church Himself, they knew Vance Smith to be honest and scholarly and an excellent choice but then again he ought not to be among the company. Why not hold the matter over for later discussion?

Winchester was amazed by all this. Should they say that the bishops had debated the matter and that they could not make up their minds on the doctrine of their Lord's Godhead?

This question scared the Bishops. They agreed 10 to 4 with 4 abstentions to his motion that 'in the judgement of the House it is not expedient that any person who denies the Godhead of the Lord Jesus Christ should be invited to assist in the revision of the Scriptures; and that it is also the judgement of the House that any such person now a member of either Company of Revisionists should cease to act therewith'.

The Bishop of London, presiding in Tait's absence, for the Archbishop was still unwell, remarked that since no one had intended Roman Catholics or Socinians to be covered by the original resolution they might have left the Companies alone in reliance upon their more careful administration in the future. If anyone wanted by a side wind to get rid of the Committee of Revision the passing of Wilberforce's motion should have achieved his object. He was not alone in this gloomy opinion.

Next day, Thursday, 16 February, Bishop Thirlwall of St David's waited only for the Bishops of Ely and Lincoln to decide whether they should speak of Dean Stanley's 'invitation' or of his 'notice' to the Unitarian before giving the discussion a sudden twist. At their March discussions of a scheme of Revision he had seconded the original fifth resolution because he thought the inclusion of some Dissenters among the Revisers 'an essential condition of our success'. If the Bishops now asserted that certain theological tenets, 'call them heresy or whatever name they pleased', rendered a man's scholarship unavailing for the work, then he would have to register his total disagreement by resigning from the Revision Company. Though he later was persuaded to withdraw his resignation Thirlwall was reckoned by Stanley to have 'contributed more than any single person to the harmonious retention of the principles on which they had begun',[46] and though Stanley himself has a claim to that eminence, certainly Thirlwall's intervention changed the whole direction of the debate in the Upper House. That honest indignation could go so far took most of the bishops quite by surprise and, with the Bishop of Gloucester and Bristol recovering courage enough to second him, Thirlwall had unanimous support for his resolution:

That, notwithstanding the restriction introduced into the fifth resolution, this House does not intend to give the slightest sanction or countenance to the opinion that the members of the Revision Companies ought to be guided by any other principle than a desire to bring the translation as near as they can to the sense of the original texts, but, on the contrary, regards it to be their duty to keep themselves as much as possible on their guard against any trace of preconceived opinions or theological tenets in the revision of the work.

However, while this turn about was being made in the Upper House the Lower House received the previous day's work from the Bishops. Despite Dr Jelf's push for conservative orthodoxy, Stanley brought the House to agree to the return of Winchester's motion with a request that the Bishops postpone any decision on any matter connected with the Revision until the Committee presented the finished work.

---

[46] STANLEY, *Times*, article on 20 July 1881.

On Friday, 17 February, the Bishops accepted this way out of all their difficulties and, after some further 'discussion and pleasantry',[47] they all went home.

Those who would maintain that it is unjust and unwise to expect theological leadership from those entrusted with a pastoral care, and that it is university divines that we should consult at such times, can derive small satisfaction from the activities of Anglican scholars at this crisis. Of course those careful exegetes concerned in the Revision made no claim to theological competence, that was, as Westcott warned Hort, 'wholly out of our province',[48] but it is remarkable how easily Lightfoot and Westcott held themselves apart from the theological scuffles of their Church. Hort urged Lightfoot that he might 'do the greatest good by discussing the matter, and telling elementary facts *coram populo*, in the tone and with the authority that belong to few except yourself',[49] but Lightfoot did not care to take a public part in the business. So Hort wrote to Westcott urging that someone say something: 'Are you sure that in the turn things are now taking it is right to keep total silence?'[50] Westcott, though he did not think he ever was more grieved and amazed as at the Bishops' failure to keep faith, told Hort that he had freed his soul by writing to Bishop Magee after the rescinding of the fifth resolution.[51] Once the Lower House had put an end to the debate Westcott could write to Hort:

I have no doubt that our duty is to say nothing more now. Lightfoot quite agrees with me.[52]

Hort, though the most intelligent and sensitive of the three, always looked to the others for leadership, and Westcott and Lightfoot were content to repeat their cosy performance at the *Essays and Reviews* crisis, telling one another again that they had been so right to keep quiet.

[47] Cf. *Times* report, 18 February 1870.
[48] Westcott to Hort, 1 July 1870, *Westcott*, I, 393.
[49] Hort to Lightfoot, 1 September 1870, *Hort*, II, 140.
[50] Hort to Westcott, date unknown, summer 1870, *Hort*, 140.
[51] Westcott to Hort, 16 February 1871 and Westcott to his wife, same date.
[52] Westcott to Hort, 22 February 1871, *Westcott*, I, 395.

Since Stanley, 'the cause of the evil', as Wilberforce described him,[53] alone among those Anglicans placed well enough to make an effective defence of that principle of communion which the Bishop of Gloucester and Bristol had once declared, possessed the strength and will and wit to speak out, and since his speaking-out effectively silenced the objectors in the Lower House, his mode of argument must be of interest.

Stanley was not a theologian and the more exact Jowett felt often uneasy at his friend's happy deployment of sign and symbol and image, but Stanley's enthusiasm was communicative. He rejoiced in the freedom he experienced through his reading of the New Testament and his hope for others was that they might become aware of the spring of divinity in the language. 'Why', someone asked F. D. Maurice, 'are things tolerated in Stanley which would not be pardoned in anyone else'? 'Because', was the reply, 'Stanley has done more to make the Bible a reality in the homes of the people than any living man.'[54] And it was in intuitive appreciation of the Revision as a means of enlarging the biblical faith of the people that Stanley celebrated the Communion. For him scholarly matters were not of huge importance. Hort remarked Stanley's fighting 'for every antique phrase which can be defended'[55] at the sessions of the New Testament Company. What Stanley wanted of the Revision was that it would produce a version of the Scriptures which would set the imagination tingling with an excitement akin to that of its original lively language.

He termed this language 'parabolic'. Admittedly oriental and suited to rude, childlike minds, it was yet the dominical language. 'It was the language in which profound doctrines were most likely to be preserved for future ages, distinct from the dogmatic or philosophical turns of speech, which, whilst aiming at forms which shall endure for eternity, are often the most transitory of all, often far more transitory than the humblest tale, or the simplest figure of speech.'[56]

It was the unhappiness of western and sophisticated men in the past to take their example from Jesus' first insensitive hearers, and to

---

[53] Wilberforce to Liddon, 16 July 1870, *Wilberforce*, III, 352.
[54] Cf. R. P. PROTHERO, *Life and Correspondence of A. P. Stanley*, 1893, I, 477.
[55] Cf. Hort, II, 137.
[56] STANLEY, *Christian Institutions*, 91.

bring down his elevating figures 'to the most vulgar and common-place meaning'.[57] It was the happiness of nineteenth century Englishmen to respond to their vocation to renew religious language. 'No age', he said in his obituary sermon for Charles Dickens, 'has developed like this the gift of speaking in parables, of teaching by "fiction".' He pointed to Dickens' work, 'that long series of stirring tales now closed' as the proclamation of the 'Christian and Evangelical truth' that 'the Rich Man and Lazarus lived very near and close to each other'. Dickens, he said, brought men to understand themselves as a community. 'He helped to blot out the hard line which too often severs class from class, and made Englishmen feel more as one family than they had ever felt before.'[58]

The reality of this family as a kinship before the Father was revealed in that language of Scripture which it was the task of the Revisers to make open, so that in reading Scripture the people might recognise themselves as a people of God. Then they would wish to share as the Revisers had shared already in the celebration of their unity. The Revision and the Revisers' Communion belong in the same order. But it was not an order that Stanley felt he could declare in Convocation.

On the first day of the February 1871 debates Stanley deployed three concepts of keeping faith. He began by appealing to his fellow-clergy's sense of what was due to themselves and their honour in the world. They had agreed long since that scholars should be invited for the Revision without regard 'to whatever nation or religious communion they may belong'. He himself had obtained a change from 'communion' to 'body' so as to include Jews as well as Unitarians. There's overkill for you, as Humpty-Dumpty might have said. There could be no doubt that the House had pledged itself to this resolution. The accommodations of the Companies had been furnished on the faith of this resolution, they have been living, travelling, feeding and entering into contracts on the basis of this pledge. Men had subscribed for the work in the belief that it was to be an ecumenical venture. They would have to keep faith with their generous countrymen of all denominations after so manifest a giving of their word.

[57] Ibid., 92.
[58] Cf. Report in *Times*, 20 June 1870.

Stanley then considered the necessity of keeping faith with the work, of observing the honesties of scholarship. The written Word of God must be honoured with our best obedience and no human theological limit be placed on those who were to serve in the clearer presentation of the divine meaning to men:

> If there be anything which is important in translating the Holy Scriptures it is that the persons concerned in it should not be supposed to be actuated by theological partialities or antipathies of their own.

He came lastly to the orthodox argument that 'the honour of our Lord' demanded that his clergy should break faith:

> Alas! and has it come to this? that our boasted orthodoxy has landed us in this hideous heresy! Is it possible that it should be supposed that we can consent for a moment to degrade the Divine attributes of our Lord Jesus Christ to the level of a mere capricious heathen divinity? Can we believe that anything but dishonour can be conferred on Him by making His name a pretext for inconsistency, for vacillation, for a breach of faith between two contracting parties?

He thus moved his argument of an hour through appeals, as he said, to an assembly of 'English gentlemen', of 'learned scholars', and of 'Christian clergy'.

Thus far Stanley on the first day of debate. His arguments on the second day were concerned not with the defence of a Unitarian having a part in the Revision, but with the participation of Nonconformists and others in the Communion.

He began by making it clear that nothing the House could rule would compel him to act on any other principle than that on which he had acted, and that the House should recognise his freedom within the law. From law he passed properly to authority. He revealed that it was at the suggestion of the Cambridge men and on the advice of the Bishop of Gloucester and Bristol that he had arranged the Communion, and that Bishop Ellicott had known quite well that it was a Unitarian minister who knelt next to him. Only the clamour of ruffians had scared the Bishop from his former self. And he reminded the House that it was the zealous Bishop of Winchester himself who had proposed the original fifth resolution which let in the offending Unitarian. 'I appeal then', he said, 'from the Bishops of Winchester and Gloucester in a panic, to the Bishops of Winchester and Gloucester when they were sober.'

Grumbling amid the laughter that followed this sally, Archdeacon Prevost complained that it was 'very painful to hear persons we so much love and respect so spoken of', and Stanley, who had much experience of the traditionalists' whining for lost courtesies as they sought to impose their opinions, replied with some force: 'It is painful to me to have this resolution brought down for our acceptance.'

The kind of clamour made against the Communion first and then the whole scheme of Revision, he went on, was of interest to them all. It came from those who had in the past by their most ungenerous taunts alienated many Christian brethren from the English Church, and it was directed towards keeping these brethren alienated still. And from this recall to their responsibilities for the unity of Christians in England, Stanley went on to persuade the members of the Lower House to be attentive to the needs of the whole Church. He urged them to consider how it was generally acknowledged that eucharistic communion did not depend upon doctrinal agreement. He presented here an argument which is familiar from later conflicts:

> during the great war which has lately been raging in Europe I have read with delight and edification how German Protestants on the battlefield received the Sacrament at the hands of Roman Catholic priests, and Roman Catholic soldiers received the Sacrament at the hands of Lutheran pastors, no doubt with every conceivable kind of "mental reservation"; but under circumstances which were, I doubt not, to them the most touching and edifying of their lives.

Stanley's references to the existing law, the character of the present opposition, the current unease at the Church's relations with Nonconformists, the incidents of the Franco-Prussian War, have that relation to the immediate case of things which characterised his every argument and practice, but the open-endedness of Stanley's eucharistic action offers no justification at all for Liddon's remark that he had made the Holy Communion 'a mere complement offered to those with whom we differ on fundamental questions, when we wish to be on good terms with them'.[59] For Stanley the Revisers' Communion expressed not an accidental comradeship but the vitality of that fellowship brought about by the love of Christ. And he was assured by his experience that such a vitality was communicated through the Anglican liturgical celebration. He knew himself a better man through his participation in this fellowship. And he supposed that others knew themselves better through their various celebrations: 'to the more enlightened members of all Churches the idea is never altogether absent that the main object of the Eucharist is the moral improvement of the communicants'.[60] It was this object that he discerned to be the motive of the Elizabethan Settlement, 'here at least Luther and Zwingli might feel themselves at one',[61] for here all dogma was demonstrably of secondary importance.

And Stanley read the disputes among Anglicans that kept the nineteenth century Court of Arches so busy as a gradual clearing of the way for the communion of all Englishmen in one eucharist. After the Bennett judgement he wrote in the *Edinburgh Review*:

> Again and again in the course of the decision the toleration of the Lutheran or Roman doctrine of the Eucharist is based on maxims laid down for the toleration of the Calvinist doctrines of Baptism, of the free critical interpretation of the Scriptures, and of the Origenist doctrine of Future punishment. It is the last and crowning triumph of the Christian latitudinarianism of the Church of England.[62]

Yet he seems not have taken any opportunity in the controversy to articulate his appreciation of Christ. And his account of the Westminster Communion was quite unacceptable to those for whom the particularity of the revelation made in Christ demanded the careful response of particular praise. 'The whole controversy', as his first biographer noted, 'was one in which the contending parties never stood on common ground. . . . Hence it was that Stanley made no answer to his critics.'[63]

---

[59] Liddon to Wilberforce, 6 July 1870, BD, I, C 201.
[60] STANLEY, *Christian Institutions*, 141.
[61] Ibid., 112.
[62] *Edinburgh Review*, July 1872.
[63] *Stanley*, II, 220.

To a friend in the summer of 1870 Stanley explained himself quite simply:

> It was with very great thankfulness that I was able to be the means of gathering together in remembrance of our common Lord those various persons, being convinced that in doing so I was obeying His command to His disciples, that they should love one another, and following His example by joining in the same good work, and in the same Holy Communion with persons of the most various opinions.[64]

He found others more concerned at the variety of opinion and less certain of there being anything in common. When on his coming to Westminster he offered the High Church leaders their first opportunity to preach 'our common Christianity' in the Abbey with liberal Anglicans, Pusey replied:

> Alas! I do not know what the common Christianity of myself and Professor Jowett is. I do not know what single truth we hold in common, except that somehow Jesus came from God, which the Mohammedans believe too.[65]

and Liddon sent a similar refusal:

> A legal (rather than a moral) bond retains us within the same communion – or, rather, God's providence does so, I hope and pray, with a view to future unity of conviction, however improbable that may seem at present.[66]

Those who accepted Tait's first appeal to inclusive law and his last expectation of eschatological unity could yet remain divided in their between whiles description of the Church. It became clear during the debate that only within a careful discussion of the nature of the Church could the consideration of intercommunion make sense.

What became clear to others had been clear to Stanley at the outset. And he was willing enough to present a less than complete apologetic in Convocation because he was already articulating his demand for a renewal of the Church's self-understanding in a more significant

[64] Ibid., II, 221.
[65] Pusey to Stanley, 28 February 1864, *Stanley*, II, 163.
[66] Liddon to Stanley, 8 March 1864, *Stanley*, II, 168-9.

controversy. Some members of Convocation might not appreciate a reference of his account of the Revisers' Communion to matters they were discussing on other days, but some certainly did remark a necessary association.

Hort remarked to Westcott that summer that he supposed the stir about Vance Smith to be in part the consequence of the Trinity being thought in England 'the merest dogma'. 'It has been killed, one fears, by that hapless *Quicunque vult*, and its substitution of geometry for life.'[67] Manifestly Stanley understood as well as Hort the connection between the clamour against the Westminster Communion and the fashion, as Pusey would not have said, for reciting the Athanasian Creed. He conducted his theological discussion of intercommunion precisely within a debate about that Creed.

In September 1870 the Ritual Commission of Convocation, of which Stanley was a member, published its Fourth Report. It recommended that something be done about the public recital of the *Quicunque vult*. The dispute which centred on this proposal was necessarily one in which the impulse towards liturgical celebration and the impulse towards credal definition had to be considered together. Tait and Pusey and Stanley were, at the time of the Communion debate, engaged in a wider exploration of what it means to be a Christian.

That those who wished to speak appropriately of the Revisers' Communion could take little interest in the administrative squabbles of the bishops and the isolationist stratagems of the scholars, but rather employed their energies in consideration of the propriety of dogmatic regulation of Church membership, has a significance for the discipline of later discussion of intercommunion, but that, as Scheherazade might have said, is another tale for which there is now no time. . . .

[67] Hort to Westcott, Hort, II, 140.

BIOGRAPHICAL NOTE

JOHN AUSTIN BAKER *is chaplain and fellow of Corpus Christi College, Oxford. He is also a university lecturer in Divinity. He is the author of the widely acclaimed book* The Foolishness of God (*London 1970*).

5 Behaviour as a Criterion of Membership

JOHN AUSTIN BAKER

IN CERTAIN CLEARLY DEFINED CONTEXTS IT IS QUITE simple to talk of behaviour as a criterion of membership. A doctor or solicitor, for example, may be 'struck off' the register of his profession for conduct which experience has shown to be inimical to the proper fulfilment of his professional obligations. From one point of view excommunication from the Christian Church is like this. But a discussion of the grounds for putting people out of communion is perhaps not quite what is wanted in a conference devoted to the subject of Intercommunion – unless we were to consider, let us say, the delicate question whether it is right to make the high walls of doctrinal difference still higher by adding the battlements of teetotalism.

Nevertheless there is a serious point here which cannot be joked or trivialised away. If we look at the matter from the position of a non-Christian, it can be said (and often is): 'You behave like that, *and you call yourself a Christian!*' Our society at any rate, even if it does not often look for positive virtues from Christians, still thinks that there are certain things more shocking in a Christian than in someone else, either because of the element of hypocrisy involved, or because of a feeling, however vaguely formulated, that Christians ought to be better than other people. *C'est leur métier.* And if, looking at the whole Christian community from the outside, it is possible to say that there are certain marks of behaviour, albeit negative ones, by which one can tell whether a person is 'really' a Christian or not, then surely these marks constitute a factual bond? People who satisfy these criteria would seem to be *de facto* members of a common category, regardless of other differences between them.

There are, however, two fairly obvious counters to this move; and in making them we are taken a good deal further into the heart of our tangle. The first is this. There is no way of assessing a community from the outside except by its behaviour. Even the 'atmosphere' of the group comes under this head, since it is generated, admittedly in the subtlest of ways, by the conduct of the members to one another. But from inside everything may look and feel very different. Christianity is, after all, Gospel first and Law only second – and even then Law with its character transformed by Gospel. And one of the fundamental difficulties with which Christians have always been encumbered is that 'Gospel' of its very nature is something you understand only when you are 'inside'; so much so that it is hard to deny that once you have truly understood and accepted (perhaps the two events are spiritually indistinguishable?) the Gospel, you *are* in some sense 'inside'. Hence all the theological ructions about belief and initiation from which we may here legitimately and with relief abstract. The outsider, therefore, identifies the members of the Christian community by the criterion of Law, and not merely of Law but of Law uprooted from its Gospel environment. But the insider knows that the community is created and sustained by the divine 'word' of the Gospel, and that one of the cardinal features of this Gospel is the promise of forgiveness and fellowship to the penitent who himself remains loyal to fellowship by forgiving others. But if this is a constitutive principle of the community, then specific items of behaviour, failures in this or that respect, can never by themselves be a sufficient index whether any given individual is a member or not. This understandably seems pretty scandalous to the outsider. It means that Christians can apparently always rely on eating their cake and having it. The bona fides of a penitent and forgiving disposition can be infallibly checked by none but God. To men they must remain invisible.

The second counter is a more complex one, though easy enouhg to sum up in a straightforward question: can we legitimately speak of a specifically Christian kind of behaviour at all? Is there such a thing as a Christian ethic? or is there only 'ethics', a human science (or art or philosophy)?

Obviously, if there were no overlap at all between the behaviour enjoined upon Christians and that approved by other kinds of people, there would be no problem. The difficulty arises because conduct such as caring for the poor, telling the truth, keeping faith, being temperate in one's appetites is something which a wide variety of people agree in approving, and something which can anyway be argued about on common ground by adherents of many religious faiths or of none at all. Equally there would be no problem if Christianity consisted in, let us say, observing certain rituals and believing certain metaphysical propositions, and involved no ethical positions whatever, Christians being told that ethics was wholly autonomous and that their conduct must be determined by non-religious considerations. But again, this is not the way it is. Christians do not deny the worth of purely pragmatic or philosophical arguments for behaviour; but they also claim that their religion involves them in approving certain kinds of conduct and reprobating others.

One obvious way in which this is done is by appeal to the words and example of Jesus in his earthly life. This, however, can run into serious difficulties. What would Jesus have said, how would he have acted, in the changed circumstances of our world? How did Jesus himself intend his sweeping directives to be used? A man who came to Jesus complaining that his brother would not divide the inheritance with him was simply told to beware of covetousness, and that Jesus had no intention of being a judge or arbitrator. Does this mean that Jesus would have disapproved of Paul's suggestion that the Corinthian Christians have their own courts, to avoid the need to litigate in front of heathen judges? Today, there is the further problem of the historicity of the Gospels. If we adopt a sceptical view, we can never be sure that in appealing to any particular saying we are invoking the authority of Jesus. But equally, if we accept the record lock, stock and barrel, we find ourselves faced not with a tidy system of ethics but with an ethically complex and highly individual person, some of whose ideas may even be repugnant to us. In every one of these situations we have to have recourse to ordinary ethical argumentation independent of specifically Christian assumptions. Indeed, if we did not bring some sort of prior ethical judgement to bear on the tradition about Jesus, we would have no grounds even for considering the question whether he was a good man or not.

Another approach makes a kind of analogical use of statements from the Christian 'story' or Gospel. Thus, St Paul encourages the Corinthian Christians to subscribe to the collection for the Jerusalem church in the words: 'You know the grace of our Lord Jesus Christ, that though he was rich, yet for your sakes he became poor, that you through his poverty might become rich' (2 Cor. 8:9). There are two creative factors in the 'argument' here. First, value-judgements have been injected into something which in a pure metaphysical form would be ethically neutral. If there are to be any pointers in the story for our guidance, then the terms of the story have already to assume that, for example, the enmanning of God involved him in surrendering bliss to embrace sacrifice and suffering, and that his doing so has achieved for us a passage from such things as sin, bondage, fear, and death to holiness, freedom, love, and eternal life. And this, in its turn, presupposes that there are good general human grounds for assessing human existence in a particular way, without reference to the story. Secondly, however, there are certain theological syntheses which would be incompatible with Paul's presentation. The Church early discovered this in the fight against dualism. Later St Augustine, in a well-known passage, tells us how he found that there was no room for this Gospel even in his beloved Platonists: 'But that *the Word was made flesh, and dwelt among us*, I read not there.' The problem is still with us today. But to say this is also to say that there is already a creative ethical component in the very formation of theological systems. The kind of God we believe in is in part dictated by our convictions on good and evil; and these, being prior to faith, must be ones we share at the natural level with other men. In short, which ever way we approach the matter, ordinary human moral discourse is an indispensable precondition of arriving at Christian belief. If that belief is in any way rational, it cannot throw away the ladder by which it has climbed; and so, inevitably, Christian faith and life not only have many moral assumptions and conclusions in common with non-Christian views of existence, but they could never even have come into being if they had not done so. We shall expect, therefore, that Christian distinctiveness will lie rather in selection, in the stress laid on particular models and principles, in the higher value attached to this or that motivation or style of living, than in any great novelty of prescription. And what is perhaps most important of all, we shall be alert to look for these moral stances not simply as lessons drawn from the faith (*didache* deriving from *kerygma*), but as assumptions integral to the faith and helping it to develop in a particular way.

Let us turn first, then, to the question of fundamental theological theory. We are concerned with belief in God as Creator, as the One ultimately responsible for the way things are. We are concerned too with this God as a moral being. But we are also concerned that God's morality shall not be totally alien to our own. When we say that God is good, we want to use that word in a sense which we can accept as proper, even if we do not necessarily embrace it with enthusiasm. 'Good', when applied to God, must not connote what we human beings call 'evil'.

It is generally accepted, even by those who believe strongly in the exercise known as 'natural theology', that arguments for the existence of God inevitably fall short of full demonstration. It is part of our concept of God that he cannot be completely described. It is also necessary, if an argument is to be valid, that what it proves shall be completely described. Hence it must always be logically impossible – as St Thomas well knew when he cunningly framed the Five Ways to construct an argument which will prove the existence of everything which we mean by the word 'God'. The most that rational thought can do is to establish that God is a reasonable hypothesis, and indicate certain things that must be true about him if he is to be truly God.

If then we are to make a proper use of natural theology, respecting its true capabilities and limitations, we shall confine ourselves to answering the following question: if there is a God, what must he be like? Nevertheless, to answer this question by the light of Reason is an absolutely essential exercise even for the adherents of a 'revealed' religion. For if Revelation tells men that God is this or that, even though she tell them three times in the loudest possible voice, if this

'this' or that 'that' is in plain contradiction of the facts of life, then only the silliest and feeblest of mankind will believe her for long. The liberating effect of Revelation, true Revelation, is to verify and confirm what for unaided Reason must always remain a hypothesis. She may do this by adding new knowledge, such as the fact of the Resurrection; but what she does add will always be congruous with the insights of right Reason, and will be properly interpreted only on those terms.

One of the most crucial issues in this interplay of Reason and Revelation is the moral one. Is there any pattern of goodness, which we can call good, which can plausibly be ascribed to the God who made this world of wonder and woe in which we live? I have tried to argue through this one at length elsewhere.[1] Here I can do no more than summarise the conclusion which I there attempted to justify on as wide a basis as possible. If we examine the world as it is, we see that no one moral value or ideal is adequate by itself to make the best of it. We need a complex structure of guiding moral ideas, in which the more obvious goods are practicable only if they are supported by other, less obvious and less attractive ones. Thus, happiness is a good thing; the world provides many ways and opportunities of being happy; God presumably then is in favour of happiness. But, given the way things are, happiness for all depends on the concern of all for the needs and fulfilment of their fellow-men; and this concern is mere emotional indulgence, if it does not have an undergirding of rigorous justice, realism, and truly pragmatic wisdom. But even this is not enough. In the last resort, and not infrequently, wisdom and realism will show us that justice can be created only by seeming injustice – injustice toward ourselves; that we have no way of achieving what we know to be the best save by sacrificing our own happiness, possibly even our own lives. Logically, therefore, the world is ordered in such a way that to maximise happiness we have all of us to be open to self-sacrifice, extreme if need be. An anecdote may be in place here. Once, during a Mission to Oxford University, we held a meeting in College at which four of the Fellows acted as a kind of panel to talk over questions raised by the audience, and to discuss them with them. The four were a

---

[1] *The Foolishness of God*, 1970, Chapters 1–6.

Roman Catholic physicist, an Anglican mathematician, an agnostic philosopher, and myself. Inevitably the problem of suffering came up; and on one aspect of it I put forward suggestions on the lines just described. The philosopher, while agreeing that one could not but whole-heartedly admire those heroic people who gave up everything to help the poor and starving and diseased all over the world, remarked: 'You seem to me to be saying that the world has to be as it is for there to be heroism. Well, what I say is, To hell with heroism, I want happiness.' Quite: so does God. Indeed, 'in thy right hand are pleasures for evermore' (Ps. 16:11). But it would seem, looking at the world, that God, if he exists, does not say, 'To hell with heroism'. His conception of goodness is that we should cultivate both – and so, unless he is just a celestial Duke of Plaza Toro, he is presumably prepared to actualise both in himself, thus presenting metaphysicians with quite a problem. As I said earlier, God's kind of goodness might turn out to be one which we could accept as proper, though we would hardly embrace it with enthusiasm.

There are, of course, many different ways of building this kind of value-structure in detail. For example, the world is dangerous; and many human beings are the sort who find deep happiness in defying danger. This being so, then either they must sacrifice their happiness to spare those who love them agony of mind or premature bereavement; or their loved ones must sacrifice their happiness to let such people be themselves. Or again, there is the painful and costly necessity of forgiveness, which accepts the evil consequences of other men's acts as the raw material from which to build a new good. But why should we? Why should we put the happiness of others before our own? Here Reason is at a stand. It can say: this is the way to attain this end. It cannot prove that we ought to take it. The attitude which embraces these demands as the ultimate goodness, on which all else depends, is a naked choice, a leap in the dark; and this choice, this act of faith, is what all men call Love. Along every logical sequence in morality we come back sooner or later to this point. The world requires it. And so, presumably, if there is a God, he requires it. This is what the word 'good' means when applied to him.

Now, as my philosopher friend rightly pointed out, there can be more than one view about this. We may decide that this is not true goodness. That the world would have been a morally better creation if there had been no intolerable danger, pain, or loss, and so no demand for this sort of virtue. If we hold this view, then we might in theory still believe in a Being who was responsible for the existence and nature of the universe, but he would not be our *God* because he would in our eyes be our moral inferior. Alternatively, if we found such a belief nonsensical, then we would have to conclude that there was no God, no ultimate Being at all, at any rate of the theistic kind. In short, if we wish to believe in God in any rational fashion, then we have to decide first, on purely moral grounds, in favour of the kind of value-structure I have tried to describe.

This is our modern version of the scandal that faced those who first heard the Gospel. They did not have to be argued, most of them, into theism – certainly not the Jews, and not in any fundamental way the poly- or heno-theistic pagans. But they did find the assertion that this was God's scale of values, the principles indeed on which by embracing suffering he had acted, either offensive or absurd. 'We preach Christ crucified; to the Jews a stumbling-block, to the Gentiles foolishness' (1 Cor. 1:23). God did not, could not will the moral anomalies. His values were those of my philosopher friend, of all naturally right-thinking men. Hence the conviction in Judaism that he would eventually remove the anomalies, either in this life if only men would keep his Law, or in the world to come for those who had kept it. For those who realised that the anomalies were inescapably part of this world-order, of sheer materiality with its seeming downward pull on the spirit, its degradation and torment of all that was best in Man, the answer was a spiritual religion of escape: Gnostic, Manichaean, Platonist, or, if Christian, then adoptionist or docetic. Six hundred years later we find solid commonsense again asserting itself in the clear-cut simplisms of Islam. But to affirm the world, to declare that God meant the whole animal, miserable mess as the necessary raw material of perfection – how could anyone in his senses believe that?

So long as men's minds were still dominated by sheer theistic conviction, by the assumption that, whatever else proved illusory, the existence of a divine Somewhat was assured, this was the form the conflict took. Of course there was a God; the dispute was over his purposes, demands, behaviour. Today that conviction, that assumption have dissolved. The believer in our society has constantly to justify his very starting-point. (Weariness with the aridity of the conventional methods of doing so is perhaps one of the factors behind the current trend toward apophaticism and reliance on self-authenticating mystical experience; but these are dangerous solutions, if used as a substitute for rather than a corrective of theological thinking.) But though the scandal may be the same, it presents itself the opposite way round. Now the position is that only if we can affirm the kind of goodness which the creation postulates can we go on to believe in God. The outcome is the same. But the foundation article of belief is now not the metaphysical but the moral. Or at any rate it must be if Reason is to have any part in our religion.

This brings us to the second part of the discussion: the practical implications. It will be apparent that the facts we have been considering make a significant transformation in the relation of the Church and the world. In the early centuries, because both Christians and non-Christians breathed the common atmosphere of a theistic world-view, the primary distinction was between those who worshipped false gods and those who worshipped the true God; and here the use of credal affirmations provided a clear and legitimate line of demarcation. In an atheistic age the crucial division runs differently. Those who cannot give formal assent to the creeds of the Church, or even to belief in God, may nevertheless be differentiated among themselves by their attitude to the moral issue which we have been examining. There are those whose moral and ethical outlook makes belief in God irrational, and so places at least a very serious barrier between them and the Christian community; and there are those whose moral values are so far in line with those of God himself that they may be said to have, again at the very least, a predisposition to belief. The really vital *praeparatio evangelii* has already taken place in their hearts. Their personality has already received what may properly be called a Christian conformation.

There are quite definite concrete situations in which this fact ought to have a direct bearing on our conduct. There has in this century been a growing appreciation among Christians of a truth which indeed has never been entirely forgotten, that the church is among other things the servant of the world, and that she can and must co-operate, without 'strings' or proselytising, with all men of goodwill in the pursuit of justice and the practice of works of mercy, simply because these things are God's will for the world which his Son came to save. But in the final analysis such co-operation is, I suggest, possible only between those who share God's approach to the moral paradoxes of life in the world. If that common stance is not present, the practical decisions on particular questions will always work out differently. We see this clearly over such issues as violence, the sanctity of life, and now, rushing upon us, the use of natural resources. Ultimately, I believe, it underlies the conflict between liberal and totalitarian political systems. It is therefore urgent, if our service of mankind, our essentially priestly and sacrificial service, is to be as effective as possible, first that we spell out clearly that natural morality which the Incarnation, Cross, and Resurrection verify as divine, and secondly that we recognise that those who share with us commitment to that morality, even though they have not arrived at faith in the revelation, are in some sense, which I shall try to define more precisely in a moment, within the ambit of the Christian community. The church, I believe, does not today have those hard edges which in a religious age were defined reasonably enough by the credal formularies. It is of the most vital importance that the cells of the church should be in living interchange with the surrounding tissue; or, to put it another way, that there should be a genuine continuum between the body of professing believers and some of those for whom profession is not sincerely possible.

Here another reflection may be in point. On all sides we see today the break-up of the smooth surface of apparently uniform belief within the very churches themselves. It becomes apparent that the extent to which individual Christians have been able to make their own the full faith of the church to which they belong varies enormously. There is, of course, nothing new in this. The phenomenon of sectarianism has always witnessed to the existence of this difficulty. Within the catholic tradition it has long been permissible to accept genuine desire or intention to believe what the church believes, a will to associate oneself with the *pisteuomen* of the ecumenical symbols, as sufficient, even where there were doubts or perplexities about individual articles. But with the present freedom of expression and publication on the part of authoritative figures the problem has been sharpened to a point at which, if we are not courageous and honest, there is some risk of scandal. Not the so-called scandal that those who hold responsible teaching positions should canvass difficulties with integrity; that is not a scandal but a reason for sober confidence. No, the scandal I have in mind is this: that at initiation the churches require of the new entrant a more rigorous commitment than will apparently ever be demanded of him there-after. In my own church it sometimes seems that an initial statement that one has no doubts or agnosticisms is the price one is expected to pay in order to be allowed to have very nearly as many as one likes.

We must ask: what is a Creed? Is it a basic minimum, without which one cannot be called a Christian? Or is it a condensed sum-mary, a series of chapter headings to an account of a full and mature faith? If I may speak personally, the fact that I can now make *ex animo* assent to virtually everything in the eucharistic symbol is the result of years of growth in understanding some small part of the many, many truths, moral, spiritual and religious which underlie each of its propositions. It is that total corpus of experience and insight to which I give my assent. And I suspect that most of my fellow-Christians would say the same. The faith of the community is something into which we grow by virtue of being incorporated into the living Body of Christ. 'What hast thou which thou hast not received?' Nothing. But my point in stressing this is simply the very platitudinous one that the continuum of growth does not stop at the door of the church. Or, to use a different illustration: the proper dia-gram is not one showing an ascending slope which levels off to a plateau when the Christian community is reached, but a continuous upward line throughout, ending beyond this life altogether, in the vision of God. What I have tried to argue is that in our present atheistic society those humanists, or whatever they may be, who embrace the moral position central to both Reason and Revelation are already on that continuous upward line, while those who reject it are not.

But the moral criterion operates in another context also. It serves in some degree to identify those particular beliefs which are of primary importance to the faith. We all appreciate that it is necessary to be very careful here. Christian theology has an ineradicable tendency toward coherence and systematisation, as the groaning shelves of our libraries bear witness. But we can, I think, legitimately say that there are certain beliefs which are primary because they give any synthesis its distinctively Christian character. And it is the moral argument which seems to provide the most satisfactory rational basis on which to define this character. Thus, if what has been said about the underlying value-structure is true, then we are pressed in a particular direction in our statements about God. It is not enough that he should prescribe a suffering world for our perfection, and dwell himself, like the deities in Lucretius, 'where there is neither snow nor rain nor any hail'. If these are his moral ideals then to be worthy of them he must live them. This is not a precise enough criterion to enable us to say that there had to be an Incarnation of God, and that nothing else would have done. But it does suggest that, given reason to believe that there was an Incarnation, in the full, traditional import of the term, that doctrine is absolutely central, because it is the only element in the Christian faith which satisfies the moral demand one hundred per cent. Any attempt to replace this with a concept of Jesus as the Man who perfectly reveals God's character, or as the perfect human being in God's image, or as the One who was supremely open to God, is in fact falling short. Such language tries to preserve all that is of essential significance, while avoiding the age-old and notorious intellectual problems connected with the classic doctrine; but it fails, because it does not meet the crucial requirement, namely that God submits himself to what as Creator he has deemed to be best. Without the Incarnation Christianity is both incoherent and inadequate; and with the Incarnation Christianity shows up the incoherence and inadequacy of non-incarnational theism. Moreover, linked inseparably with this belief are the Cross and Resurrection as the revealed historical indicators of its truth – in fact almost the whole christological middle section of the ecumenical creeds. These things are primary in a definitive, determinative way; but this primary character is illuminated most clearly by our understanding of the moral character of the universe.

Perhaps enough has been said to suggest how this approach might be extended to other elements in the creeds. Rather than pursue this in detail, I would like to press on to the general implication. Because Christians are first of all human beings, the moral criterion we have described also operates as a criterion of relations between members of the universal Christian company. Wherever the moral demand of God's world leads men to acceptance of those affirmations of the faith which the very demand itself shows to be central, there surely the Spirit of God and of Christ is present, the Body of Christ lives in the world, the Kingdom comes in its unique power. To refuse intercommunion where these conditions are met is simply to deny, and by denying help actively to destroy the already existing facts of what God has done.

But this at once raises severe practical problems. A moral structure is not something that can simply be approved with the mind, as one might tick the right answer to a sum in arithmetic. Of its very nature it involves commitment in practice – not just moral theory but behaviour. And how, in heaven's name, are we to define what behaviour is indicative of membership? Would it even be desirable to try? The Old Testament Law is probably the finest attempt there has ever been to provide a detailed description of behaviour as a criterion of membership – and, moreover, to supply that description with a moral structure and a theological context – but even this created more problems than it solved. Essential as rules are for the true fulfilment of human life, we know by now that a comprehensive code, even if, *per impossibile*, it could be agreed, would not offer a practicable way forward.

Two thoughts may here be of help. Let us begin simply by tabling them, and then see whether and how they may serve to complete our total picture.

The first thought is that the Church is not a meeting of the Ethical Association. We may find it useful or even necessary to engage from time to time in abstract moral pattern-making in order to clear our minds or see where we are going and how one thing relates to another. But the moral life of the Christian community starts not from generalised statements but from Jesus and the record of his doings and of his particular, concrete ethical teaching. The declaration, 'Jesus is Lord', is as proper in the moral as in the religious sphere; and if the Church does not make that declaration the starting-point of her moral and ethical thinking, then she has no distinctive contribution to make or character to display.[2]

The second thought is that a style of morality can be soundly evolved only by getting to grips as a community with concrete moral problems. (It is really rather funny that the once sinister and disreputable science of casuistry became respectable overnight when someone changed its name to 'situation ethics'.) Any attempt to make the moral foundations of belief anything more than mere theory will have to take the form of an ongoing corporate discussion of current ethical issues; for only in this way do abstractions take on life and reality.

Perhaps now we can begin to see how our practical problems might be solved. We can state fairly simply the basic moral principles which make our faith rational and possible. We can show that in the particular situation of his own individual life, death and resurrection, and in his teaching, Jesus gives us working examples of these principles, and in the end vindicates and verifies them. Because of this we affirm Jesus as Lord in the moral sphere. But we bring to bear on our own situation a great deal more than this. First, there is the living tradition within which his teaching and example have been understood and applied since the Resurrection – a process which we can see already under way in the New Testament itself. Secondly, there is our growing knowledge of God's world, and our constantly extending experience through history, which is also a mode of God's creative activity. By being open to all these three elements in shaping our means and our ends we give reality to the affirmation that Jesus is the Logos by whom all things were made, the light that lightens every man, and the ultimate Lord of history. Only in the moral sphere, in the actions that are determined by its

---

[2] To say this is, of course, to assume a certain answer to one of the most fiercely argued of theological questions today, namely, can we know anything with reasonable certainty of the historical Jesus? It is obviously out of the question to discuss so vast and complex an issue here. It must suffice simply to come clean about my own personal conviction: that we can from the N.T. evidence form a substantially accurate idea of Jesus's characteristic positions and lines of teaching; that if we could not, then Christianity ought in all honesty either to put up the shutters or call itself by another name; and that the numerous bizarre contemporary realisations of Jesus ('Superstar', 'Che Guevara', etc.) are, like the repulsive child of the ancient apocryphal infancy Gospels, simply the kind of fantasies that have always rushed in to fill the vacuum created by ignorance of or indifference to the highly individual figure of the Gospel record.

underlying God-given structure, do these affirmations impinge effectively on the life of the world.

The fulfilment of this task calls for the participation of all who by their acceptance of this central core of faith have received from God the communion of which ecclesiastical intercommunion is the outward expression. In a sense they are already one at a fundamental level, whatever the regulations may say. But to refuse them outward intercommunion is to put serious practical obstacles in the way of that vital task to which they have all been called by God. The capacity of the Church to witness in our world to the saving power of the Gospel is severely restricted by social and cultural limitations. Too many Christians look at the world in a particular rather narrow way because they all come from the same secular origins. We cannot afford to throw away any contribution we can scrape together, which will help us to explore the meaning of the Gospel for mankind at large, with all its variety of cultural forms and spiritual insights. It is my belief that such co-operation can exist effectively only where there is open acceptance and fellowship. Given the way things are, this must be based on some hard core of common commitment; and this, I have tried to argue, is at bottom a moral insight. In this sense behaviour is the most basic of all criteria for intercommunion; but behaviour not along the old lines of success in keeping the rules but in the more creative form of commitment to the spirit of holiness plus-forgiveness.

But this intra-Christian dimension is not the only one. Remembering what we said earlier, it now becomes necessary to ask whether those outside the Christian community who accept the moral structure underlying the faith are not in fact saying, 'Jesus is Lord', in the moral sense, even though they cannot yet say it in the religious. I am not thinking here of those fortuitous and superficial alliances where Christians work with others to achieve a particular goal which all happen to want but for widely differing reasons. In the light of what we noted, first about the relation of so-called 'Christian ethics' to ethics in general, and secondly about the way in which Christian theology is rooted in certain broad but distinctive moral attitudes which it is open to all men to adopt to their world on the basis of their own observation, I would argue that there will always, in every generation, be those who can say, 'Jesus is Lord', in the sense of 'the normative guide and model of my dedication to goodness'; and that common experience constantly brings us into touch with people who by their words and lives show that this is true. To work with such is in no way a superficial alliance; it is a shared exploration on an agreed basis into God's will for our Here and Now. As Christians we hope and pray that this moral commitment of theirs will lead them on to an awareness of the full reality of God. But we put obstacles in the way of that awareness by blocking them from organic connection with the community in which faith in God and love for God are men's daily bread. Very often such people, working with Christians in a secular context in a joint vocation of service to the world, would value some form of association with the Church which, while not pretending to be closer than it really was, would acknowledge the great and fundamental things we have in common, would come clean and admit that these things are *Christian*, and that in them all concerned have a factual bond of fellowship which gives them a most significant common *persona* within the world. This is not to reduce the faith to a system of morals; it is to give that morality which is in harmony with God the best possible chance to grow into faith in God and into the joyful awareness of his love, and at the same time to double its power to work within the world for the world's redemption. This, I believe, is what ought to be meant in practice by the idea of an 'open Church' in organic unity with the world Our Lord came to save. In this context behaviour – again, let us stress, understood as Christians understand it, not as legalistic achievement but as commitment to holiness within an environment of unwearying forgiveness – can and should be seen as a proper criterion of membership not merely within the circle of Christian 'denominations' but reaching out beyond them; and this not as a substitute for faith but as the natural and reasonable approach toward that faith, the fullness of which none of us, even within the baptised and eucharistic community, will attain until faith itself is swallowed up in the vision of God.

BIOGRAPHICAL NOTE

LOUIS JACOBS *is the Rabbi of the New London Synagogue. He lectures in the Talmud at the Leo Baeck College for the training of rabbis. He has published many books, including* Principles of the Jewish Faith, Studies in Talmudic Logic and Methodology, Jewish Values, *etc.*

6 Judaism and Membership

RABBI LOUIS JACOBS

MY KNOWLEDGE OF CHRISTIANITY IS ADMITTEDLY SCANTY but it seems to me that the main difference in the concept of membership between Christianity and Judaism lies in the nature of the entity to which the member belongs. In Christianity he belongs to the Church, a community of individual believers. In Judaism he belongs to a people. I am quite prepared to be told that this is a gross over-simplification, that Christian believers have a corporate life, a mystical body, and that the individual believer counts for much in Judaism. Very true, but the point I wish to make is that Judaism has no such concept as a Church. There is no such thing in Judaism as 'The Synagogue' with a capital 'S'. Whenever membership is discussed by Jewish thinkers the meaning is always membership of the covenant people. One way of expressing this idea is to say that there is a nationalistic element in Judaism but there are so many difficulties in the idea of a Jewish 'nation' that, for our purpose, it is better if we keep to the term 'people'.

With this reservation in mind – and it must frankly be said that it is a reservation that renders precarious any comparison between the two faiths – I submit for the consideration of my Christian colleagues in this symposium what membership means in Judaism. Three basic questions require to be answered: (1) How is membership attained? (2) What does membership involve? (3) How can membership be forfeit?

1. How is Membership Attained?

According to traditional Jewish law, as it had developed at the beginning of the Christian era and as it is still maintained by Jewish Orthodoxy today, there are two ways in which a person becomes a member of the Jewish community – by birth or by conversion.

Membership by birth means that a child born to a Jewish mother is automatically Jewish. Why the status of the mother and not that of the father should be decisive is far from clear. Various explanations of the phenomenon have been made from time to time – from the improbable suggestion that it is a hangover from a matriarchal system to the importance Judaism attaches to the role of the mother or that paternity contains an element of doubt which maternity does not – but these are no more than guesses unsupported by any real evidence. The Talmudic sources simply state the law without giving any reason for it.[1] But in these sources there is complete unanimity so that if a Jewish man marries a non-Jewish woman the children of the marriage are not technically Jewish whereas if a non-Jewish man marries a Jewish woman the children of the marriage are technically Jewish. (The Liberal movement in this country departs here from traditional law and holds that where either of the parents is Jewish the children are Jewish provided that the parents are willing for the children to be brought up as Jews.) It should be noted that birth is determinative of the child's status without any further rite or ceremony. Although male children have to be circumcised and circumcision is the 'sign of the covenant' (Genesis, Chapter 17) yet failure to have the child circumcised does not affect his status as a Jew.

Membership by conversion involves the acceptance by the convert of the basic tenets of the Jewish faith and a firm resolve to keep

---

[1] The sources are: Mishnah, Kiddushin 3: 12, English translation in H. DANBY, *The Mishnah*, Oxford, 1933, p. 327; Babylonian Talmud 68b, English translation in *The Talmud*, ed. I. Epstein, Soncino Press, London, 1936, *Kiddushin*, pp. 344–6. These sources are discussed in the collection of answers by 43 Jewish scholars who replied to David Ben-Gurion's question: 'Who is a Jew?' The answers are published under the title: *Jewish Identity*, compiled Baruch Litvin, ed. Sidney B. Hoenig, Feldheim, New York, 1965.

the Jewish laws and customs.[2] Here a formal act of initiation is required before membership of the Jewish people becomes a reality – immersion in a ritual bath (the *mikveh*) and circumcision for a male convert, immersion for a female convert. (Reform Jews do not demand immersion for converts.) Once he has acquired membership of the community the convert is the equal of any other Jew. He can refer in his prayers, as other Jews do, to the Patriarchs as his 'forefathers' because, now professing the Jewish faith, he is their spiritual heir.[3] The practices of his non-Jewish past, that he ate forbidden food, for example, must never be held against him.[4] All the Biblical injunctions to love the 'sojourner' (*ger*) and care for him as an equal to the 'citizen' (*ezrah*) are applied to the convert. For the Rabbis the *locus classicus* for the acceptance of converts is the book of Ruth: 'For whither thou goest, I will go; and where thou lodgest, I will lodge; thy people shall be my people, and thy God my God' (Ruth 1: 16).

A good indication of how the Jewish teachers understood membership by conversion is provided by the letter of Maimonides (1135-1204) to Obadiah, a convert to Judaism from Islam.[5] Obadiah's teacher had stated that Muslims were idolators and when Obadiah was moved to protest the teacher insulted him, called him a fool. Maimonides was incensed, first because it is simply untrue to say that Muslims are idolators and secondly because a convert has to be welcomed not insulted. Among other warm expressions of encouragement, Maimonides writes to Obadiah: 'You should know how great is our obligation to strangers who are converted to Judaism. We are commanded to honour and respect our parents and we are commanded to obey the prophets. It is possible for a man to respect and to honour and to obey someone for whom he has no

[2] The conversion procedures are given in the Babylonian Talmud, Yevamot 46a–47b, English translation in the Soncino Talmud, pp. 300–14. A comprehensive account of the legal position is given in Hebrew in *Encyclopedia Talmudit*, vol. II, Tel-Aviv, 1954, pp. 253–89. In English there can be consulted the far from adequate collection of essays: *Conversion to Judaism*, ed. David Max Eichorn, Ktav, New York, 1965.
[3] The sources for this, the accepted ruling, are given in *Encyclopedia Talmudit*, loc. cit., p. 258 note 104.
[4] Mishnah, Baba Metzia 4: 10, English translation Danby, pp. 354–5; Babylonian Talmud, Baba Metzia 58b, Soncino, p. 348.
[5] *Responsa of Maimonides*, ed. Joshua Blau, Jerusalem, 1960, No. 488, Vol. II, pp. 728–835.

love. But with regard to strangers we are commanded to love them with a great love coming from the heart just as we are commanded to love God. God Himself in all His glory loves the stranger, as it is said: "He loves the stranger, providing him with food and clothing" (Deuteronomy 10: 18). As for his calling you a fool, I am utterly astonished. A man capable of leaving his father and his birthplace and the protection afforded by the government of his people; a man capable of so much understanding as to attach himself to a people, which today is despised by others and is a slave to rulers, because he appreciates that theirs is the true religion; a man capable of so understanding the ways of Israel as to recognise that all the other religions have stolen from this one, one adding, the other subtracting, one changing, the other lying and attributing to God things that are not so, one destroying foundations, the other speaking topsy-turvy things; a man capable of recognising all this, pursuing after God, passing through the way of holiness, entering under the wings of the Divine Presence, casting himself at the dust of the feet of Moses our teacher, head of all the prophets, on whom be peace, and desiring God's laws; a man whose heart has led him to come near to the light of life, to ascend the degrees of the angels, and to rejoice and take delight in the joys of the righteous; a man capable of casting this world from his heart, not turning to lies and falsehood; shall such a man be called a fool? No fool has God called you but wise, understanding, upright, a pupil of our father Abraham who left his father and his birthplace to go after God.'

Before leaving the question of how membership is to be attained, some reference must be made to the Rabbinic doctrine of 'the precepts of the sons of Noah'. The doctrine runs that in addition to the Torah given to the Jewish people there is a Torah for mankind in general. This involves the keeping of seven rules – 'the seven precepts of the sons of Noah'. The usual formulation of these is: (1) Not to worship idols; (2) Not to commit murder; (3) Not to commit adultery or be guilty of incest; (4) Not to steal; (5) Not to blaspheme; (6) Not to eat a limb torn from an animal while it is still alive; (7) To have an adequate system of justice. A Noahide (i.e. any human being) who keeps these precepts is held to be one of the 'righteous among the nations of the world' and he has 'a share in the World to Come'. The doctrine means that, as Judaism sees it, a person can find his 'salvation' without necessarily becoming a member of the Jewish people. The choice is open to him to belong to the Noahides by keeping the seven Noahide rules.[6]

2. What Does Membership Involve?

For the Talmudic Rabbis and their successors, membership of the Jewish people involves the keeping of the precepts (*mitzvot*) of the Torah. The emphasis is undoubtedly on deeds rather than on beliefs but this is not, as is sometimes assumed, because Judaism does not hold beliefs to be important. A discussion of the role of dogma in Judaism is beyond the scope of this paper.[7] It is sufficient to note that the practices are based on the central dogma that the precepts are ordained by God. They have been revealed as what it is that God would have the Jew (or, in the case of the Noahide rules, mankind) do. Although for the purpose of legal classification the precepts are divided into 'light' and 'severe' the ideal is for the Jew to keep all the precepts.[8] But disregard of the precepts does not cause a Jew to forfeit his membership of the Jewish people. The Jew who offends against the rules is a sinner but he remains a Jew.

There are many sayings in the Rabbinic literature in which are expressed the tensions between the ideal picture of an entirely faithful community and the sober reality that many Jews fell far short of total observance. In the second century Rabbi Judah and Rabbi Meir debated whether Jews are still called God's children (Deuteronomy 14:1) even if they are sinners.[9] A third century Palestinian teacher said that even the sinners of Israel are still as 'full of *mitzvot* as a pomegranate is full of seeds'.[10] Another third century

---

[6] A comprehensive account of the Noahide laws is to be found in *Encyclopedia Talmudit*, Vol. III, Tel-Aviv, 1951, pp. 348–62. For the whole question see RAPHAEL LOEWE, 'Potentialities and Limitations of Universalism in the Halakhah' in *Studies in Rationalism, Judaism and Universalism in Memory of Leon Roth*, ed. Raphael Loewe, Routledge and Kegan Paul, London, 1966, pp. 115–50.

[7] The essay by SOLOMON SCHECHTER, 'The Dogmas of Judaism' in his *Studies in Judaism*, Philadelphia, 1945, Vol. I, pp. 147–81, is still very valuable. Cf. my *Principles of the Jewish Faith*, Vallentine, Mitchell, London, 1964, Introduction, pp. 1–32.

[8] See AVOT ('Ethics of the Fathers') 2:1: 'And be heedful of a light precept as of a weighty one, for thou knowest not the recompense of reward of each precept' (Danby, p. 447).

[9] Sifre to the verse, 96, ed. Friedmann, Vienna, 1864, p. 94a.

[10] Babylonian Talmud Hagigah 27a, Soncino, p. 171.

Palestinian teacher commented on the verse (Esther 2:5) in which Mordecai, though of the tribe of Benjamin, is described as a 'Jew' (*yehudi*, i.e. of the tribe of Judah). He remarked that whoever denies idolatry is called a 'Jew'.[11] A Rabbinic homily[12] on the ingredients of the incense (Exodus 30:34–8) notes that one of these is galbanum which was supposed to have an unpleasant smell. The lesson derived from this is that a public fast-day in which the sinners do not participate is no fast-day, i.e. the prayers of the sinners are as essential as the galbanum was essential to the incense.

However, while the commission of even the worst sins does not disqualify a Jew completely from membership of the Jewish people (the children of a woman who committed such sins, for example, would still automatically be Jewish) yet an unrepentant idolator is partially disqualified, that is to say, for some purposes he is treated as a non-Jew. If he killed an animal for food, even though he did it in the prescribed ritual manner, the animal would be forbidden to Jews.[13] (If a non-Jew performs such an act the animal is forbidden on the grounds that only the act of a person to whom the law applies is valid.) Similarly, he cannot help to form the quorum of ten (the *minyan*) required for public prayer, any more than a non-Jew can. This was extended to the Jew who publicly profanes the sabbath.[14] Since the sabbath is a testimony to God as Creator, its public desecration is held to be akin to idolatry. This latter rule was a source of acute embarrassment in the last century when some Jews did profane the sabbath and everyone knew of it but who certainly considered themselves to be Jews and frequented the synagogue. A famous ruling by the German legal authority Rabbi Jacob Ettlinger (1798–1871) has it that the old law was directed against those whose open sabbath desecration was a public defiance of the Jewish religion, a declaration that the offender had no wish to be considered to be a Jew. 'Nowadays', he argued, 'the very fact that the sabbath

---

[11] Babylonian Talmud Megillah 13a, Soncino, p. 74, quoting Daniel 3:12: 'There are certain Jews. . . .'
[12] Babylonian Talmud Keritot 6b, Soncino, p. 45.
[13] Babylonian Talmud Hullin 5a, Soncino, pp. 15–20, but see the interesting discussion in this passage that, in opposition to the ruling, R. Anan said in the name of Samuel: 'In the case of an Israelite apostate in respect of idolatry, we may eat of his slaughtering'
[14] Hullin, loc. cit.

desecrators do frequent the synagogue and look upon themselves as Jews is sufficient demonstration that their sabbath desecration is no act of defiance but is due to their lack of appreciation that the offence is so very serious. By no means can their offence be equated with idolatry.'[15]

On the question of belief the matter is much more complicated. Would a rejection of basic Jewish beliefs result in the partial disqualification we have mentioned? The truth is that there is no ruling anywhere in the classical sources that, for example, a Jewish atheist cannot help to make up the quorum for public worship. But that, as Solomon Schechter has rightly said,[16] is because such a bizarre notion as a Jewish atheist attending the synagogue for prayer was beyond the imagination of the Jewish teachers. It remains true, nevertheless, that no tests of belief are applied to applicants for synagogue membership. It is assumed that the desire to become a member of a synagogue and to participate in its services is evidence enough that, albeit in a very vague manner, the applicant assents to the basic Jewish beliefs.

It must also be said that, because of the emphasis in Judaism on practice, considerable lattitude was given to Jewish thinkers in their interpretation of the basic Jewish beliefs. Maimonides drew up his thirteen principles of the Jewish faith and his ruthless logic led him to declare:[17] 'When all these principles are in the safe keeping of man, and his conviction of them is well established he then enters into the general body of Israel, and it is incumbent upon us to love him, to care for him, and to do for him all that God commanded us to do for one another in the way of affection and brotherly sympathy. And this, even though he were to be guilty of every transgression possible, by reason of the power of desire or the mastery of the base material passions. He will receive punishment according to the measure of his perversity, but he will have a portion in the world to come, even though he be of the transgressors in Israel. When,

[15] Responsa, *Binyan Tzion Ha-Hadashot*, Vilna, 1874, No. 23.
[16] 'The Dogmas of Judaism', op. cit., p. 156.
[17] *Commentary to the Mishnah*, Sanhedrin 10: 1, *Helek*. This section of Maimonides' writings has been translated into English with an Introduction and notes by J. ABELSON in *Jewish Quarterly Review* (Old Series), Vol. 19 (1907), pp. 24f.

however, a man breaks away from any of these fundamental principles of belief, then of him it is said that he has gone out of the general body of Israel and he denies the root of Judaism. And he is termed "heretic" (*min*) and "unbeliever" (*epikoros*) and it is obligatory upon us to hate him and cause him to perish, and it is concerning him that the Scriptural verse says: "Shall I not hate those who hate Thee, O Lord?" (Psalms 139:21).'

But a statement such as this of Maimonides is most atypical. While it would be untrue to say that Judaism knows nothing of heresy and heresy hunting (Maimonides himself was ironically dubbed a heretic by those who disliked his extreme rejection of all anthropomorphism) there was no machinery in Judaism by which an official body could declare a man to be a heretic. There was to be sure a kind of consensus of opinion among believers as to which beliefs a Jew was expected to subscribe but in the absence of any close and accepted definition (there existed no synod or similar body to do this) the net result was that – provided the thinker was observant and accepted the Torah revelation in general terms – a thinker was free to interpret the beliefs as his reason saw fit. (His views would be declared heretical by those who thought they were but there was very little they could do about it.) In this connection the case of Gersonides (1288–1344) is instructive. Gersonides laid it down as axiomatic that the Torah does not compel us to believe that which we know to be untrue, 'untrue' meaning here contrary to reason. Unlike the majority of Jewish thinkers in the middle ages Gersonides did not believe entirely in the doctrine of *creatio ex nihilo* but believed with Plato in the eternity of a formless hylic substance upon which God imposes form. He also believed that God only knows the future in a general way but does not know how a man will choose in a given set of circumstances. These views, especially the latter, were extremely unconventional and for his pains Gersonides' book *The Wars of the Lord* was called *The Wars Against the Lord*. But his book was not placed on any 'Index' (there was never any such thing in Judaism) and he is studied today by the Orthodox even if they do not agree with all his opinions. No one ever suggested that because of his unconventional beliefs Gersonides should not have been allowed to help make up the quorum for public prayer.

3. How Can Membership be Forfeit?

The legal answer is – never. Once a person is a Jew he is a Jew for the rest of his life and nothing that he does, not even conversion to another faith, can ever change his status. This was not always the official Jewish view. The passage from the Talmud quoted in support of the view was originally no more than a simple homily on the lines of the passages we have quoted earlier that even a Jew who sins is still a Jew. The passage in question[18] is in the nature of a comment on the verse: 'Israel hath sinned' (Joshua 7:11). The comment is to the effect that since the verse does not say: 'The people hath sinned' it follows that 'even when he has sinned an Israelite remains an Israelite', i.e. he does forfeit the high title 'Israel'. But in mediaeval France, in all probability as a counter-measure against Jewish conversions to Christianity, the Jewish teachers declared that the meaning of the passage was that even if he had 'sinned' (i.e. converted to another faith) a Jew remains a Jew. This became the official position as stated in the standard Codes of Jewish Law.[19]

In the State of Israel the problem of defining a Jew has been the source of much debate and of no little confusion. In the Father Daniel case – that of a Jew who became a Christian monk but who wished to be registered in Israel as a Jew – the court decided that he could not be registered as a Jew. Although the traditional law is clear that he is, in fact, a Jew, the Israeli court felt that it was not called upon to interpret the traditional law but rather what was in the minds of those who framed the Law of Return. It was argued that while Jews consider as such all who are such either by birth or conversion they do not consider a convert to another faith to be a Jew. Whatever the traditional law says, this appears to be the opinion of the majority of Jews today. The paradox which results is that the secularist Jew is held to be a Jew while the Jew who believes in God but who is a Christian or a Muslim is not considered to be a Jew. In view of the history of the whole concept of membership this attitude is very easy to understand. In the one case there has been no formal repudiation. In the other there has been a deliberate choice of

---

[18] Babylonian Talmud Sanhedrin 44a, Soncino, pp. 285–6.
[19] This topic has been keenly analysed by JACOB KATZ: 'Though He Sinned, He Remains an Israelite' (Hebrew) in *Tarbiz*, Vol. 27 (1958), pp. 203–17.

another faith, a choice that involves, so far as Judaism is concerned, an act of apostasy.

The problem of separatist groups within the Jewish community has exercised the minds of the Jewish teachers. The earliest of these was that of the Samaritans who, on the Rabbinic view, were originally heathen who were 'converted' to Judaism. The Rabbis debated whether their conversion was an authentic one, many of them deciding that it was and that, indeed, while the Samaritans did not keep all the laws, those they did keep they observed with greater zeal than the Jews themselves. Eventually, however, they were declared to be outside the Jewish community. Legend has it that some of them were discovered worshipping the image of a dove (!) on Mount Gerezim, whereupon they were declared to be out and out idolators.[20] The legend expresses, of course, the eventual schism between Samaritans and Jews. There are still some hundreds of Samaritans in Nablus who offer up each year the Paschal lamb in a ceremony on Mount Gerizim. They consider themselves to be the only true Jews but are not considered to be Jews by the rest of the Jewish community. The Sadducees, on the other hand, were considered to be Jews even by the Pharisees.[21] The whole Sadducean movement vanished, however, from the Jewish scene so that no practical considerations became involved. The break with Christianity came early on but, as we have seen, the problem of whether a Jew who became a Christian was still a Jew was acute in the middle ages.[22]

The Karaite movement in the middle ages repudiated Rabbinic tradition and claimed to go back to the plain meaning of Scripture. For a long time, and despite the fierce debates between the Karaites and the followers of the Rabbis, the Karaites were held to be Jews. Some of the Rabbinic authorities permitted intermarriage between their followers and the Karaites. Even those who forbade it did so on

---

[20] Babylonian Talmud Hullin 5b–6a, Soncino, pp. 21–4.

[21] On the joint membership of Sadducees and Pharisees in the Sanhedrin see HAIM COHEN, *The Trial and Death of Jesus*, Harper and Row, New York, 1971, pp. 26–8 and the references given in the notes.

[22] See JACOB KATZ, *Exclusiveness and Tolerance*, Studies in Jewish-Gentile Relations in Mediaeval and Modern Times, Oxford, 1961, and the references given by Raphael Loewe, op. cit., p. 147, note 6.

other grounds, that since the Karaite laws of marriage and divorce were different from those of the Rabbis there was the possibility of bastardy. The bans by Rabbinic authorities in the 18th century on the followers of the pseudo-Messiah Sabbatai Zevi (1626-76), the followers of Jacob Frank[23] (1726-91) and the Hasidim,[24] were precautionary measures, an attempt at keeping the 'sinners' from contaminating the innocent rather than declaration that they were not Jews. There are no Sabbateans and no Frankists left today. The Hasidim managed to still the suspicions of their opponents and are today in many ways the most Orthodox wing of Jewry.

What of the Reform movement? The major differences between Reform and Orthodoxy do not affect basic principles but are in matters of observance – how far the synagogue services should be changed, how strictly should the traditional sabbath be observed, how many of the dietary laws should be retained and so forth. It follows from what has been said earlier in this paper that Orthodoxy, on its terms of reference, could not declare the Reformers to be outside the Jewish camp. From the point of view of Orthodoxy it is, indeed, frequently said that Reform is not a legitimate expression of Judaism. In practice this means no more than that the Reformers are treated as individuals who are 'sinners'. Since a large proportion of contemporary Jewry belongs to the Reform and to other non-Orthodox movements[25] and since these Jews are completely identified with Jewish life, the kind of schism which brought about the eventual separation of groups like the Karaites from the corporate body of Israel has been avoided.

The problem for Orthodoxy today is the degree of cooperation it can permit itself with Reform. In philanthropy, work for Israel, relations with the non-Jewish community and so forth there is complete cooperation. Since Reform Jews reject some of the traditional marriage laws (the *get*, 'bill of divorce', in its traditional form, for instance) some marriages which take place under Reform auspices

---

[23] Information in English on the Sabbatians and the Frankists is provided in the studies in G. SCHOLEM'S *The Messianic Idea in Judaism*, Allen and Unwin, London, 1971.

[24] The documents against the Hasidim containing these bans have been collected in M. WILENSKY'S *Hasidim and Mitnaggedim* (Hebrew), Jerusalem, 1970.

[25] Such as the 'middle-of-the-road' Conservative movement active chiefly in the United States and to which (to declare my bias) I belong.

are invalid so far as the Orthodox are concerned but that is not because they are Reform marriages but because, from the Orthodox point of view, there is legal impediment. The same applies to some Reform conversions. Reform Rabbis are obviously not held by the Orthodox to be qualified to give decisions on laws the Reformers do not consider binding. But it is incorrect to say that this means that the Orthodox look upon the Rabbis of the Reform movement as 'laymen'. The truth is that there is no special priesthood in Judaism so that all Rabbis are 'laymen' or, if it be preferred, all Jews are priests. Some Jews today seem to favour a more clear-cut division between Reform and Orthodoxy but there are powerful tendencies, on the contrary, towards greater cooperation between the two groups. Orthodox Rabbis have been known to preach in Reform synagogues and *vice versa* but one cannot pretend that so far, at least, Jewish 'ecumenism' has moved very far in this direction. At all events, it is totally misleading to think of the differences between Orthodoxy and Reform as being a Jewish parallel of the differences between Catholicism and Protestantism in Christianity. The two are much closer than any such analogy would warrant.[26] Precisely because of this the obstacles in the way of greater cooperation are more stubborn. In the history of religious controversy it is like which is suspicious of like.

To sum up, and if the comparison is not too banal, Judaism is like the philosophy of a club with a particular purpose over and above the purely social. The club's founder members all belong to one family as do the majority of its present-day membership but membership is open to all who accept the club's particular philosophy. Full membership is granted to these after an initiation ceremony. The club's constitution contains a large number of strict rules. Some of the members adhere lovingly to these and tend to look askance at those members who disregard the rules. Other members press for a revision of the rules and still others quietly neglect some of them. Once a

---

[26] Solomon Schechter delivered an address at the dedication of a new building of the Reform College in Cincinnati. In this he compared Orthodoxy and Reform to the two parties in the British Parliament. Schechter, here and elsewhere, stressed the essential unity of what he calls 'Catholic Israel'. See the address: 'His Majesty's Opposition' in SCHECHTER'S *Seminary Addresses and Other Papers*, Burning Bush Press, New York, 1959, pp. 239–44.

person has become a member he is held to be a member for life even if he no longer pays his dues, attends meetings or obeys any of the rules. He is a member *in absentia* and will always be welcomed back. It is only when he joins a club which has a contrary philosophy that his fellow-members consider his membership to have lapsed.

BIOGRAPHICAL NOTE

ERIC J. SHARPE *is a Senior Lecturer in the Department of Religious Studies of the University of Lancaster. He has written* Not to Destroy but to Fulfil *(1965), and is at work on a study of caste as it affects the Christian Church in India.*

7 Church Membership and the Church in India

ERIC J. SHARPE

The Problem of Caste

IT IS, I THINK, SIGNIFICANT THAT A CONSULTATION ON the problems of Church membership and intercommunion should be prepared to devote a proportion of its time to some consideration of these problems as they appear in an explicitly non-Christian milieu – that is, in a milieu dominated not by Christian or secular forces, but by religious traditions of a distinctively non-Christian and moreover non-Western character. Exclusive concentration on the situation and prospects of the churches as they appear in our own Western milieu may be necessary at times, but inevitably brings with it a measure of distortion in the long run. The Church lives and works in the *oikumene*, and we all ought to know (even though we may sometimes forget) that Christianity is by no means exclusively a Western phenomenon; indeed, there are some who are becoming convinced that in future, the geographical centre of gravity of Christianity may well shift more and more towards the Third World – Africa, Asia and Latin America. And despite what the apostles of secularisation are telling us, the situation of the Church in those parts of the world is not yet identical with its situation in the West. Eventually it may become so; though for a variety of reasons I do not believe that this will be soon. In the meantime, the problems of how individuals and groups become and remain Christian are quite distinctive in those areas. Exactly how distinctive they are in one of the largest of them, India, I hope to be able to show, though I would disclaim at the outset any hint at comprehensive treatment.

Briefly what I shall try to do is to concentrate on the most outstanding of India's religio-social phenomena, viz. caste, and against this background to locate the Church's membership problem.[1]

It is, however, necessary to stress at the very outset that generalisations about the situation of the Church and the churches in India are never to be trusted. Not only are the Christian bodies in India themselves of considerable diversity (almost as diverse, as a result of, among other things, piecemeal missionary work over the last three and a half centuries, as the Western churches in which the missions originated); but India itself is equally a country of vast diversity – geographical, racial, social, linguistic and religious. Thus as R. W. Taylor has recently pointed out with regard to India's religious traditions,

> In the study of religions, as in the social sciences, it is simply impossible to arrive at very many useful middle-level generalizations that apply to *all* of India. There are vast differences between regions and sects. Within each region and sect there may be great differences between groups with different placement in the caste/class structure and between those still caught in tradition and those caught up in modernity and between those engaged in sanskritazation, those engaged in westernization and those (perhaps the most important in the long run) engaged in reinterpretation.[2]

Similar statements might well be made about each and every aspect of the problem under consideration. I am going to assume that Christian diversity in India needs no demonstration from my side;

---

[1] There is no comprehensive treatment of caste as it affects the Christian Church in India at present in print; one is, however, in preparation by Duncan M. Forrester and the present writer. Most books on Christianity in India contain at least some reference to the caste problem. Among recent articles, special mention may be made of DEVANANDAN, 'Caste, the Christian and the Nation in India today', in *The Ecumenical Review* XI/3 (April 1959), pp. 268–81.

[2] *Religion and Society*, XVI/1 (1969), p. 6f.

the facts are presumably well enough known. But the facts of the Indian situation may be relatively unfamiliar, and I should like to take a little time to reinforce Taylor's point, particularly in view of the circumstance that generalisations about India, about Hinduism and about caste, are still rather common in some quarters.

In the first place, there is a tendency in the West to assume that because over 80 per cent of Indians are known to be Hindus, and because we have long been accustomed to talking about an apparently monolithic religion called 'Hinduism', therefore upwards of 400,000,000 Indians are adherents of substantially the same religious tradition. This is true only in the vaguest of senses. The trouble is that Western scholarly convention has taken what is primarily an ethnic and geographical, and only secondarily a religious term (Hindu), and reified it by adding the ubiquitous suffix '-ism'. As far as the accurate understanding of the Indian situation goes, the result has been disastrous. I agree completely with Wilfred Cantwell Smith, that '. . . the term "Hinduism" is . . . a particularly false conceptualisation, one that is conspicuously incompatible with any adequate understanding of the religious outlook of Hindus'.[3] Even the most cursory study shows that this capacious terminological umbrella is capable of sheltering virtually every type of expression that the religious life of mankind has ever seen; but that does not make it a unity.[4] And the deeper one's study goes, the more the essential diversity reveals itself; Hinduism, so far from being a unified phenomenon, is shown to be an infinitely complex network, or honeycomb, of religious traditions, bound together in some ways, but entirely separate in others. Certainly some modern Hindu apologists, such as ex-President Radhakrishnan, have made far-reaching claims about the homogeneity and universality of Hinduism; but these claims can easily be shown to be valid only in respect of an ideal, not in respect of the facts of the Hindu situation. Time does not however, permit a closer examination of these facts. It must suffice to point out that for our purposes, the milieu in which the

[3] *The Meaning and End of Religion* (Mentor ed. 1964), p. 61.
[4] Cf. ibid., p. 63: '. . . the mass of religious phenomena that we shelter under the umbrella of that term [Hinduism], is not a unity and does not aspire to be. It is not an entity in any theoretical sense, let alone any practical one.' Cf. also HINNELLS and SHARPE (eds.), *Hinduism* (1972), pp. 1ff.

Christian Church in India operates is characterised not by one homogeneous religious pattern, but rather by a great variety of possible patterns.

We must pass briefly over the racial and linguistic diversity of India, pausing only to note that in the matter of language, there are more than a dozen major indigenous languages, and over two hundred minor ones, not counting dialects, and that there is a gulf fixed between the north and the south of India in this regard. The major languages of the north are Sanskrit-based, the major languages of the south, Dravidian-based, and this is far more than a matter of dialect – which may help to explain the persistence of English as a language of all-Indian communication.

We must turn now to the main subject of this paper, the problem of caste. It is a matter of common knowledge that socially, and perhaps religiously, India is, and always has been, dominated by the institution of caste; but there are ample opportunities for misunderstanding here due to the presence of certain stereotypes, and we must consider this phenomenon a little more closely as it is in itself, before moving on to its Christian implications.

The misunderstanding to which I refer arises partly out of the type of outdated textbook approach to the religious traditions of India which concentrates on questions of genesis rather than on questions of function. In many of these books one will read that some time in the second millennium B.C., fair-skinned Indo-Europeans from the north entered India, and created the caste system as a kind of primitive *apartheid*, in order to keep themselves and the aboriginal Indians firmly separate.[5] Originally, we read, there were four castes, or *varnas* (significantly for this theory, the word *varna* means 'colour'): a priestly, a warrior, an artisan and a serf caste. Now this is all very well as far as it goes. The Hindu lawbooks (e.g. *Mānavadharmasāstra*) are quite explicit on the point that there are four castes, and only four. But the most authoritative of

---

[5] A typical statement would be that of FARQUHAR, *The Crown of Hinduism* (1913), p. 158: 'The differences between the tall, white Aryans, with their advancing civilization and noble religion, and the short, black aborigines, with their coarse habits and degrading superstitions were so great that cultured Aryans could not fail to shrink from close contact with them: intermarriage was unthinkable, and even social intercourse was impossible.' No such view would, or could, be held by scholars today.

these law-books were put together more than two thousand years ago; and a great deal has happened in the meantime to change the picture. To be sure, the four *varnas* are still recognised in a theoretical way; but each one (better called 'class' than 'caste', incidentally) has since been subdivided and otherwise modified many times. The boundaries between the lower classes in particular have been flexible; with the result that the present-day institution of *jāti* (the commonest word for caste; it means 'birth') now exhibits a startling variety.[6] There are literally thousands of castes and sub-castes. There are the Brahmin castes (several hundred of them); there are the rest of the castes, which by now have come to combine features of the medieval guild, the extended family and the trade union; and then there are the outcastes – or scheduled castes, or depressed classes, or *Harijans* – groups, which originally formed no part of the system, but which now often have strong caste features themselves. In the cities, some of the traditional caste prohibitions and tabus are being relaxed and others have been the subject of fairly recent legislation; but over the greater part of India, basic caste structure – with all its infinite regional variations – survives virtually intact.

Caste as a purely social institution might not have been such a difficult hurdle for the Christian Church to surmount, but caste is more than this to the orthodox Hindu – it is in equal measure a religious ordinance, an essential aspect of the given order of creation. We have spoken of the vast variety of Hindu traditions; but one Hindu religion concept is virtually universal – the concept of *dharma*, which means both cosmic law and the religious and social law binding on the individual. The Hindu terms for what we call 'Hinduism' usually involve the word *dharma*, qualified in some way or other: *sanātana dharma*, *arya dharma*, *hindū dharma*, *varṇaśramadharma*. A Hindu, in Hindu terms, is someone who observes a *dharma*, or rather 'the' *dharma*, which regulates his place in society, his position in the eternal round of transmigration and rebirth, and his hope of ultimate salvation (*mokṣa*, release from rebirth). Now it is

---

[6] There are of course a number of modern studies in which this point is made. Useful introductions are HUTTON, *Caste in India* (3rd ed. 1961), and MANDELBAUM, *Society in India* I–II (1970). The latter work in particular has a most comprehensive bibliography on all aspects of caste. Cf. also ZINKIN, *India changes!* (1958), esp. pp. 79ff.

within the framework of caste that *dharma* operates. Each caste has its own *dharma*; but since every *dharma* is an aspect of universal or cosmic *dharma*, to be a member of a caste is to be a Hindu – neither more nor less. Thus the only way in which one can become a Hindu is to be born into a caste, the only way in which one can cease to be a Hindu is by ceasing for some reason to be a member of a caste. To be a member of a caste is to have and to acknowledge one's true place in the universe (a place determined by the inexorable operation of the law of *karma*). That is why, for instance, the *Bhagavad Gītā* stresses that it is better to perform one's own *dharma*, however badly, than another person's however well:

> Better a man's own duty, though ill-done, than another's duty well-performed; better it is to die in one's own duty – another's duty is fraught with dread.[7]

Now as far as the recent history of Christianity in India is concerned, the institution of caste for the most part has been regarded as a very great barrier to church membership. On the one hand, Christian missions have considered it their sacred duty to persuade Hindus to accept Christian baptism and thus automatically to break caste – which means, of course, separating them from their *dharma*, as well as from their families and their social settings. Alternatively, they have concentrated on outcaste groups, who technically speaking have had no caste to break, and for whom the concept of *dharma* has been relatively unimportant. And questions of Church membership have been bound up with the caste question to a quite extraordinary degree as a result. But before we go on to examine in slightly more detail some aspects of Christian policy over against caste, it will be necessary to consider briefly the kind of impression which caste has made on the Western Christian mind, since for better or for worse, it is from the West that the Christian Church in India has derived many of its attitudes.

Before about 1800, Western Christians, Catholic and Protestant alike, were on the whole not terribly disturbed by the institution of caste, and were prepared even to allow converts to perpetuate their

---

[7] *Bhagavad Gītā*, III: 35 (tr. Hill).

caste distinctions fairly openly. After all, did not the doctrine of the Great Chain of Being mean that all creation had been organised by an all-wise Creator on hierarchical lines?[8] Why, then, should there be any objection to a social system which simply recognised that fact? Political observers, whose attitude in matters religious was often limited to a general desire to perpetuate the *status quo*, tended to praise, rather than to condemn, caste. Take, for instance, this statement by the historian William Robertson, from the last years of the 18th century:

> Under a form of government, which paid such attention to all the different forms of which society is composed, particularly the cultivators of the earth, it is not wonderful that the ancients should describe the Indians as a most happy race of men; and that the most intelligent modern observers should celebrate the equity, the humanity, and the mildness of the Indian policy.[9]

Of course, it was believed by this time as a matter of practical politics that to meddle with caste, or with any other form of Hindu religion, would probably result in some kind of insurrection; which was why missionaries were long regarded with such disfavour, and why the East India Company saw nothing ludicrous in keeping out Christian missionaries with one hand while paying large sums of money for the upkeep of Hindu temples with the other.[10]

There had of course been a Christian missionary presence in India for some two centuries already (leaving the Syrian Christians out of the reckoning for the moment). The mission of Francis Xavier and his successors to the west coast of South India was the first in the field; here high-caste and low-caste converts had been kept firmly apart, and there were even eventually different missionaries appointed for work among the different caste groups. The most celebrated among these, Roberto de Nobili, virtually became a Brahmin

---

[8] See LOVEJOY, *The Great Chain of Being* (1936) for an account of the impact of this idea on Western thought.

[9] *An Historical Disquisition concerning the Knowledge which the Ancients had of India* (1791), p. 268, quoted by BEARCE, *British Attitudes to India, 1784–1858* (1961), p. 16f.

[10] For this strange episode, see RICHTER, *Indische Missionsgeschichte* (2. Aufl. 1924), pp. 199ff.; MAYHEW, *Christianity and the Government of India* (1929), pp. 145ff. Summary in SHARPE, *Not to Destroy but to Fulfil* (1965), p. 27f.

for the sake of attempting to win Brahmins – though his extra-ordinary initiative led before long to bitter controversy.[11] The Lutheran Danish-Halle missionaries in eighteenth-century Tranquebar attempted at first to ignore caste altogether, but in time rigid caste distinctions were to be observed in the Christian communities, not least since in this part of India there were both caste (*shudra*) and outcaste Christians.[12] At various times, separate church buildings were used, and separate chalices at the Eucharist. Thus at first in both Catholic and Protestant camps, the criterion of church membership was kept for the most part separate from caste membership: to be baptised did not necessarily involve making a clean break with caste and since the outcaste, by definition, causes ritual pollution to the caste Hindu by touch, a middle wall of partition (theoretical, and sometimes physical) was erected between different groups of Christians. They might be members of the one body of Christ, but there were a whole range of things that they could not do together: they could not eat together, even at the Lord's table, and they could not physically worship together.

After about 1800, though, the underlying altitude which had begun to rise to this situation began to change, and change radically. Partly as a result of the French Revolution, new winds were blowing through secular Europe; partly as a result of the Evangelical Awakening, new winds were blowing through the missions, at least on the Protestant side. Within a remarkably short space of time, it became axiomatic that the Christian witness in India should involve an energetic witness against the caste system as a whole and all it involved, and that no one ought to be allowed to become or remain a

---

[11] On de Nobili, see e.g. RICHTER, op. cit., pp. 64ff.; CRONIN, *A Pearl to India* (1959); BRUCKER, 'Malabar Rites', in *The Catholic Encyclopaedia*, IX (1910), pp. 558ff.; and articles 'Nobili' and 'Akkomodation, Missionarische', in *Jesuiten-Lexikon* (1924), cols. 1299f. and 24ff.

[12] On the Tranquebar Mission, cf. RICHTER, op. cit., pp. 110ff.; FENGER, *History of the Tranquebar Mission* (1906); ESTBORN, 'The Tranquebar Mission', in Swavely (ed.), *The Lutheran Enterprise in India 1706–1952* (1952), pp. 1ff. In later years, the Tranquebar missionaries were criticised severely for some of their attitudes, not least to caste; see e.g. BEACH, *India and Christian Opportunity* (1904), pp. 155, 159, 180. 'These and other societies, who looked upon caste as a matter of indifference to the Church . . . ignored the fact that caste was . . . bound up with a system of philosophy with which Christian faith was in hopeless antagonism.' FINDLAY and HOLDSWORTH, *The History of the Wesleyan Methodist Missionary Society*, V (1924), p. 136.

Christian who insisted on retaining any shred of respect for caste and its observances.[13]

On the home front, we find William Wilberforce informing Parliament in 1813 that

> Our religion is sublime, pure and beneficent. Theirs is mean, licentious and cruel. . . . Equality . . . is the vital essence and the very glory of our English laws. Of theirs, the essential and universal pervading general character is inequality, despotism in the higher classes, degradation and oppression in the lower.[14]

The caste reference is very plain. In this same year, 1813, the revision of the Charter of the East India Company permitted for the first time Christian missionaries something like free access to the Company's territories. These new missionaries were enemies of caste, almost to a man (and woman); but then they were enemies of 'heathen darkness' in equal measure. And whereas the previous century had been able to regard caste as a social rather than a religious ordinance, the Evangelical missionaries were able to make no such concession. Hinduism they saw clearly, was all of a piece, and should be combatted as a totality.[15] What was required of any convert henceforth would have to be nothing less than a total rejection of what Alexander Duff called this 'old, pestilent religion'. Caste, as it happened, formed a very convenient focus of enmity; for whereas it was difficult to know what was going on in a convert's mind and heart, the open renunciation of caste and acceptance of Christian baptism could be insisted on, and observed when (or rather if) it took place.

There is no lack of evidence of the distress caused to Hindu families, particularly of the higher castes, when one or other of their number felt inwardly impelled to accept baptism, and the social

---

[13] Thus we find in *The Report of the Wesleyan Methodist Missionary Society* for 1858 (p. 155), the typical statements that caste laws are 'a lie against nature, against humanity, against history', and that caste itself is 'the bane of India'.

[14] Quoted by BEARCE, op. cit., p. 82.

[15] Perhaps the most consistent attempt to devise a missionary strategy in accordance with this view was made by the educationalist Alexander Duff. See SHARPE, op. cit., p. 65: 'It [Hinduism] seemed to be essentially a whole, and Duff believed that to attack and undermine any one part was to attack and undermine the whole.'

ostracism which was the inevitable consequence. But this was not the only source of distress. A less well-known aspect of the history of the Indian Church concerns the impact made by non-Lutheran missionaries on previously Lutheran missions, particularly in South India. For instance, the anti-caste zeal of the Anglican Bishop Daniel Wilson in the 1830's and 1840's decimated many of the formerly Lutheran Tranquebar congregations. Wilson encouraged his missionaries to attempt to root out every vestige of 'heathenism' from the Christian community, forbidding as well as caste, the use of Tamil music, Tamil marriage customs, and the use of some Tamil names. In 1847 he introduced the practice of 'love feasts', which rapidly became shibboleth occasions, since to take part was to proclaim one's freedom from caste prejudices. Later observers have noted, not without reason, that the harsh legalism of this kind of approach was not really evidence of pastoral concern, since it set such great store by external observances.[16]

This same insistence on some outward and public break with caste could be documented from a variety of sources. I will take one fairly typical example, from the work of the German Leipzig Mission in South India in the 1850's.

In 1854 it was proposed to ordain one of the mission's two first ministerial candidates, a certain Nallatambi. However, the missionaries were not agreed among themselves as to the wisdom of this step, since one in particular was related by marriage to an English missionary who was very much anti-caste. This English missionary proposed to the Lutherans a practical test of the ordinand's freedom from caste prejudice; he should be invited to take tea with the missionary before his ordination. Nallatambi's reply to the invitation was: 'Preserve me from your ministry and your teacups. I don't want either of them, and I shall be quite happy to remain a catechist.'[17] However, it ought to be said in all fairness that the Leipzig missionaries, good Lutherans as they were, did not impose such strict rules on catechumens as they did on ordinands, and that

---

[16] See SANDEGREN, *Kast och Kristendom i Sydindien* (1921), p. 197: 'The Reformed missionaries' legalism and lack of pastoral patience had a very harmful effect on the lives of the congregations.' The Swedish book from which this quotation is taken is very valuable for our subject; regrettably, it has never been translated.

[17] Ibid., p. 209.

they insisted that no distinctions of caste should be observed in church, though they were prepared to accept caste customs which had to do with rank and social standing.[18] The difficulty arose, needless to say, when it came to deciding precisely which customs these were.

Most Evangelical missionaries were not prepared to make even these concessions, and for the remainder of the nineteenth and a good part of the twentieth century caste continued to stand as a symbol of everything to which Christianity was opposed. A symposium published in 1929 as *The Christian Task in India* will serve as well as any as source of later statements along these lines. In it we find, for instance, a leading Indian Christian, Bishop Azariah of Dornakal, writing that

The essence of sin, according to Jewish prophets, was oppression of the poor; the essence of all true religion and virtue was 'to do justly, to love mercy, and to walk humbly with thy God'. These are what the Indian philosopher consistently ignored. Else, the age-long tyranny of caste would have been unknown.[19]

An American missionary, S. Higginbottom, accuses caste of limiting and restricting occupation and therefore contributing to poverty, of failing to develop the best in each individual, and of perpetuating servility and inequality. And another, J. F. Edwards, dismisses caste, untouchability and communalism as all 'a plain denial of Christ's principle of brotherhood'.[20] Such examples might easily be multiplied.

Thus in the period of most spectacular Christian advance in India – the nineteenth century – it had gradually become axiomatic that to become a member of a Christian church meant two things: to accept Christian baptism and to renounce caste; and from this it followed that the higher the caste of the Hindu, the less likelihood there was of his being converted to Christianity. It is true that as long ago as 1850 an act was passed, the Caste Disabilities Removal

[18] Ibid., p. 219f. Cf. above, n. 13, for the way in which missionaries of the Calvinist (Reformed) tradition reacted to this attitude on the part of the Lutherans.
[19] MACKENZIE (ed.), *The Christian Task in India*, p. 32f.
[20] Ibid., p. 173.

Act, which removed – at least in theory – some of the more severe penalties imposed by any caste on those persons who converted to another religion.[21] But although it is an open secret that the teachings of Jesus held considerable appeal for many Hindus, open conversions from the higher castes were always very few and far between – and this despite the fact that the Christian missions devoted a good deal of their resources to the attempt to reach these upper castes, particularly through education.[22]

One inevitable result of the social ostracism which accompanied such individual baptisms was that the missions were forced to undertake the support of their converts in the much-maligned 'mission compounds', or 'mission villages'. 'All over India', wrote Bishop Stephen Neill in the 1930's, 'are scattered mission villages created for the reception of those who, with exceptional courage, have acted as individuals, and have braved the contempt of their fellows in order to follow Christ. The experiment has only rarely been a success'.[23] This is true, though I am not really persuaded that the mission compound or village was the *wholly* negative phenomenon that later commentators have sometimes assumed it to be, it has to be admitted, however, that this essentially *ad hoc* solution to a pressing social problem ensured the perpetuation of Western habits of mind among Indian Christians and that the 'mission compound mentality' was not always in the Church's best interests.[24]

But the mission to the upper classes was not the whole of the story. The last quarter of the nineteenth century was the period of the great mass movements into the Church. The trend began in the 1860's and continued unabated for several decades. The figures of

[21] The Act has been called 'a considerable victory for religious freedom', though it may be questioned how effective it in fact was. SINHA, *Secularism in India* (1968), p. 14.

[22] A 'respectable Hindoo' was recorded in the *Report of the London Missionary Society* for 1834 (p. 39) as saying that 'Others, as well as myself, are convinced of the truth of Christ's religion; but caste is like an iron chain about our necks.' Cf. O'MALLEY, *Modern India and the West* (1941), p. 673. On the educational enterprise, see SHARPE, op. cit., Chapters 2 and 3.

[23] *Builders of the Indian Church* (1934), p. 45.

[24] For a negative view of the 'mission compound' and its mentality, see MCCORKEL (ed.), *Voices from the Younger Churches* (1939), p. 25. But cf. MCGAVRAN, *Bridges of God* (1955), p. 47: 'As we look back on the last hundred years, it seems both necessary and desirable for there to have been this approach. With all its limitations, it was the best strategy for the era.'

increase in membership of the Christian community between 1861 and 1910 provide startling reading: 1861 – 52·3 per cent, 1871 – 61·6 per cent, 1881 – 86·1 per cent, 1890 – 34 per cent, 1900 – 52·8 per cent, 1910 – 72·2 per cent.[25] Characteristic of mass movements is that whole families, groups, villages, are received simultaneously into the Church, as a result of a collective decision, that they are baptised collectively, and that the process of Christianisation is held to be an ongoing process, begun by elementary instruction and baptism, but not ended by it. A further characteristic, as far as India is concerned, is that the greater part of the mass movements involved the conversion not of caste Hindus, but of outcases – socially the lowest of the low. Occasionally these groups might be located within an urban complex, but for the most part they were to be found in the villages.

It is important to recognise that the converts in mass movements aroao were not by any means a *tabula rasa*, either religiously or socially. Their religion was one or other variety of what is generally known as 'popular Hinduism', 'animism' or 'primitive religion' – though none of these titles is very appropriate; their social structure broadly 'tribal', though with a good deal of the characteristic insistence of the caste system on purity and rank.[26]

Now what kind of requirements concerning membership were the churches in a position to make of these people? In reality, little more could be required than a good intention. They could not be required to renounce caste, since for the most part they had no caste to renounce; and it is not easy to legislate against 'superstition'. If the group were prepared to accept some elementary instruction in the Christian faith, to submit to baptism, to build a church, and undertake the partial support of a minister or catechist for their further instruction and the regular provision of Christian worship, then the mission or Indian church could do no more. An act of incorporation into the Christian Church had taken place, and a sacramental pattern had been established. But what went on beneath or outside

[25] The figures are taken from *Encyclopaedia Britannica* XVIII (11th ed. 1911), p. 595.
[26] 'Popular' Hinduism has been remarkably little studied, in comparison with the so-called 'Higher' Hinduism. See, however, e.g. WHITEHEAD, *The Village Gods of South India* (1916), and ELMORE, *Dravidian Gods in Modern Hinduism* (1925). Among more recent studies, see DIEHL, *Instrument and Purpose* (1956) and DE SMET and NEUNER (eds.), *Religious Hinduism* (3rd ed. 1968), pp. 95ff., 136ff., 154ff., 163ff., 172ff.

this pattern could neither be checked nor altered. Their God had a new name; but the remainder of the divine hierarchy – lesser deities, spirits, ghosts, demons – survived. The social conditions under which they lived changed only gradually, or not at all, and such is the force of tradition and the power of a people's collective representations that a whole mass of pre-Christian attitudes and practices simply continued undisturbed. It has done so to this day.

This is almost certainly one of the reasons for the phenomenon, so common in Indian village Christian communities, of what one might perhaps call half-way membership, in which individuals, although they have been baptised, have never been confirmed or otherwise received into the full membership of the Church. This is, however, a complex phenomenon; it may be suspected that the desire to avoid making a complete break with traditional culture plays some part in this situation; but in some cases it may be, too, that there is official unwillingness to admit to full communicant membership those who have not given evidence (*inter alia* by giving up caste observances) of living a full Christian life.[27]

We may perhaps refer in this connection to the study published in 1965 by Bishop Carl Gustav Diehl of the Tamil Evangelical Lutheran Church: *Church and Shrine: Intermingling Patterns of Culture in the life of some Christian Groups in South India* – a study which, as its title suggests, subjects the actual life of some South Indian (Lutheran) Christians to critical scrutiny. Diehl allows that very many Christians in the villages are inevitably still profoundly involved in the Hindu culture of which they have previously been part, and he gives numerous examples of the ways in which this involvement takes place. His final summing up is, however, curiously double-edged. On the one hand, he writes,

> In most cases registered the Christians have fulfilled their obligations as members of the Church. It can be taken for granted

---

[27] There is precedent for this in the history of the Church: in the Middle Ages the custom of *prima signatio* was resorted to by those who wanted to be associated with the Christians, without becoming fully committed to the Christian way of life. See RIMBERT, *Vita Anskarii* 24; also SVERDRUP, *Da Norge ble kristnet* (1942), p. 115. Attention might also be drawn to the New England Puritan institution of the 'Half-Way Covenant', proposed in 1662 as a form of membership for those who had not had a 'converting experience'. BOORSTIN, *The Americans: The Colonial Experience* (1965), p. 40.

that they have with reasonable regularity attended Sunday services. When the pastor visits the congregation, they have willingly admitted him into their house for prayers. The local teacher will have had little difficulty in persuading them to bring their newborn babies to baptism. Marriages and funerals have been celebrated in the Christian fashion. . . .[28]

But on the other hand, since 'Christian activity' is something super-imposed on previous patterns of life, and something to which the Hindu pattern has no precise equivalent, the old patterns persist when the individual has need of them – seemingly very often. Thus:

> Temptation to make use of the old ceremonies comes to an in-dividual Christian, if his own religious situation is considered, either because the Church has not substituted Christian means of the old ceremonies, or because he has not grasped the full signi-ficance of evangelical freedom. He may of course also take to the old customs when he thinks that the Christian rites fail, or when he feels the need of more tangible means of securing what he wants.[29]

It seems that what Bishop Diehl is saying here is that although the formal requirements of Church membership are observed, there is another wide area of human need which is not sufficiently catered for by these patterns of observance. If an ex-Hindu (in the formal sense) continues to act in a distinctively Hindu way at certain decisive moments in his life, it is because he needs to do so. A very similar observation was made in 1959 by P. D. Devanandan, when he wrote that 'something like the caste group consciousness' had developed in the Indian Church partly, but only partly, as a carry-over from previous patterns of behaviour. In addition,

> . . . we must also concede that this group consciousness is due to the individual's continuing need for social security, for com-munity belonging, for collective strength and for prestige of association. Also in the case of the less advanced members of the Church there is need for some sort of social control. They ask for

---

[28] DIEHL, *Church and Shrine* (1965), p. 178.
[29] Ibid., p. 179.

social directives which will give positive guidance in making individual decisions on social conduct.[30]

Two other recent books in which problems of this kind are discussed in considerable detail, and against the background of field-work studies are Victor E. W. Hayward (ed.), *The Church as Christian Community* (1966), which contains three separate studies of North Indian churches, one in an urban milieu, one rural and one tribal; and P. Y. Luke and John B. Carman, *Village Christians and Hindu Culture* (1968), which is based on intensive studies in one rural area of the Medak Diocese of the Church of South India. It would be wrong to say that the tone of these studies was altogether pessimistic, but there seems throughout to be the feeling that previous generations of Christians, whether missionaries or not, have seriously underestimated the depth of the problems that surround the attempt to establish Christianity, particularly in rural India. Ernest Y. Campbell's study of the Church in the Punjab, for instance, notes that

> In many cases only the exceptional village Christians can even live as Christians in the rural environment. In their families and groups, in their life and thinking – without benefit of literature or ceremony or Christian tradition – rural Christians are governed almost exclusively by the age-old village traditions and pre-Christian thought and behaviour patterns. Christianity which is only vaguely or briefly known can be little more in most cases than a thin veneer over habitual patterns of thinking and doing, which are the villagers' inheritance in a non-Christian culture.[31]

It is fatally easy for the outside observer, particularly if he should be altogether outside the Indian situation, to say that from the Christian point of view, it is permissible to extend membership of the Christian community only to those who are prepared to accept a certain minimum standard of Christian behaviour. But difficulties arise just as soon as one begins to try to decide exactly what these criteria are to be. Baptism, certainly; but there is little unanimity as to what else might be a criterion. The outward renunciation of caste, particularly on the part of a group, would be a theoretical

---

[30] DEVANANDAN, in *The Ecumenical Review* XI/3 (April 1959), p. 276.
[31] HAYWARD (ed.), *The Church as Christian Community* (1966), p. 217.

possibility, but little more. There are examples on record, however, of attempts being made in this direction. For instance to look back into the last century, in the 1880's, the brethren of the Cambridge Mission to Delhi (an Anglican society, of which C. F. Andrews was once a member) working among the Chamar (Leather-Workers) caste, attempted to secure a collective renunciation of certain common practices among them. In the first place they built a square of eight houses, which were to be let to such Chamars as professed themselves willing to observe three simple rules:

1. To observe Sunday as a day of rest.
2. To use Christian rites exclusively at times of birth, marriage and death.
3. To abstain from the use of *charas* (a drug).

And when friction occurred between the regenerate and the unregenerate among the Chamars (as it inevitably did), a caste council or *panchayat* was called in order to give the Christians the opportunity to break decisively with their non-Christian fellows. Significantly, those who wished to remain in caste fellowship were required to affirm this on a pot of Ganges water (or what was reputed to be such). Five Christians did so ('openly and wilfully denied their Lord'), but eight families apparently broke the caste bond once and for all, in public. I say apparently, because G. A. Lefroy, the missionary who recorded all this, was forced to admit that after it all, 'for the present at any rate they continue in just their old connection of friendship and fellowship with the Chamars', and among the missionaries, 'very varying are in the views taken . . . of the extent of their surrender'.[32]

So far we have been looking at the Hindu institution of caste as a focus of Christian opposition in the modern missionary period of the Church in India, and we have seen that despite this opposition, the Christians' break with traditional patterns of culture has been far from complete. A (not altogether separate) further facet of the caste problem concerns the resestablishment of the caste spirit, or what has been called 'casteism' within the Christian churches. This has been very frequently commented on by missionaries and other

[32] LEFROY, *The Leather-Workers of Daryaganj* (Cambridge Mission to Delhi Occasional Paper No. 7, 1884), p. 22.

observers of the Indian scene. Thus, to take one example, we find J. N. Farquar commenting in 1913 that caste

> . . . has overtaken and poisoned every Hindu sect that has tried to escape from it, and . . . has infected, at least in some degree, every community in India, numbing with its venom great groups of Muhammadans, little circles of Jews, and even certain Christian churches.[33]

Leaving aside the language of this statement, the plain fact has been that Christian communities in India, perhaps because they have been expected by Hindus to behave like castes, have done precisely that, not only over against non-Christian communities, but even over against other Christian groups. It seems from studies carried out at various times over the past few decades that 'casteism' – involving the deliberate cultivation of social distinctions between groups, to the points of refusal to interdine, intermarry, and the like – is common, even endemic, among Christians in various parts of India. Technically it is distinct from the problem we have been discussing so far; but its roots are similar, and it appears to be equally difficult to combat.

An an example of this trend we may perhaps refer to Ninan Koshy's recently published study of caste relationships in the Christian Churches of Kerala. In this area there are two distinct Christian groups: on the one hand the Syrian Christians, with traditions going back at least to the fourth or fifth centuries, and conceivably even as far back as the first century and to the Apostle Thomas himself; and on the other hand, bodies of recent converts, usually from an outcaste background. The caste problem in Kerala, then, takes the form of exclusiveness as between these two groups. It is not a new problem; indeed, it has been in evidence for over a century. But a couple of quotations from Koshy's report *Caste in the Kerala Churches* (Bangalore 1968) will make plain the present range of the problem:

> Casteism is one of the most serious problems that confront the Kerala churches. It is now more than a century since conversion from backward classes to the Christian Church began in Kerala.

---

[33] FARQUHAR, *The Crown of Hinduism* (1913), p. 176.

In spite of the passage of a century and more, there are separate places of worship, separate congregations, separate cemeteries, etc., for the different caste sections within the Church in various parts of Kerala (p. 23). . . . The most dominant characteristic and chief contributing factor of inter-caste tensions in the Kerala Church is the exclusiveness of the Syrian Christians as a distinct caste and their apparent determination to perpetuate this.[34]

The same report also makes clear that most Syrian Christians believe that differences between themselves and backward class Christians should and will continue.

A similar caste-type exclusiveness may even affect Christians belonging to two nominally outcaste groups: an example would be the relationship between Mala and Madiga Christians in central India, as reported by Luke and Carman. For a variety of reasons, the Malas consider themselves the superior group, and although in church Malas and Madigas will sit and worship together, and take Communion together, in their own villages they neither mix nor take water from the same well. In one village, Achampet, a Mala evangelist has served a Madiga congregation for years, always taking a Mala woman of the village as his personal servant, and reserving the 'mission well' for his own use and for the use of other Malas, all of whom in that particular village are non-Christians. It is further recorded that the Malas in that village have refused to become Christians simply because they have no desire to mix with Madigas; twice in the history of that particular congregation, however, the Malas have considered becoming Christians, but have apparently been dissuaded by Malas in other villages.[35]

In both these cases – and in others which might be added – there is nothing which can be done on any kind of official level to remedy the situation since all the parties are formally Christians in good standing. There may be exhortation; there may be disapproval; but there is little else.

In what we have said thus far, the problem of church membership in the Indian Church has centred on caste: first, as what we might (not altogether accurately) call a Hindu 'survival' in the midst of

[34] KOSHY, *Caste in the Kerala Churches* (1968), pp. 23, 51.
[35] LUKE and CARMAN, *Village Christians and Hindu Culture* (1968), pp. 78ff.

Christianity, and secondly, as a means by which social barriers have been set up between different groups of Christians. In becoming a member of a Christian church, it is generally expected, as a matter of practical theology, that the individual will cease to be in the formal sense a member of a caste; but at the same time, it is recognised that the theological ideal and the social actuality may be far removed from each other. This in itself constitutes a problem of no small order. But at this point a further problem obtrudes, which might be phrased in the form of a question: Is it *right* for the Christian Church to insist on such an acute separation of the Christian from Hindu social order? Or alternatively, were the Evangelical Christians and their successors right to make the renunciation of caste virtually the sole condition on which the individual might be received by baptism into the fellowship of Christ's Church?

For almost a century, a small section of liberal Christian opinion in India has in fact held to the position that *formal* membership of the Church is always unnecessary, and doubly so in a country like India. Among missionaries, mention might be made of William Miller of Madras Christian College, who on one celebrated occasion confessed bitterly that insistence on baptism had caused great harm to the Christian cause in India, and that for his part,

> . . . because I daily see the terrible harm which this state of matters is working throughout India, . . . I have put, and while life lasts shall put, openness of heart to God and truth, and willingness to learn of Christ, emphatically in the first place and baptism emphatically in the second.[36]

A decade or so later, the LMS missionary Bernard Lucas, in a series of books, among them *The Empire of Christ* (1907), *Christ for India* (1910) and *Our Task in India* (1914), urged that in concentrating on proselytism rather than genuine evangelism, the Christian witness in India had become fatally obscured. The third of these books in particular contained a powerful indictment of proselytising methods as having contributed materially to the exotic character of Christianity

[36] Quoted by BAAGÖ, *Pioneers of Indian Christianity* (1969), p. 77. Baagö himself, a Dane and former missionary, is well known as an exponent of this type of view. See also his monograph *The Movement around Subba Rao* (1968).

in India, and to the false impression which many Hindus had gained
of Christianity as a foreign religion.

If we wish to dissociate ourselves (he wrote) from the proselytising
impression current among Hindus, we must make it perfectly
clear and evident that, as regards ourselves and our work, mere
accession to organised Christianity is not our primary object. We
must frankly face the issue, and ask ourselves whether we are content to spend our lives in ministering to the religious life of India,
even though the result of our labour is never represented by a
single accession to organised Christianity.[37]

Baptism was certainly not dismissed by Lucas; but he was insistent
that it was the function of the Indian Church, and not of the
missionary-evangelist, and that premature baptisms, injurious both
to the Hindu community and to the life of the individual, should be
avoided at all costs.

Attitudes like these were shared by some Indian Christians; and
their number increased as time went on – as may be seen, for instance, by referring to that powerful Indian Christian manifesto of
the late 1930's, *Rethinking Christianity in India* (1938). And it needs
scarcely be pointed out that still more recent developments in
Western theology – secular Christianity, religionless Christianity,
and the rest – have merely served to reinforce, in the minds of those
in a position to receive such impulses, that 'churchianity' is a bad
thing, and that baptism in particular, since it imposes illegitimate
theological tests and sets the convert apart from his Hindu fellows,
is perhaps the worst thing of all.[38]

This general attitude, of impatience with the whole question of
church membership in the Indian setting, has of course been further
reinforced by recent concentration on 'dialogue' as the only appropriate mode of encounter between Christian and Hindu. Although
dialogue itself is a notoriously vague term, it clearly rules out of
court any attempt to *persuade* anyone of the truth of any position
whatever; and when it is allied to the equally vague impression that
the Hindu may be in some sense an 'anonymous Christian', then the

[37] LUCAS, *Our Task in India* (1914), p. 105. On Lucas, see BAAGÖ, op. cit., pp. 78ff.
[38] On this general problem see SHARPE, 'The problem of Conversion in Recent
Missionary Thought', in *The Evangelical Quarterly* XLI/4 (1969), pp. 221ff.

problem of church membership retreats still further into limbo.[39]
Needless to say, the Christians who hold positions on this wing do
not represent a majority, nor do they speak for the mass of Indian
Christians. But their voices are increasingly being heard, inside and
outside India.

It should be remembered, however, that the Hindu attitude to
caste has not remained static and unchanged throughout our period.
Certainly in the villages, where the Christian Church at present has
a great deal of its membership, changes have been minimal; but in
the better-educated section of the population, particularly in the
cities, many of the views of the missionaries have been echoed by
Hindu reformers, albeit on other grounds. In fact caste is one of the
Hindu institutions most frequently attacked as archaic and destructive by Indian progressives.[40] This is not a development which we
can discuss in detail here, though it is certainly one of the features
which would need to be understood in a fuller study of the Church's
situation in India. It may suffice in this context to give only one
example, from the early years of the century and from the pen of
Rabindranath Tagore:

> The regeneration of the Indian people, to my mind, directly and
> perhaps solely depends upon the removal of this condition of
> caste. When I realise the hypnotic hold which this gigantic system
> of cold-blooded repression has taken on the minds of our people,
> whose social body it has so completely entwined in its endless coils
> that the free expression of manhood, even under the direst
> necessity, has become almost an impossibility, the only remedy that
> suggests itself to me is to educate them out of their trance. . . .[41]

[39] The 'anonymous Christian' attitude towards Hindus is far from irrelevant to the
complex of problems with which we are concerned, but space prevents a full discussion
of this side of things. The most accessible statements – by Roman Catholics – are
HILLMAN, *The Wider Ecumenism* (1968) and PANIKKAR, *The Unknown Christ of Hinduism*
(1964). The whole idea is open to serious theological objections.

[40] A lecture heard by the present writer in Madras in 1969 was entitled 'The Raja, the
Monk and the Mahatma', and criticised Rammohun Roy, Vivekananda and Gandhi for
their equivocal attitude to caste; the lecturer was a 'modern' Hindu, a prominent Civil
Servant. Cf. SHAH and RAO (eds.), *Tradition and Modernity in India* (1965), p. 31:
'. . . the caste system as practised in the past and as it is still in practice is indefen-
sible. . . . On such a view of the human situation, Indian culture cannot command
respect. There is room in it neither for dignity nor for freedom of man.'

[41] Quoted by FARQUHAR, *The Crown of Hinduism*, p. 175f.

Numerous Indians, as citizens of what is nominally a secular state, would echo these sentiments in these days. And as long as the Christian keeps his sights set on the higher levels of Indian society, it might seem as though the caste problem is fast disappearing.

But on the village level – where the greater part of the membership of the Christian Church is currently to be found – the problems of secularisation, indigenisation and dialogue are not the major problems. The greatest sources of practical difficulty have to do with the ministry, with the provision of Christian teaching, and with pastoral oversight. Often it is felt that if these problems could only be solved, the caste question in its various aspects would eventually solve itself. Perhaps this is so, although it would be unwise to be too categorical on this point. It would seem, at least, as though the present disproportion in some areas between confirmed and simply baptised (and therefore non-communicant) Christians could be remedied if only better teaching were available.

But not all membership problems can be solved so easily. For instance, in present-day India there are forces which actively discourage membership of Christian churches, particularly on the part of former outcastes. Of late outcaste groups (*Harijans*) in India have been given a certain amount of Government aid. But Christians are technically speaking not *Harijans*. So it was that in 1954 a group of Madiga Christians were told that they could not have a share of Government lands, although their non-Christian Madiga neighbours could – unless they were prepared to renounce their Christianity, at least temporarily, by submitting their Hindu, rather than Christian, names to the officials. Some (but not all) did precisely this. The dilemma facing these Christians was expressed by a village Christian in 1959 in these words:

One cannot get on well in the world if he tries to live a truthful and honest life. We have been undergoing great hardships from the time we became Christians, and have been suffering great loss. Last year we nearly resigned our church membership in order to avail ourselves of the privileges and concessions offered to the Harijans by the Government – wells for drinking water, house sites and housing materials, lands for cultivation, scholarships for Harijan children attending Government schools, a reserved seat for a Harijan in the local village panchayats, and a supply of bullocks. . . . How can we afford to lose all these benefits from the Government? We are still wondering if we have made a mistake in accepting Christianity.[42]

Precisely the same point is made, with respect to Kerala, by Koshy, *Caste in the Kerala Churches* (Bangalore 1968), though with the added twist that backward class Christians '. . . feel that the Syrian Christians and their leaders who have great influence in the state have not done anything to get their legitimate grievances redressed'.[43]

I do not propose to attempt a summing-up of the points raised in this paper. My aim has been to draw attention to problems – with all the distortion thereby entailed – rather than to suggest solutions. Perhaps I might, however, revert finally to my first point, about the infinite variety of India. No one part of India is representative of the whole of the subcontinent, nor is one Christian problem representative of the whole of the Christian Church. All one can say is that the caste problem (which has in fact far more ramifications than we have been able to deal with here) is still typical; in it is embodied the essential encounter, on the practical, grass-roots level between the Church and traditional Hindu culture. On the intellectual level, on the secular level, on the level of pure spirituality, there are doubtless other problems and other perspectives; and I do not wish to claim an authority I do not possess in predicting what might happen next in any of these areas.

May I end, then, by quoting a few lines from a recent field study of a Christian Church in North India:

It may be . . . that the rural church in the Punjab today is set in the Punjab of today to 'be' rather than to 'do'; to survive rather than to grow; to reach down into the soil of India – a thing it could not do perhaps under missionary tutelage – rather than to send out visible branches of new membership and the added foliage of new groups and classes. It is possible that only when

[43] KOSHY, op. cit., p. 27.
[42] LUKE and CARMAN, op. cit., p. 68f.

these new indigenous roots find solid purchase in Indian rural culture will a fresh and vital expression of Indian Christianity spring forth to mobilise the aspirations and energies of the many Christians who are now un-committed and unenthusiastic.[44]

[44] The words of ERNEST Y. CAMPBELL, in Hayward (ed.), *The Church as Christian Community*, p. 217.

BIOGRAPHICAL NOTES

DAVID CLARK *is a Methodist Minister working in a Presbyterian/Methodist team ministry in Greenwich, London. He is secretary of the Methodist Sociological Group and editor of the bulletin 'Community'.*

8 Community, Membership and the Church

DAVID B. CLARK

THIS PAPER FIRST EXAMINES THE SOCIOLOGICAL MEANING OF community and its expression through different types of social and especially ecclesiastical organisation, particular attention being paid to the concept of church membership. It then sets out to establish criteria for assessing the quality of community and ends by suggesting features of any church hoping to match such criteria. The subject is a large one but I felt it of most value to undertake a comprehensive, even if at times rather rapid, survey of the field.

The Essential Nature of Community

'Community' is a word today over-used yet rarely defined. I employ it here to indicate that essential ingredient without which all, repeat, all social units would disintegrate. As MacIver states, 'Life is essentially and always communal life. Every living thing is born into community and owes its life to community'.[1] Simpson writes, 'Without the presence of community men could not will associational relations'.[2] But what is the nature of this vital social ingredient?

---

[1] R. M. MACIVER, *Community*, London 1924, p. 209.
[2] G. SIMPSON, *Conflict and Community*, New York 1937, p. 11.

Simpson continues, 'Community is no circumscribed sphere of social life, but rather the very life-blood of social life. Community is not simply economic, nor simply political, nor simply territorial, nor simply visceral. Nor is it all these special elements added together. Ultimately, it is a complex of conditioned emotions which the individual feels towards the surrounding world and his fellows . . . It is to human beings and their feelings, sentiments, reactions, that all look for the fundamental roots of community'.[3]

However, it would be inaccurate to describe the phenomenon of community as *a* sentiment. Rather, as the words just quoted rightly imply, community is a complex of sentiments that contribute towards a wider whole. Sociologists, amongst others, have directly or indirectly spent a good deal of time and effort trying to decide which of this complex of sentiments are most important. A good deal of research, especially in the field of (so-called) community studies, reveals two as basic.[4] These I call the 'essential' elements of community, all other sentiments of communal note being embraced by them.

The first essential element can be termed 'a sense of solidarity'. It is a sentiment very much akin to what MacIver and Page call 'we-feeling' which they define as 'the feeling that leads men to identify themselves with others so that when they say "we" there is no thought of distinction and when they say "ours" there is no thought of division'.[5] Solidarity is by far the most commonly accepted ingredient of community and it is this sentiment which writers have in mind when they refer to social unity, togetherness, social cohesion, a sense of belonging and so forth.

Unfortunately preoccupation with solidarity has led to the neglect of the second essential communal element, 'a sense of significance'. This is very similar to what MacIver and Page term 'role-feeling', i.e. 'the sense of place or station' experienced by group members 'so that each person feels he has a role to play, his own function to fulfil in the reciprocal exchanges of the social scene'.[6] That

[3] SIMPSON, op. cit., pp. 71 and 97.
[4] See the discussion in D. B. CLARK, *Community and a Suburban Village*, Unpublished Ph.D. thesis, University of Sheffield 1969, Chapter I.
[5] R. M. MACIVER and C. H. PAGE, *Society*, London 1950, p. 293.
[6] MACIVER and PAGE, op. cit., p. 293.

significance must stand side by side with solidarity is emphasised by Klein when she writes, 'Not infrequently in practice people want a show of appreciation more than they want affection'.[7] Again significance is made up of a complex of subordinate sentiments (such as social superiority, pride, a sense of achievement, a sense of fulfilment, etc.) all contributing to the larger whole. I return to these two essential components of community later.

Although a sense of community is necessary for any social group to survive, community is expressed in and through numerous social forms – through many different kinds of social interaction and social structure. Where men are satisfied with these forms of expression a very strong sense of community can exist, for its actual intensity must be measured in relation to the attitudes of the group members and not against some exterior standard. As Gans writes of an American town, 'If Levittowners report that they find their community satisfying, as they do, their opinion ought to be respected. Although the suburban critics insist that these satisfactions are spurious and self-deceptive, they offer no valid evidence, so that their charge only indicates their differing standards for the good life'.[8] In fact a wide variety of groups throughout history have experienced a very strong degree of community even though, to the eye of the outside observer, they may appear in other respects to have suffered extreme deprivation – witness the early Christian Church. Witness too in recent times the people of Biafra during the Nigerian civil war.

Such satisfaction can remain for several reasons – for example, because members of the group concerned have never seen the possibility of any other way of life. Writing of northern England in the 1930s Orwell makes a similar point: 'Talking once with a miner I asked him when the housing shortage first became acute in his district; he answered, "when we were told about it", meaning that till recently people's standards were so low that they took almost any degree of overcrowding for granted.'[9] But if the social environment so changes that people are introduced to the possibility of greater

[7] J. KLEIN, The Study of Groups, London 1956, p. 118 (footnote).
[8] H. J. GANS, The Levittowners, London 1967, p. xxvi.
[9] G. ORWELL, The Road to Wigan Pier, Harmondsworth 1962 (first published 1937), p. 57.

communal satisfaction, then the end of old patterns of social activity and social structure are very much in view.[10]

This century has seen in English society such a situation of flux. Social expressions of community which at the parochial level at least had basically remained stable through, or reasserted themselves even after, the early upheavals of the industrial revolution have of late undergone fundamental and far reaching changes. There are many reasons for this, and none can be designated the prime cause, but without doubt one of the outstanding agents of change has been the phenomenon of mobility. The latter has three interrelated aspects. There is spatial mobility, where people have above all moved their place of residence, but also referring to the regular movement they are involved in to and from school, work, the shops and centres of recreation (including holidays abroad). There is social mobility, in a far more open society than existed even thirty years ago. And, related to both as cause and effect, there is what can be called 'cognitive' mobility, characterised by an ability and eagerness to assimilate and to reflect critically upon a wide range of experiences from beyond one's immediate social and cultural environment. It is particularly the great increase in the number of cognitively mobile people in society that has brought such thoroughgoing changes in the social expression of community.

Using the criterion of mobility, two dominant types of social interaction and structure can be distinguished. Following Merton, these can be called the 'local' and the 'cosmopolitan'.[11] I have already discussed these two types at some length elsewhere;[12] suffice it to say here that the local is a person who throughout life has remained spatially, socially and cognitively immobile. Such would be certain of the residents of a mining parish in Yorkshire where I worked, who were born and bred, had worked and died, in the same village. The cosmopolitan is a person who has been spatially, socially

---

[10] See the pertinent discussion in D. A. SCHON, *Beyond the Stable State*, London 1971.

[11] R. K. MERTON, *Social Theory and Social Structure*, Glencoe 1957 (revised edition), pp. 387–420.

[12] D. B. CLARK, 'Local and Cosmopolitan Aspects of Religious Activity in a Northern Suburb', in *A Sociological Yearbook of Religion in Britain, No. 3*, London 1970. D. B. CLARKE, 'Local and Cosmopolitan Aspects of Religious Activity in a Northern Suburb: Processes of Change', in *A Sociological Yearbook of Religion in Britain, No. 4*, London 1971.

and cognitively mobile. Such are many residents of the London borough where I now live.

In sociological terms these two categories form ideal types and as such are applicable to only a limited number of actual cases. Very many people fall in between and one comes across those who might be called, for example, 'uprooted locals' or 'nostalgic cosmopolitans'. What must be emphasised is that both locals and cosmopolitans can experience an equally strong sense of community *as measured by their own expectations*. Here sociologists as well as others have often gone badly astray. Even Ferdinand Tönnies, who wrote the classic study of community, slips into the error of associating *Gemeinschaft* (akin to our locally oriented life-style) with the presence of community and *Gesellschaft* (akin to our cosmopolitan life-style) with its absence. Thus he writes of late nineteenth century Germany: 'The entire culture has been transformed into a civilisation of state and *Gesellschaft*, and this transformation means the doom of culture itself if none of its scattered seeds remain alive and again bring forth the essence and idea of *Gemeinschaft*, thus secretly fostering a new culture amidst the decaying one.'[13] The temptation to assume the rural village represents the zenith of community and urban society its nadir must be resisted.

Local and Cosmopolitan Expressions of Christian Community

The emergence during this century of a cosmopolitan expression of community which has in many places overwhelmed the local is a feature not only of English society at large but also of its various institutions, amongst which is the church. I want, therefore, to turn now to local and cosmopolitan expressions of Christian community. Particular attention will be given to the concept of church membership. Within and behind this discussion lies a changing approach to authority, in its turn having an important bearing on our understanding of the relationship of man to God.

Those participating in locally oriented religious institutions often do so because it is part and parcel of their local cultural heritage. They are baptised as infants and though confirmation later in life may give the semblance of a choice, it either occurs at such an early

[13] F. TÖNNIES, *Community and Association* (translated and supplemented by C. P. Loomis), London 1955 (first published 1887), p. 270.

age (from seven onwards in some churches) that it precludes mature judgment or is something so expected that it happens as a matter of course. We are several centuries past the days of Richard Baxter when he with other boys were confirmed at random in the churchyard as they ran out to greet the bishop, but a similar approach to such ceremonies lingers on.[14] Entry into the religious organisation is seen by the local as of a piece with his total way of life – to join the church is to affirm both his solidarity with and identity amongst his own people. His membership is dominantly of a social nature. Any minister who has witnessed the break up of a locally oriented congregation knows this only too well. Of the total number of very regular worshippers of one small Methodist church which I saw shut down only half made any effort to link up with other churches of Methodist or any other denomination.

Where churches of a local type exist in a social milieu which to them is both acceptable and accepting, conditions of membership tend to be left relatively undefined. Because people know by upbringing to which denomination they belong there is little attempt to mark formal boundaries with strong sanctions. In this situation the question of at what precise point a person becomes a member of the church is not a pressing one – it simply happens as part of the normal run of things. Where locally oriented congregations find themselves in a culturally foreign or hostile environment, then the need to preserve a distinctive life-style becomes much more acute and conditions of entry are more definite.[15] For example, churches desiring evidence of dramatic conversion as a condition of acceptance usually come into this category.

What needs to be stressed is that in all cases the local type of church demands that in the final resort its members owe prior allegiance to it amongst all the other groups to which they may belong. In some cases (as amongst certain Free Church congregations) this manifests itself in members giving virtually all their spare time to church activities. 'I never know why we don't take our beds and sleep there!' commented one Methodist lady to me about her own church involvement. Where participants seem to be rather less actively involved, the church of a locally oriented kind can still be distinguished

---

[14] M. PERRY, (ed.), *Crisis for Confirmation*, London 1967, p. 18.
[15] R. ROBERTSON, *The Sociological Interpretation of Religion*, Oxford 1970, p. 123.

How much of this was a late Victorian phenomenon?

by its explicit or implicit assumption that the total life of members is ultimately its responsibility.

The local type church is typified by the set pattern of its life, Sunday by Sunday or throughout the year. Members know just what happens, when and how to respond on each occasion, again something that makes membership a process of slow learning and considerable practice. The insider is aware that there are almost as many subtle procedural variations within the so-called simple Nonconformist service as within the ostensibly more complex Roman Catholic liturgy. Typifying such a situation is the embarrassment felt by many locals if they are inadvertently evicted from their regular pew by unsuspecting strangers.

The organisation of the locally oriented congregation is highly structured though usually according as much to an informal as official code of rules. Each person has his role however humble to play, whether it be giving out the hymn books, seeing to the flowers, making the coffee, ordering the church posters or collecting in the jumble. The members of the locally oriented church gain a sense of significance in these and many other ways. But status is not just achieved, it is also ascribed; for example, because of longevity of service rendered to the cause. Typical here was the respect shown by all the members of one northern Methodist church to its caretaker (a postman by occupation) who had served them for thirty years and his father thirty-six years before that.

The stable, sometimes almost static, nature of the local type church means that the first, and often second, response to change is defensive. Members are controlled by very strong informal pressures to conform to a traditional way of life which in numerous cases are exerted not only through people being well known to one another but actually related. In one of my own Yorkshire churches a split in the Leaders' Meeting meant a split in several families. In fact, the locally oriented congregation has many similarities to an extended family. It has much the same ethos and its view of authority is of the same sort. It often looks to the 'head of the family', usually a person of considerable local standing, to give the lead. This may be the local priest, especially if he has been resident in the area for some time, but in other cases, notably in the Free Churches, it is frequently a local layman and not the minister who fulfils this role. To such persons – symbolic figures representing the established cultural and social traditions of the congregation – members look for the maintenance of their particular religious life-style. In trying to unite two Methodist churches still sited only a few hundred yards from each other some forty years after Methodist union at the national level, I was taught forcibly that members will not dare to move unless their informally chosen leader gives the word. Ecumenists be warned!

The cosmopolitan expression of Christian community presents a very different picture though as yet it is still very much a developing phenomenon. Consequently whilst it is fairly easy to point to clear-cut examples of locally oriented English churches, the cosmopolitan religious life-style is still found growing out of or existing alongside the local. By definition the cosmopolitan is a highly mobile person. He has left his place of upbringing many years before and his desire to associate with a worshipping congregation is no longer simply a matter of course. Once away from the mores of his native Christian group he often experiences little pressure to join a church. He now transfers or takes up his membership through personal choice rather than custom. Like the organisation man in Whyte's Park Forest, he shops around not only between congregation and congregation but between denomination and denomination. In Whyte's case-study the factors deciding choice of church were in order of preference – the minister, the Sunday school, the location, the denomination and the music.[16] As in Park Forest, the cosmopolitan's choice is more utilitarian than social in the sense that he places his own preferences, based on a discrimination born of wide experience, before the expectations of the folk back home.

As yet there are few English churches which have adapted their conditions of membership to suit the true cosmopolitan. If he wishes to associate he still has to pay lip service to the traditional practices and formulae of the locally oriented church. But in reality, minister and congregation know membership means a very different thing to the cosmopolitan than to the local. There is little attempt to demand total allegiance from him, there being a tacit understanding that for the cosmopolitan the church can only be one amongst many

[16] W. H. WHYTE, *The Organization Man*, Harmondsworth 1960 (first published 1956), p. 339.

organisations that have the right to claim his loyalty. If a local is missing from worship one week there are immediate enquiries as to whether he is ill or indisposed; if a cosmopolitan is away for several weeks it is assumed that he is busy with the garden, away yachting, absent on business or visiting friends. Furthermore, because the cosmopolitan is attracted to the church as a religious rather than social institution, he sees little point in being involved in church activities over and above those which have a demonstrable religious content. Worshipping once a Sunday is quite sufficient to meet his needs.

The cosmopolitan church member appreciates order in religious affairs, for his is an organised way of life, but is not greatly perturbed if the time of mass is altered or the Sunday School Anniversary is cut from two Sundays to one. As long as the church provides what he basically wants, he is ready to accept innovation, for example, on the liturgical or ecumenical front, though he draws the line at things which begin to encroach on the time and energy he has deliberately allocated to the religious sphere.

Where dominantly cosmopolitan congregations do exist, the organisation and running of church affairs is a means to an end rather than an end in itself. All know the minimum number of tasks which must be undertaken to keep the church operational and members, necessarily interchangeable or replaceable in a mobile population, are fitted into the essential jobs according to their skills and experience. Unlike in the locally oriented congregation, person and role rarely become synonymous. 'Am I on duty this morning?' cheerily remarked a cosmopolitan deacon arriving at a London church four minutes before the service began: any local in such a situation would have blushed for shame! Cosmopolitan office holders achieve status more because of the quality of the expertise they can contribute to the organisation than because of their relationship to other members or length of conscientious service. 'A good effort' or 'loyal support' take second place to getting the job done.

In the cosmopolitan situation change is an everyday part of the social scene. The immediate response is interest in and examination of new ideas rather than spontaneous resistance. In the cosmopolitan congregation there is little attempt to put pressure on members to conform to past traditions; innovations are judged pragmatically. In Whyte's Park Forest the young cosmopolitan suburbanites, despite opposition at national level, quite happily, indeed enthusiastically, set up a new United Protestant Church embracing members of five major denominations.[17] It seemed the obvious step to take in their new surroundings.

All these things have some bearing on the attitude of the cosmopolitan to authority and leadership in the church. He views leadership as dominantly a functional matter to be accepted or rejected according to its effectiveness and efficiency. His model of church life is more akin to the business organisation than the extended family. He is not greatly attracted by symbolic leadership in religious affairs unless it produces what Whyte calls 'meaningful activity' at the periphery where his very transience often keeps him. He looks on church leaders as facilitators (and perhaps administrators) rather than guardians of the faithful. If he himself does decide to take up a leadership role in the church (as layman or priest) he expects to be quickly accepted, employed according to his merits and not to have to prove his worth simply by clocking up the years.

Community as a Quality

If the local and cosmopolitan are the two most obvious expressions of Christian community manifest in English society at present, the question which must now be posed is whether the church should seek to foster the one or the other – whether the church should look for something entirely different? This raises the further fundamental issue as to whether there are any criteria by which the *quality* of communal life typified by local and cosmopolitan churches can be assessed.

In seeking an answer we must go back to our discussion of the meaning and expression of community at the societal level, as opposed merely to the ecclesiastical level. It was stated earlier that, *from the point of view of the participants*, a very strong sense of community could be experienced within groups characterised by many different patterns of social activity and structure. Using the yardstick of the actual sentiments of the group members it would be quite impossible, without looking in detail at specific situations, to say whether locals or cosmopolitans enjoyed a stronger degree of

---

[17] WHYTE, op. cit., p. 340.

community. Even then, wider inferences about either type would be empirically dangerous.

But the point of view of the participants is not the only thing to be taken into consideration when trying to define what criteria decide the quality of communal life. As was mentioned before, the participants themselves may be quite unaware of the possibility of wider horizons and richer experiences. There is nothing unjust about those outside the situation making personal judgments as to whether they feel group members have still to realise their potential level of solidarity or significance. I am quite aware that at this stage we are stepping out of the strictly scientific field into the realm of moral, ethical and theological debate. Yet I am sure that unless such a step is taken much sociological analysis remains a mere catalogue of dry bones. Further I am convinced that sociologists amongst others, if they can now and then throw off what Theodore Roszak calls 'the myth of objective consciousness'[18], can suggest things of use to those dealing with the larger questions of meaning and value.

The two essential components of community were defined as a sense of solidarity amongst and a sense of significance for members of any given group. Turning first to the matter of social solidarity, the criterion I suggest by which its *quality* should be judged is that of 'comprehensiveness'. In other words, the qualitative criterion is the extent to which man, whilst retaining an intense sense of belonging at the level of the small group, can feel solidarity with increasingly wider circles of humanity. MacIver, in his well-known study of community, puts the point as follows: 'Our life is realised within not one but many communities, circling us round, grade beyond grade. The near community demands intimate loyalties and personal relationships, the concrete traditions and memories of everyday life. But where the near community is all community, its exclusiveness rests on ignorance and narrowness of thought, its emotional strength is accompanied by intellectual weakness. Its member becomes the slave of its traditions, the prisoner of his own affections. Without the widening of the gates – nay, without the breaking down of walls – there is no progress.'[19] Simpson puts the matter this way: 'It is the

---

[18] T. ROSZAK, *The Making of a Counter Culture*, London 1970. See especially pp. 216–17.

[19] MACIVER, op. cit., p. 260.

problem of carrying over the ideals of the primary or face-to-face group which is the most easily communalised, to the larger groups, and ultimately to nations and international action . . . There has latterly been much discussion of the need for a return to primary groups. But what is needed is a return to the ideals of the primary group in such a shape and so adjusted as to be capable of application to cosmopolitan conditions. Otherwise, a sort of return to the communal womb is being urged, a nostalgia for the infantile. To apply these ideals of the primary group to a world where large-scale industry has atomised the individual a structure for relationships must be erected so that the promulgation of these ideals may reap the fruits of sympathy, understanding, and togetherness, rather than rendering them abortive.'[20] All this may be relatively easy to assert; to attain this goal is what mankind has been about since its emergence. History demonstrates over and over again how easily men have failed to glimpse or have lost sight of this measure of the quality of solidarity and how often the stubborn retention of an exclusive sense of belonging has wrecked havoc with hopes of establishing the wider community of man.

The criterion by which I suggest the quality of man's sense of significance must be judged is that of 'autonomy', the realisation of his unique human individuality. Autonomy as used here has two interrelated facets. On the one hand, it is closely associated with what Jenkins calls 'excellence'[21] – the realisation of man's capabilities within a society where his skills and aptitudes are fully developed, utilised and appreciated by others. On the other hand, autonomy has an important moral dimension. It refers to that state where man is able and willing to stand, if need be, alone in taking full responsibility for his own moral decisions. In recent years educationalists have termed this second aspect of autonomy 'moral maturity'. Despite debate as to the exact stages through which man passes en route to moral maturity, there is wide agreement that the latter has not been reached if his behaviour is motivated by selfishness, by fear of some external authority (often manifest as guilt), or by fear of losing the approval of the crowd (often manifest as shame). To quote Bull, the morally mature person is one who has attained 'an emotional

[20] SIMPSON, op. cit., p. 39.
[21] D. T. JENKINS, *Equality and Excellence*, London 1961.

autonomy that is personally independent of others; a rational autonomy that follows inner principles rather than external conventions; a behavioural autonomy that makes its own moral judgments in applying those principles to concrete situations'.[22] Yet such judgments must always be made in the context of that comprehensive sense of solidarity already discussed as the other component of communal quality. As Robertson writes, 'In essence, individuality is only meaningful in a situation which is in some sense cohesive; individuality only makes sense in the *relation* of one individual to another.'[23] To summarise then, community at its richest is found in those social groupings where men experience the most intense *and* comprehensive degree of solidarity *consistent with* the realisation of the autonomy of each.

Theological comment on this definition of communal quality must be left to those with more expertise in that field than I. Suffice it to say here that many theologians today would argue that the Gospel is very much about man's quest, alongside his fellow men of religious belief or none, for solidarity and significance, and that the Christian is called to take these basic essentials of community more not less seriously than others. Some would argue further that the Christian is one who recognises that where a sense of solidarity and significance of real quality are experienced, there the kingdom of God is to be found. Thus, for example, holy communion is by no means an exclusively ecclesiastical phenomenon but community realised as holy.[24] Thus, as Dom Sebastian Moore states, 'a Christian is not a special sort of man. He is what man in the divine plan *is*'.[25] From the Christian point of view, this adds a further crucial dimension to our definition of the quality of community. It means that man's sense of solidarity depends ultimately on mankind being 'one in Christ', and that his sense of significance is attained not through independence but through mature dependence on Christ. In this context the vine is very much the Christian's symbol of community at its zenith. The church's distinctive contribution is to point to the sacred in the midst

[22] N. J. BULL, *Moral Education*, London 1969, p. 121.

[23] ROBERTSON, op. cit., p. 203.

[24] See J. A. T. ROBINSON, *The Difference in Being a Christian Today*, Redhill 1972, p. 53.

[25] S. MOORE, in ed. P. JEBB, *Religious Education: Drift or Decision?* London 1968, p. 250.

of the secular not as something empirically distinct but as that which adds an all-important dimension to communal quality. The church is *not* here to impose a particular brand or expression of community on society; it exists to make manifest by word and deed the latent presence of Christ in all creative expressions of communal living.

Future Expressions of Christian Community

How can the quest for community in its full Christian context be pursued? Taking the definition of communal quality just discussed, I shall in this final section use it to throw light on the communal life of the church especially in its local and cosmopolitan expressions.

The first thing to be noted is that the church, despite the Christian ideal, in practice reveals as many different levels of communal quality as other social institutions. At a time when 'man comes of age' is the observation of some, others can still speak of the church as 'little more than an infant . . . recently weaned'.[26] Rosemary Haughton comments that 'the church does not consist of fully mature human beings. At any time only a minority will have anything like a full understanding of the free nature of the truly Christian response to authority'.[27] Because one is dealing with an institution whose members often have a sense of solidarity which is superficial or exclusive and a sense of significance which is restricted or infantile, compromise is inevitable. Goffin pertinently writes that 'a completely pure religion for the few would be no religion for the many'.[28] What is more, to ignore or to cast off the many is simply to export the problem, with which all Christians should be involved, of trying to build a society and indeed world of a communally rich kind. For example, the church neither acts with a sense of responsibility for others nor deepens its own communal life by the outright refusal of Christian baptism or marriage to infrequent attenders. It is an immature church which puts all the onus on the irregular visitor to educate himself in the meaning of Christian community. On the other hand, to baptise or marry indiscriminately is colluding with society in its own childish view of things Christian. Likewise with the question of disestablishment. It is far more important for the

26 J. M. TODD, in *Objections to Roman Catholicism*, London 1964, p. 72.
27 R. HAUGHTON, in *Objections*, op. cit., p. 132.
28 M. GOFFIN, in *Objections*, op. cit., p. 35.

Church of England (and other denominations) actively to help ordinary men and women, churchgoers and nonchurchgoers, to grow out of an infantile view of the function of religion than it is to spend a great deal of time and energy on constitutional change. As society grows to a more mature understanding of the nature of Christian community the disestablishment question will solve itself. But in all this the church must start with people – outside and inside the institution – where they are and not at the point where it thinks they ought to be.

In relation to the first major component of communal quality, the church should be seeking within its own membership and beyond to establish an intense and comprehensive experience of social solidarity. There is no doubt that on the matter of intensity the locally oriented expression of community has much to offer. Whatever else, the church must not lose the depth of human relationships which can be found in many local type congregations. The locals teach us in this context that good roots are very important for enduring communal relationships. There may well be eight or nine million people watching the televised services every Sunday but this can never replace the experience of solidarity found within many local type congregations.

The commonly observed warmth of locally oriented expressions of Christian community is seen in the enjoyment and vigour with which locals usually celebrate the major events of the church year. Sunday School Anniversaries in Methodist churches of the Midlands or church bazaars in those of the north have to be witnessed to be believed! The cosmopolitan rarely finds himself caught up in this sort of ethos and is in many ways communally the loser for it though here and there he is attempting to recapture the spirit of the past. In Notting Hill Norwyn Denny writes of the team ministry there that their aim has been 'to bring back joy to community life' through the palm processions, the street parties, the wedding feasts, the community organisation pageants, the free participation of the congregation, the spontaneity within liturgy (and) the baptismal jamborees'.[29]

On the other hand the intensity of the local's sense of solidarity is, as we have noticed, often due to the exclusiveness of his group.

[29] N. DENNY, 'Group Ministry and Community', in *Community No. 3*, Summer 1972.

Because members share a common heritage based on years of living in proximity, 'incomers' find acceptance a slow business. If the quality of community is to grow in church and world, these boundaries have somehow to be pushed outwards – something only possible as cognitive mobility, typical of the cosmopolitan, increases. This is what the ecumenical movement is really all about. Ecclesiastically it means the hard slog not to break down loyalty to the smaller Christian group but to find the means by which this can be freed from restriction to one place or one people. It is quite impossible, therefore, for any church to mean business ecumenically if it sees itself as *the* only genuine or model Christian community.

Nor can the Christian quest for wider experiences of solidarity allow for community to be tied to secular units of an exclusive kind. Here a major issue is that of church-state relations. Though in a mainly locally oriented society nationalism can still play an important part in binding together a wide variety of smaller groups each having an intense communal life of its own, it too must give way to a more comprehensive concept of community as mobility increases. Folk religion has its place in the communal development of man and its vital social nature must not be forgotten, but it is becoming increasingly clear that any church remaining closely bound to secular groupings (national, political or economic) of an exclusive sort has misunderstood the crucial contribution of the ecumenical movement to our time.

All this means that the church has to work for much greater openness at the boundaries of its own and other organisations. The criterion of church membership, for example, must be of a kind that facilitates the creation of a strong sense of solidarity in a wide variety of situations. Because a mobile population now encounters many different expressions of community, this would seem to indicate the emphasis being taken off locally oriented values and organisation (e.g. the need to attend worship every Sunday, to give generously to the upkeep of the local church, to accept readily the ethical pronouncements of one denomination and so forth) and placed on those essential things which all Christians have in common. In other words, we need now to spend every effort to define the heart of the matter and not worry so much about the boundaries.

This heart of the matter is very much the theologian's province but two comments may be of help here. First, the wider community extends and the more diffuse the edges become, the clearer and firmer must be the centre. Here the locals again have something to offer in the value they have attributed to symbolic people (and indeed to symbolic place as anyone trying to close a church knows only too well!). As the church moves towards a more cosmopolitan understanding of community, it will have to take a good look at such symbols. For in and through them cohesiveness finds expression. The problem is that symbols of a local type can so easily become concrete or narrow. Though one would agree with Davis that 'the chief function of the eucharist is to unite and express the full community of the church',[30] the sad fact is that in many cases it can become mechanistic or individualistic. Has Goffin a point when she writes, 'Whatever the distinctions of the more accurate theologians, the delicate minuet played by the separation, the manoeuvering, the bringing together of opus operatum and opus operantis, the average Roman Catholic is conditioned to think of God's grace as channelled through pipes?'[31] In all denominations, however, urgent consideration needs to be given to what the eucharist is meant to symbolise in *communal* terms.

In a different context, and remembering what has been said before about the ecumenical movement, one would agree with Valerie Pitt in her Memorandum of Dissent to the Report of the Archbishops' Commission on 'Church and State'[32] that the Crown, as a symbol of *Christian* community, is now quite out of place. A world developing a cosmopolitan ethos demands a church which has freed itself from such locally oriented views of community.

Perhaps our world is asking for symbols of a very different type. Maybe we are at a time when community must be its own symbol. So when the small Christian community at Taizé is during the spring and summer of 1971 visited by 42,000 young people from 75 countries one must pause for thought.

The second point that needs to be borne in mind is that any attempt to define what lies at the heart of Christian commitment will have

---

[30] C. DAVIS, *God's Grace in History*, London 1966, p. 69.

[31] GOFFIN, op. cit., p. 28.

[32] V. PITT, in *Church and State* (*Report of the Archbishops' Commission*), London 1970. See especially pp. 72–5.

to take very seriously the partial nature of the institutional church as an expression of man's experience of community. The days of Christendom are gone for ever. At the other end of the scale, the local's demand that man give his all to the local Christian congregation has an increasingly hollow ring about it. Men live and love within many groups – for the church as an organisation to claim the whole of a man or even the prior loyalty of man is to de-socialize and de-humanize him. The concept of membership must somehow be refashioned to enable man to experience a deep sense of belonging to the Christian community without either weakening that sense of solidarity he should be able to experience elsewhere or destroying his own autonomy.

The Christian's search for autonomy, the second essential element of communal quality, likewise brings into question certain aspects of the local and cosmopolitan ways of life. Without detracting from the importance of nurturing the young in the Christian way of living, a mature Christian community can only exist where members, with as much knowledge and understanding as they are capable of, have deliberately chosen to associate with the church. The difficulty in the locally oriented church is that one finds oneself in unless one makes a real effort (with the inevitable social recriminations) to opt out, a situation which many cosmopolitans feel dishonest or resent. White in his survey of public school religion quotes one boy as saying, 'At the age of fifteen my housemaster suggested to me that I should be confirmed . . . to me confirmation was a part of the routine life at college, comparable to taking "O" and "A" levels. . . . I suppose I am one of those whom many despise since I do not know whether God exists neither do I have the slightest interest.'[33] Such a comment again stresses that what people are really being asked to choose or commit themselves to needs much thought.

Man's autonomy, as discussed earlier, is in part a consequence of the opportunity society gives him to develop fully his skills and aptitudes. The church then should be to the fore in actively striving for a world where all have equal opportunity for personal development. If this sounds trite let us remind ourselves how even today the church so often colludes with government in keeping men in a state of subservience. But freedom to attain autonomy must be

33 PERRY (ed.), op. cit., p. 24.

available within the institution too. Where the locally oriented tradition fails to exploit the potential abilities of its members or the cosmopolitan tradition in its hurry passes them by, the church itself is preventing growth. Rice writes, 'If they do not feel any responsibility for task performance, then individuals and groups are forced into dependent, child-like roles. Though some may welcome such roles in some circumstances, those with aspirations to adult maturity must feel either guilt in accepting dependence or resentment at its imposition.'[34]

This last comment also emphasises that autonomy is not just a question of the full realisation of talents but that it has a moral dimension too. As the Christian sees it autonomy can be summed up as mature dependence on Christ. In this context man's sense of significance has two aspects. On the one hand, the church declares that man, whatever his achievements or failures, can rely on Christ as utterly dependable. Here the local type of Christian church at its best has much to commend it for it ascribes value to members not just because of what they can contribute but because they are members of the family. The love and caring shown by many locally oriented Christians towards even less attractive members of their congregations is at times a deeply moving thing to witness. The cosmopolitan with his more functional approach to life can all too easily devalue the less talented members of the group.

On the other hand dependence must be *mature*. On this score the church, especially the locally oriented church, has a great deal to answer for. The Christian's relation to his own institution (and thus so some would argue to God) has in many places and for many centuries remained at an immature level. For example, the Christian is not being *maturely* dependent if he remains motivated mainly by fear of some external authority however apparently righteous. For, as Rosemary Haughton writes, 'When an external code is regarded as an absolute good, even when divorced from personal understanding and acceptance, the personality is fixed at a stage of immaturity, and generally makes a virtue of it.'[35] One of the most critical tasks now facing the church is to rid itself of this type of so-called 'virtue' and to enable its members to grow towards real autonomy. Likewise the

[34] A. K. RICE, *The Enterprise and its Environment*, London 1963, p. 252.
[35] HAUGHTON, op. cit., p. 127.

Christian is held back whilst his church, be it local or cosmopolitan, retains fear or favour of the crowd as the overriding sanction. The church is in this case open to the Durkheimian critique of accepting the group, writ large or small, as its god. Typical of this situation was the extreme distress I witnessed within one local type Yorkshire congregation when the daughter of a deeply involved family refused to get married in church because she felt it would for her, as an agnostic, be quite dishonest. But as Whyte shows only too clearly when discussing organisation man, the cosmopolitan also can become dominated by and subservient to the ethos and sanctions of the group. To move from social conformity towards self-awareness and self-determination is a struggle for both local and cosmopolitan alike.

Finally, an examination of autonomy in all its different aspects indicates that the relationship of laity to clergy is one of the utmost consequence. It must be admitted that as yet there seems little indication that the mainly local type pattern of clerical dominance is on the wane. The church has for so long undervalued its laity that it is little wonder they either remain passive followers within the institution or, as they become increasingly cosmopolitan, leave it altogether in many instances. The future leadership of the church, whilst steering between being authoritarian on the one hand and being weakly 'non-directive' on the other, will have to give far more scope for all members to offer their distinctive contributions to the whole and to share fully in decision making at every level.

BIOGRAPHICAL NOTE.

BIOGRAPHICAL NOTE

ROBERT TOWLER *is a lecturer in sociology in the Department of Sociology at the University of Leeds, where he graduated in Psychology-Sociology in 1964 and subsequently did doctoral research on the attitudes of men in training for the Anglican ministry. He contributed 'The Role of the Clergy' to* The Christian Priesthood, *the 9th Downside Symposium (1970), ed. N. Lash and J. Rhymer. He is publishing* Homo Religiosus: Sociological Problems in the Study of Religion *with Constable in 1973.*

9 *Inter-Church Relations:*
A Sociological Comment[1]

ROBERT TOWLER

THE ECUMENICAL MOVEMENT IN THE CHRISTIAN CHURCH
has become a dominant concern of Christian leaders since the Second
World War. Because of its essentially domestic nature it has attracted
little attention from sociologists, who have been more interested in
investigating such things as the relationship between people's formal
religious affiliation and their voting behaviour, the size of family
they produce, their annual income and similar matters. It may be that
the cause of this neglect has been that the internal affairs of churches
have been judged to be of little importance in themselves but it
seems more likely that it has been due to a preoccupation with social
variables more amenable to quantification, since those who have
conducted surveys, either academically or commercially, have been
ready enough to include items about religion in their questionnaires.
If religion is to be studied seriously, however, the internal workings of
a religious system must be accorded high priority, even though
they appear to be of an organisational character bearing a strong
resemblance to secular enterprises. And the few sociologists who have

---

[1] By kind permission of the publishers of the present volume, this paper appears as a
chapter in the author's forthcoming book with Constable.

considered the ecumenical movement have in fact concluded that it is very significant for the proper understanding of the contemporary churches, though they have differed in the conclusions they have drawn from it.

The ecumenical movement is generally regarded as having originated with the first world missionary conference held at Edinburgh in 1910, although the formation of the World Alliance for International Friendship Through the Churches in 1915 and the first meeting of the International Missionary Conference in 1921 also contributed to the interest which finally took shape in the Faith and Order Conference held in Lausanne in 1927, the first gathering explicitly called to promote the cause of Christian unity.[2] While the movement is interesting in itself, of more obvious importance is the impact which it has had in making ecumenism a popular ideal in most Christian churches. Ecumenism itself, i.e. the attempt to reunite churches, predates the movement by many centuries as may readily be seen, for example, from the attempted *rapprochement* between the Latin and the Orthodox churches at the Council of Florence in 1439 or from the various re-alignments within Methodism.[3] Ecumenism is interesting to the sociologist because it represents a reversal of the more readily understood phenomenon of the fragmentation of churches, and when, as at present, it becomes a dominant concern, it represents an entirely new development well worth close attention. The principal concern of sociologists, therefore, has been to discover why the desire for the reunion of churches, sporadic for many centuries, should have become a major interest in the twentieth century.

The account of ecumenism most commonly given by sociologists represents it as a response by churches to the diminishing number of their members and as an attempt to recover their strength by organising mergers to form a larger body. It is therefore taken to be a sign of religious decline and when, as at present, it occurs on a large scale it is taken as evidence of secularisation. It is proposed that in a period of

---

[2] See STEPHEN NEILL and RUTH ROUSE, eds., *A History of the Ecumenical Movement* (Philadelphia, The Westminster Press 1954).

[3] On Methodism, see JOHN KENT, *The Age of Disunity* (London, Epworth Press 1966), and ROBERT CURRIE, *Methodism Divided: A Study in the Sociology of Ecumenicalism* (London, Faber and Faber 1968).

religious strength a church will recruit new members and will retain the loyalty of children born to old members, and that the organisation will consequently grow in size. Being vigorous, any disputes which arise amongst the members will be argued fiercely and the protagonists will have no difficulty in finding support. Disagreements are likely, therefore, to result in small groups of dissidents splitting away to pursue their ideals independently. While the churches remain vigorous, each splinter group will continue to grow, and to develop in its own particular direction, becoming more differentiated from the others as an increased emphasis is placed on the particular aspect of belief or order which originally caused the rupture. The only circumstances in which a church will renage on its own distinctive doctrine will be either when the reasons for it have been forgotten, or else when a decline in numbers renders the church no longer viable as an independent organisation. In either case the original vitality has been lost, and readiness to compromise on principles which had once been the *raison d'être* of the church indicates that all hope of renewed strength has been abandoned. Robert Currie expresses this view at the end of his study of ecumenism in the British Methodist Churches:

'Ecumenism develops as conflict declines and as religion declines. Failing to recruit, flourishing communities become sluggish, ageing and dispirited. . . . As tolerance of persistent decline fails, the organisation seeks to replace missing "frontal" growth from recruitment with "lateral" growth from amalgamation . . . close examination of the process of reunion shows that in advanced societies ecumenicalism is the product of an ageing religion. It arises out of decline and secularisation, but fails to deal with either.'[4]

In the context of Methodism, for which Currie is able to list fourteen *major* divisions and unions,[5] the proposition has a certain validity although other factors besides the failure of recruitment might have led to the same result even for Methodism. When the same proposition is applied more generally, however, and without a detailed examination of the processes at work, it is unacceptable.

[4] CURRIE, op. cit., pp. 314 and 316.
[5] Ibid., p. 54.

There are two major objections to this seriously over-simplified account.

In the first place its logic is inadequate. It is one thing to show that churches which are declining in numerical strength, even to show that only and all such churches, manifest an interest in reunion; it is another thing altogether to show that the ecumenical interest has been caused by numerical decline. It would be just as reasonable to suppose that some third factor was causing both the decline and also the interest in ecumenism. Currie at least examines the relationship in some depth, even though he does not investigate alternative explanations. It is commoner to find some vague general principle invoked in support of the proposed explanation, as when Jacques Ellul breezily says that 'it is the tendency of all groups threatened by an external enemy to gather together, to hush up internal divisions'.[6] In the second place this common account is usually presented with a disregard for the explanations given by ecumenists themselves worthy of a nineteenth century anthropologist, and it will not do to treat an actor's own account as mere delusion even if a more cogent alternative can be provided. An ideology as strong and pervasive as ecumenism deserves careful study. If Currie is right when he says, 'much emphasis is placed on enthusiastic international conferences, while the practicalities of everyday church life are overlooked',[7] then the way in which the usurping ideas fit into a new pattern of religious thought should be seriously explored. Since the idea of reunion does indeed represent a *volte face* for the members of many denominations, we must give due attention to the way in which ideas which were previously unthinkable gained currency, rather than rest content with a general account of the causes. A cynically detached explanation will fail to convince unless it is based on an understanding of how and why people came to see things in so new a way.

The attitude which people adopt to religious organisations other than their own is dependent, to a large degree, on the nature of their own religious commitment. It is not the strength of their commitment which is significant so much as the way in which they are

---

[6] JACQUES ELLUL, *Fausse Présence au Monde Moderne* (Paris, Librairie Protestante 1963), p. 72, quoted in ROGER MEHL, *The Sociology of Protestantism* (London, SCM Press 1970) (trans. from the French edition of 1965), p. 204.

[7] CURRIE, op. cit., p. 11.

committed For the purpose of distinguishing the different ways in which people may conceive of their church membership, it will be useful to consider the types of answer one might receive to the hypothetical question, 'Which church do you belong to?' The point of interest will be not so much the answers themselves, as what the answers tell us about how the question was understood, since church membership is susceptible of several interpretations. The first type of reply might be the mention of a particular congregation: 'St. Mary's', or 'London Road Baptist' or 'the Parish church'. To the person giving this kind of answer, 'his' church is local, 'even down to stone and lime, hassock and hymn books, gowns and surplices' as a recent church report put it,[8] and his commitment can accurately be described as a *local* type of commitment. What matters to him is the integrity and identity of the local unit in all its particularity, for his sense of religious belonging is mediated through it. The fabric and decorations of the church, its forms of service, its associated organisations and clubs, these and all the other familiar details are facets of the religious universe which surrounds him, and without which the doctrine and beliefs taught in that church would be insubstantial and difficult to grasp. They are not, for him, mere objects or arbitrarily chosen ways of doing things, but symbols which have an importance and a significance in enabling him to feel at home in familiar surroundings when he confronts the uncomfortable things with which his religion is sometimes concerned: guilt, pain, bereavement, loneliness and so on. Indeed the reality of these experiences and the belief that they will not overcome him are associated so intimately with these tangible and mundane symbols that they provide reassurance enough for most of the time. This kind of religious commitment presupposes, of course, the stability of a congregation. It occurs in its strongest form when a person is born into a congregation, when he goes to the church with his parents as a child, when he is married there and his children are baptised there, when he and his family go there Sunday by Sunday, and so on throughout the whole cycle of his life. Stability such as this is becoming less and less common, but it is still true of the experience of a substantial proportion of the older church-going population; indeed it carries,

[8] Interim Report of the Multilateral Church Conversation in Scotland, *Reports to the General Assembly of the Church of Scotland*, 1972, p. 591.

if anything, added significance for them, since the church remains as one of the few elements of continuity in a world stripped of most of the features familiar from childhood and in which most other rituals of social life have either died or been transformed out of recognition. It is worth noting that this is a form of religious belonging known to only a small minority of the clergy of any denomination. Since the time they spend at any one church tends to be limited they are more aware of the elements shared in common by the various churches they have served than of the characteristic features of any particular church, and this may make them insensitive to the experience of their congregation and unsympathetic and impatient with what appears to them to be a narrow vision of the church centering round the parish pump. The desire of someone to give to the church a new stained-glass window or to pay for the organ to be restored may appear to the minister ill-conceived in the light of world poverty, whereas to the person concerned it has a symbolic meaning which puts it in a different category from a donation to Oxfam, a meaning of which the minister may be largely unaware.

To the person with this local type of religious commitment, ecumenism appears in a particular light. Recognising as a member of his own church someone from a different denomination is as un-objectionable as it is meaningless, since members of the same denomination who belong to different congregations are strangers anyway. A visitor is a visitor, regardless of which church he comes from. The introduction of bishops into a non-episcopal church is of little greater significance. The imposition of a new form of service is a more serious matter, but it is a change which may be accepted in time. To close the church building, however, or to share a minister with another church in the name of efficiency, are different matters altogether. To lose one's church building is to lose one's church. To join another congregation is to become a permanent visitor but never to be at home; to have another congregation join with one's own church is little better, since it is permanently to have a group of visitors, which is a contradiction in terms. To the person with a local religious commitment, the closure of church buildings on the grounds of rationalisation and efficiency is as meaningless as the advocacy of working for Oxfam instead of cleaning church brasses, since alternatives are being proposed which are drawn from a different order of reality. The church is the church is the church, and that's an end to it. Currie quotes a calm and unemotional letter written to the *Methodist Recorder* in 1926 which illustrates the view in a very practical way:

> 'On the one side of our Chapel within a hundred yards is a Free Methodist Chapel; on the other side is a Primitive Methodist Chapel about the same distance away. In each of these chapels are a band of eager, enthusiastic officials who have had a life-long connection with their Chapel, and sphere of work. Supposing, through Union, you close two of these chapels, what is going to become of these various officials?'[9]

To the man with this type of religious commitment, the apparently weighty matters of compromise – or *rapprochement*, according to the view taken – over church doctrine and polity are of very limited interest. He will be undisturbed by such changes and will not oppose them; but by the same token he will not lend them his wholehearted support. He is ecumenically minded already in that he has always welcomed strangers to his church with genuine warmth. He is instinctively in favour of intercommunion between churches since it is only a fancy name for what is, to him, a simple act of friendship and hospitality. If ecumenism means closing his church, however, or encouraging others to close theirs, it violates his basic notion of what belonging to the church is all about and he can be counted upon to oppose it to the last ditch.

To the same hypothetical question, 'What church do you belong to?' other people might say 'Church of England' or 'Catholic' or 'Free Kirk'. They have understood the question in a radically different way and we may infer that their sense of religious belonging is different. Readily to identify oneself with a denomination implies stability, but the stability is attached to the boundaries between religious denominations rather than the boundaries of a specific religious community. If clergy and ministers can be unsympathetic to local commitment they are much less so towards denominational commitment since it is more characteristic of their own sense of religious belonging. For the person with this *party* type of commitment what is especially significant is not the particularity of any one congregation, but the more general ethos common to all churches of

[9] *Methodist Recorder*, 16 September 1926, quoted in CURRIE, op. cit., p. 197.

the denomination, and this is frequently seen in contrast with other denominations. For the Catholic, what is significant is belief in the Mass and going to Mass every Sunday, belief in the importance of the Virgin Mary, in the authority of the Pope, the practice of going to confession and much else besides. They may or may not be things of importance in themselves, but they have an added significance as symbols of religious belonging. As the locally committed man feels at home in the familiar surroundings of a particular place, so the Catholic derives an equivalent sense of security from a set relationship with his priests, from invoking the help of the Mother of God, from the familiar ritual of attendance at Sunday mass. They are all parts of a symbolic world which is warm and known, and within which the Catholic has grown up and lived, has buried his mother and married his wife, has been sorry for getting drunk and hoped for a life beyond death. It is the institution of the Catholic Church, rather than the surroundings of a particular congregation, which forms the religious context which he knows as his own. The beliefs which he holds and the things he does in the name of religion are important not so much in themselves as because they are characteristically Catholic. To fail to go to Mass on Sunday may be a sin for the Catholic, but it is also to alienate himself from the Catholic Church and to withdraw from a world in which his mundane experiences have a special meaning which they cannot be given in any other way.

The Catholic Church is chosen merely as an example, of course, and not every Catholic has this type of religious commitment. In countries where Catholicism is virtually the only religion, such as Spain or Malta, another model of religious commitment applies, but in such areas the problem of ecumenism and inter-church relations does not arise. The party type of commitment is found in other denominations, and the very different example of the Free Church of Scotland might have been elaborated as an equally good illustration. This type of commitment has its own appropriate response to ecumenism. The man thus committed is untroubled by the closure of particular churches, even if it involves closing the church which he normally attends. Although less easy to accept, he will not be unduly shaken by alterations, even substantial ones, in the sphere of the religious symbols with which he is familiar;

Catholics accommodated themselves quite rapidly to the recent removal of a host of saints from the Calendar, to the introduction of the vernacular mass and to the abolition of Friday abstinence from meat. Mary Douglas, it is true, has questioned this ready accommodation to change,[10] and it may be that alterations to the traditional familiar practices in other churches, besides the Catholic Church, have had consequences which are yet to become fully evident. Indeed we should expect rapid and extensive changes to an established religious tradition to be difficult for the man with a party type of commitment to accept. This does not apply to changes introduced slowly over a number of years: what is anathema is for an important symbol to be lost in a compromise as a result of ecumenical bargaining with another church. Faced with a scheme for reunion with the Methodist Church, some members of the Church of England, many of them clergymen, could countenance the closure of churches and the amalgamation of parishes, but they could not accept the idea of accepting as their fellow ministers men who had not been ordained by bishops. To repeat, then, the party type of religious commitment involves a sense of belonging through attachment to the symbolic significance of an institution such as traditional beliefs, customary practices and principles of authority. The symbols are not concrete objects or particular places, but a complex institution and ideology.

Yet a third type of commitment is implied when a person answers the question 'Which church do you belong to?' by saying something like, 'Well, I go to the Methodist church'. What is implied is a provisional and qualified attitude to a particular congregation or denomination which suggests a *pragmatic* type of commitment. Although the ecumenical consequences of this type of commitment are less positive, it would be a mistake to overlook it since it characterises a significant proportion of the church-going population; a proportion which, moreover, is unlikely to diminish. It may arise in at least two distinct ways. It may be, for example, that in some area a devoted group of Congregationalists, with a local type of commitment, has shrunk in numbers to such an extent that their church has had to be closed or demolished. The remaining members then go to the neighbouring Baptist church, say, as the one which is least

---

[10] On the abolition of Friday abstinence, see MARY DOUGLAS, *Natural Symbols: Explorations in Cosmology* (London, Barrie and Rockliff, The Cresset Press 1970), pp. 3f.

dissimilar. While becoming formal members of that congregation, they continue to think of themselves, either singly or corporately, as perpetual visitors, and are thought of as such by members of the other congregation. Their sense of religious belonging remains unchanged, probably because of a life-long connection with their Congregational chapel, but they are permanent exiles in a friendly church which nonetheless cannot be home. The same situation can arise when a person moves to another area, as when a member of the Scottish Free Church moves to England and has to accept membership of a Nonconformist church there, foreign and uncongenial though it may be, as better than nothing at all.[11] For a person thus placed his pragmatic commitment has no ecumenical consequences; since his principal feeling is one of home-sickness, he will be detached from any ecumenical proposals.

An identical type of commitment, which is likely to become increasingly common, can occur in quite different circumstances. In some recent research a woman respondent, when asked, 'Do you have any religion?' replied by saying:

'No religion really. Tend to go to Catholic because my husband is, but mother's Protestant and father's Jewish. I was brought up in Jewish religion.'[12]

Had the woman said that she was a member of the Catholic Church her membership would have implied a pragmatic commitment, and the same applies to those who attend a particular church because of a spouse's commitment, because it happens to be the nearest to home, or for any other extraneous reason. As before, the attitude to ecumenical proposals is one of detachment and non-involvement since it is a matter of no consequence.

It has been necessary to summarise these different types of religious commitment because without some prior knowledge of what church membership means to different people, it is impossible to understand how the present widespread interest in church unity has arisen.

[11] The example contrasts strangely with Max Weber's agnostic experience on the occasion of a visit to the Isle of Skye, when he was asked one Sunday which service he had attended, H. H. GERTH and C. WRIGHT MILLS, eds., *From Max Weber* (London, Routledge and Kegan Paul 1948), p. 303.
[12] ROBERT TOWLER and AUDREY SMITH, 'Common Religion' in MICHAEL HILL (ed.), *A Sociological Yearbook of Religion in Britain*, No. 6 (London, SCM Press 1973).

Such notions as 'compromise' have no meaning unless one first knows what church people regard as sufficiently significant to warrant the use of the word. For some people it is the integrity of the local church which is of vital concern, for others it is the integrity of the denomination as a wider institution, while for still others ecumenism matters little. Clearly, many of those who support various schemes of reunion must be prepared to set aside certain things which matter to them deeply and be willing to acquiesce in the loss of some symbol which previously had a profound significance for them. Writing about the U.S.A., David Moberg suggested that there are three ways in which this can happen:

'One is the *dogmatic* argument that divine authority has revealed an unchanging pattern; all churches ought to accept and enter into this sole authentic version of unity. Roman Catholics, many Anglo-Catholics, and the Eastern Orthodox hold this view, each claiming to be the only valid centre for the reunion of Christendom. The second is *pragmatic*, emphasising the practical need for churches to unite and exert a stronger influence. The rank and file of Protestantism tends to take this view. There are many *idealistic* interpretations. Some like the Protestant Episcopal Church, find a strong sanction for unity in the ideal of continuity. Others are convinced that division, which is the alternative to union, involves weakness, waste and more seriously, an inherently divisive spirit and unkind deeds.'[13]

The first reason for reunion which Moberg mentions can hardly be said to lead to genuinely ecumenical relations, but it is an accurate statement of one possible stance. As a Vatican document of 1928 put it, 'There is but one way in which the unity of Christ may be fostered, and that is by furthering the return to the one true Church of Christ of those who are separated from it.'[14] That remains the formal position of the Roman Catholic Church although it has been greatly modified, in a manner characteristic of that church, by the promulgation of other statements which, when taken together, constitute a much less dogmatic position, without actually revoking

---

[13] DAVID O. MOBERG, *The Church as a Social Institution* (Englewood Cliffs, N.J., Prentice-Hall 1962), p. 257.
[14] The encyclical *Mortalium animos* (1928).

any earlier statement. Both the second and the third of Moberg's motivations amount to the acknowledgement by the parties to an ecumenical adventure of an ideal or a value to which they are willing to accord supreme importance. Each party to any such agreement must be willing to accept some new, common pattern of belief, and to alter their former doctrine and policy so that it becomes consonant with it. In this way no church is required to say that it was wrong and another was right, but all agree together that they were partially wrong and that the newly agreed formula is a better statement of the truth. This device saves any church from losing face by making concessions to another.

This process is carried on at two different levels. It is obvious in working documents used in negotiations and in finally agreed formulae; the ideals which are shared by those who initiate ecumenical discussions are rarely articulated in any formal way, however, and while they are often difficult to discover they are of much greater significance for an understanding of the process. Given the difference between independent religious traditions, the practical problem is to discover the way in which contact is established, the occasions of contact and the persons who establish it. But all the time the effective constraints which are operative must be borne in mind, whether they be the importance of a denominational tradition or the sacredness of local churches.

There have been a number of factors which have promoted ecumenical contacts, some of them specific and easy to document, others more general and difficult to disentangle from wider social processes. Four factors will be considered briefly here as being of particular importance, in order of increasing generality. In the first place, the clergy and ministers in all churches have played a key role in ecumenism; it is they who have led the ecumenical movement and who have been mainly responsible for negotiating the terms on which reunions have been attempted. Bryan Wilson has argued very forcibly that their role has been crucial in the propagation of ecumenism.[15] He points out that the clergy have often been more than mere leaders of such movements: they have been the movement's rank and file as well. Clerical enthusiasm has indeed been important, and

[15] BRYAN R. WILSON, *Religion in Secular Society* (London, C. A. Watts 1966), part 3, 'The religious response'.

he is probably correct in supposing that ministers enthuse because they are ministers, rather than because they are motivated by the same feelings and attitudes which they share with their lay people but experience more strongly. It is a mistake, however, to begin by asking why clergy are so enthusiastic about ecumenism, for reasons are usually the last things to emerge from a sociological analysis. Rather, we should start by asking what situations have led clergy to think in terms of co-operation with other churches. The layman normally meets only those who are committed to the same religious group as he is himself so far as any matters of religious significance are concerned. In his day-to-day secular occupations he spends time with people who do not share his religious commitment, and his interaction with these people is conducted on the basis of shared secular values and ideas. If a situation arises which, for him, has religious implications, it will remain a private experience, for to interpose his religious perspective would be to violate the perceptions he shares with his fellows, which are secular. Violations take place, of course, but they are attended by sanctions and the offender will be branded as a religious fanatic or a Bible-thumper and thereafter treated accordingly. It should be noted that the imputed fanaticism consists not in the offender's religious commitment but in his breach of shared values by introducing his alien perception.[16] Religion for the layman is a private matter for most of the time, and it becomes a shared, public way of experiencing and communicating only within the religious group, or some sub-group such as a man's own family. Exceptions to this general rule exist which would be worthy of micro-sociological analysis such as, for example, the place of a recognised religious department within an otherwise secular organisation such as a television company. The minister's religion, by contrast, is a matter of public knowledge, unless he deliberately mixes in society *incognito*, but much of his time is spent within the religious group. The minister who serves a group of people who are locally committed will spend much more time than they do with members of the same denomination who belong to different churches, and this, as well as his periodic movement from congregation to congregation, will help to engender a sense of commitment to the denomination rather than

[16] In a more than trivial sense the man is treated as mad: not just as if he were mad, but as mad.

to the local church. In addition to this most clergy now come into contact with clergy of other denominations. When communications were less rapid such contacts were infrequent, particularly in England where the clergy of the established church were isolated by social barriers from nonconformist ministers, who were of lower social status, and from Catholic priests, who were Irish immigrants or eccentric aristocrats or – worst of all – converts.

In certain special situations, however, contact with clergy of other churches was not unusual, especially for those working abroad in foreign missions. When two ministers of different churches met the mere fact of their meeting was in itself an ecumenical event. It could not avoid being so, for since both lived in publicly religious worlds their respective worlds could only be kept apart by playing a kind of charade. Furthermore, the clergy of all the churches were abroad for the same ostensible purpose of rescuing the natives from the darkness of the heathen night and failure to co-operate in a common endeavour meant that their shared purpose was to that extent less effectively prosecuted. It was these informal meetings, which could be called ecumenical only in the purely descriptive sense that more than one church was represented, but not in the sense that any ideas of church unity were involved, which led eventually to the Edinburgh conference of 1910. From the ecumenical activities of missionaries grew the self-conscious desire for reunion which we describe as ecumenism.

In England some contact between clergy of different churches has for some time been inevitable. Since the late nineteenth century chaplains to the armed forces have been of different denominations, as also have chaplains to hospitals and then, gradually, to many other types of institution. Such chaplaincies are not unlike missionary situations, in which some contact is inevitable and the aims of the churches are held in common. Finally the renewed concern in the post-war period with such issues as world poverty, disarmament and race relations has led to the formation of groups and organisations to articulate these concerns which from the beginning have been unselfconsciously ecumenical. Currie alleges that 'ecumenical projects are interpreted in lofty terms of "mission", with little reference to their specific motivation and origin.'[17] The specific motivation and

17 CURRIE, op. cit., p. 11.

origin of much that was to become ecumenical in fact lay in other concerns, of which 'mission' was one of the earliest and most important.

The concerns which brought the clergy of different churches together did not override the importance of their separate religious commitments, but they were occasions on which contact was made between overtly religious persons, and therefore between different religious worlds, where no such contact had formerly existed. Often, the result was that they discovered that the differences which divided them were much less wide when they discussed them together than they had supposed when they only imagined or read about them. Wilson suggests that ecumenism has become a concern because clergy are anxious to improve their collective status. The part played by the clergy in increased ecumenical co-operation seems to have been more fortuitous than that, for the motives which have led them to pursue ecumenism with such an obsessive concern have been diverse. Some take part in ecumenical talks convinced that no reunion will come about and determined to prevent any; others take part in the hope, often expressed in grandiloquent language, of helping to solve the problems of a divided world; yet others, no doubt, take part with an eye to their own career prospects. When some clergy in England are drawing benefits from the Ministry of Social Security there is as much concern with subsistence as with status. The concern for reunion between churches is nevertheless a predominantly clerical phenomenon, and something, moreover, with which the lay members of their churches often disagree. Those clergy whose congregations are opposed to ecumenism because it would close local churches often have a radically different idea of what church membership means than have their laity, to whose wishes and feelings they can be sadly, sometimes cruelly indifferent. Division of opinion between ministers and laity of this kind has been well illustrated in the Methodist Church, both in the past, as shown by Currie, and in the present also.[18] Those clergy whose congregations

[18] See MICHAEL HILL and PETER WAKEFORD, 'Disembodied ecumenicalism: a survey of the members of four Methodist churches in or near London', and BRYAN S. TURNER, 'Institutional persistence and ecumenicalism in Northern Methodism' in DAVID A. MARTIN, ed., *A Sociological Yearbook of Religion in Britain*, No. 2 (London, SCM Press 1969).

are opposed to ecumenism because it would deprive them of the church which they feel to be distinctively their's often fail to realise that their own contact with clergy of other churches has reduced their exclusive loyalty to their own church, with the result that they become insensitive to the honest loyalty of their laity, which they often despise. From all this it is clear that it is the clergy and church leaders who have been largely responsible for the ecumenical movement, and that while there have been many reasons for this, it has often expressed a simple desire to create a formal organisational unity where practical ecumenical co-operation has already been experienced.

A second factor favouring the growth of ecumenism is seen in the changes in theological thought which have recently been taking place at an accelerating pace. Rodney Stark and Charles Glock have written that:

'In part, the ecumenical dream rests on the assumption that Christians are reaching a common theological outlook, that the old differences have lost much of their force. In this view contemporary denominationalism is an organisational rather than a theological affair.'[19]

From the data they have gathered in surveys in the U.S.A. they have drawn an analysis which suggests that 'such a view is superficial'. What has happened, rather, is that old theological disputes over such questions as predestination, infant baptism and prayers for the dead, which once divided denominations, have become much less important. In their place new disputes have arisen, which have split denominations and even congregations into partisan groups, and thereby made established church divisions appear comparatively unimportant to those who are concerned with these new issues. Such evidence as we have from survey research conducted in the U.S.A., although it is far from satisfactory, suggests that the new disputes often divide clergy and laity within a denomination,[20] thus aggravating further the separation which has just been noted.

[19] RODNEY STARK and CHARLES Y. GLOCK, *American Piety* (Berkeley and Los Angeles, University of California Press 1968), pp. 24f.

[20] See JEFFERY K. HADDEN, *The Gathering Storm in the Churches* (New York, Doubleday 1969), especially Chapter 5.

The short term effect of these new disputes is to polarise people into radicals and conservatives depending on whether they sympathise with this questioning and re-evaluation of traditional beliefs or whether they react by reasserting more vehemently than ever the truth of the traditional religious symbols which they have received. This polarisation has immediate ecumenical repercussions. On the one hand the radicals read writers with whose ideas they sympathise without reference to denominational affiliation and become generally careless of established religious boundaries. Conservatives, on the other hand, whom one would expect to retreat more defensively than ever within their own churches and denominations, appear to be distressed and anxious, sometimes to the point of panic. Far from defending their religious world passively, in many places they have adopted attack as best method of defence. The absolute and unchanging truth of religious and moral ideas emerges as having higher priority than particular embodiments of that truth, and we find support coming from otherwise quietly unassuming people for such movements as the Billy Graham Evangelistic Crusades and the Festival of Light,[21] which are not so much evangelising movements as movements to express solidarity in the old revivalist tradition.[22]

Changes in theological thought, then, tend to promote ecumenism both directly through fostering inter-denominational theological debate, and also indirectly through ecumenical reassertion of the threatened traditional religion and morality. In the long term this latter response will probably be seen as a very transitory phenomenon, and the radical theology itself will either be overtaken by the fulfilment of its own prophecies, or will meet an alternative fate which Peter Berger has foreseen:

'The probable fate of secular theology, once its appeal as the *dernier cri* in religion has passed, would then be its absorption into the legitimating apparatus of the institution (which, incidentally, is exactly what happened with classical liberalism). We strongly

---

[21] On the Festival of Light in Great Britain, see ROY WALLIS, 'Dilemma of a moral crusade', *New Society*, 13 July 1972, pp. 69–72, and JOHN CAPON . . . *And There Was Light* (London, Lutterworth Press 1972).
[22] Cf. WILSON, op. cit., pp. 149f.

suspect that this process of neutralisation is already taking place as these "challenging new insights" are integrated in various ecclesiastical programs. In this process, there is nothing to prevent the "death of God" from becoming but another program emphasis, which, if properly administered, need not result in undue disturbance in the ongoing life of the institution.'[23]

Although it would obviously be wrong to suppose that theological thought is simply the product of the society in which it emerges, it is equally wrong to ignore completely the social context of any intellectual trend. Perhaps the most significant aspect of the wider social changes for recent religious developments has been the declining importance of some traditional secular divisions within society. The possibility of interaction across social boundaries which were formerly sacrosanct, whether national, ethnic or class boundaries, played a vital role in promoting both the meeting of clergy from different denominations and also the exchange of theological ideas, both of which, as we have tried to show, has had implications for the development of ecumenism.

This decline in the importance of traditional social distinctions of a purely secular kind must itself be considered as the third factor contributing directly to the growth of ecumenism, although the effects have often been felt in a complex variety of ways. In his analysis of the origins of denominational fragmentation in the U.S.A., Richard Niebuhr wrote of the 'churches of the disinherited', pointing to the way in which many churches had grown out of a working class milieu, for the lower social strata had been effectively excluded from the established churches of the affluent.[24] It has been argued that if religious differentiation had its origins in social differentiation, then the relative homogeneity of contemporary society will have the reverse effect, and promote ecumenism.[25] But even if it were possible to accept that today's society is more homogeneous than it was in

[23] PETER L. BERGER, 'The secularization of theology', *Journal for the Scientific Study of Religion*, Vol. 6, 1967, p. 15.

[24] H. RICHARD NIEBUHR, *The Social Sources of Denominationalism* (New York, Holt 1929) cf. K. S. INGLIS, *Churches and the Working Classes in Victorian England* (London, Routledge and Kegan Paul 1963), and E. P. THOMPSON, *The Making of the English Working Class* (Harmondsworth, Middlesex, Penguin 1964).

[25] ROBERT LEE, *The Social Sources of Church Unity* (New York, Abingdon Press 1960).

the past (which it is not) the process would still require a good deal of explication. The process may be seen at work in a number of different ways. Where a religious group grew up in a particular social context some of the elements of its religious symbolism will have been appropriate to that context, speaking with special force to that particular social condition. Thus the experience of chronic material deprivation may find a religious response in an emphasis on the rewards which may be expected in the kingdom of heaven by those who have been poor on earth. The example is crude, but actual religious traditions have evolved in which the complexes of symbols are subtly appropriate to the conditions of their adherents. Once established, religious traditions acquire their own dynamic, and symbols persist long after the experiences of life to which they were appropriate have passed away. Whereas once these symbols had embodied the experience of a group of people and expressed in a uniquely real way their hopes and fears and aspirations, they end up as disembodied shells. In a living tradition the religion alters to express the different experiences of subsequent generations of believers. But religious evolution is slow. It may often be overtaken by history, and when this happens a religion may become an empty set of symbols in its native land.

The same thing can happen even more readily when a religion is exported to a foreign land.[26] In the past there have been remarkable groups like the native Indian members of the Scottish Original Seceders in the Central Provinces of India, who had 'never been in Scotland, were in no sense original and knew nothing about secession.'[27] But it is the less spectacular examples which best illustrate the disembodiment of religious traditions in foreign lands. The Baptist Church in the U.S.A. was split into separate denominations in the northern and southern States of the east coast States, and each sent its respective missionaries to the frontier states in the west. There they both met the Disciples of Christ, a denomination indigenous to the frontier. In the course of time the Northern Baptists

---

[26] The useful distinction between native and foreign cases of disembodied religious traditions is drawn from P. A. J. WADDINGTON, *The Ecumenical Movement : a study in the sociology of religion*, unpublished M.A. dissertation (The University of Leeds 1970).

[27] Cited in BENGT SUNDKLER, *Church of South India : The Movement Towards Union, 1900–1947* (London, Lutterworth Press 1954), p. 36, quoted in WILSON, op. cit., p. 148.

and the Southern Baptists met in the west and found they had much in common, while their brethren back east remained separated; on the other hand the Northern Baptists and Southern Baptists in the east both thought themselves similar to the Disciples of Christ, whom their respective brethren in the west thought entirely different.[28] Disembodiment, which can occur in a native situation when a religious tradition fails to evolve as rapidly as the secular environment, becomes almost inevitable when a new religion arrives in a foreign land and the change in environment is instantaneous.

Disembodied religious traditions may persist for many generations through sheer inertia. They may even persist long enough to find new groups of adherents for whom the symbols will again come to life. While they survive, however, they remain weak and there will be little opposition to ecumenical co-operation or reunion. With clerical leadership, the rank and file members will resist ecumenism only out of stubbornness or independence, and not because of any religious convictions.

Unlike the contact between clergy of different churches and the changes in theological thought, both of which positively encourage ecumenism, the changes in secular society which render religious differences obsolete do no more than remove barriers to it. To portray this third factor in anything but negative terms would be misleading. The writers who argue that ecumenism springs directly from religious weakness assume too easily that the positive factors arise in response to this weakness, whereas it seems nearer the truth to say that it is the simultaneous but independent occurrence of certain factors encouraging ecumenical activity, and of others making it less objectionable, which together promote ecumenism. Peter Berger's analysis of 'ecumenicity' provides an elegant and attractive account of the movement towards reunion, but he, too, assumes that an explanation of what makes ecumenism possible can also serve as an explanation of why reunions take place.[29] Berger introduces the notion of pluralism as a key variable in his analysis to describe a

---

[28] RECTOR, 'Baptist-Disciple conversations towards unity' in NILS EHRENSTROM and WALTER G. MUELDER, eds., *Institutionalism and Church Unity* (London, SCM Press 1963).

[29] PETER L. BERGER and THOMAS LUCKMANN, 'Secularization and pluralism', *International Yearbook for the Sociology of Religion*, No. 2, 1966, and BERGER, 'A market model for the analysis of ecumenicity', *Social Research*, Vol. 30, 1963.

situation in which many religious traditions co-exist in a single society without any one of them being accorded a pre-eminent position. In a pluralist society no religion remains profoundly true for people, in the sense that it is related to their total experience of life – in Berger's terms each religion lacks a 'plausibility structure'. Each religious tradition alike offers something which is less than totally convincing and credible to any of its adherents. Religious pluralism, particularly as found in North America, is part of a wider pluralism which characterises the whole social structure. In western capitalist societies the movement towards pluralism is an integral part of advancing industrialism, for it arises out of the 'free' movement of population.[30] If resources are to be exploited in the most economical way then industry must be sited conveniently and the labour force move continually. The constant movement which results has the effect of breaking down the old structures, both in local communities and also in wider communities based on social class and ethnicity, within which religious traditions had previously flourished. Continuing modernisation in the West is thus responsible for the erosion of traditional social boundaries which had been of religious as well as of secular significance. The positive consequences, which are important for an understanding of ecumenism and which constitute the fourth factor, are no less obvious for something which might be very loosely termed a 'world civilisation' begins to emerge. As Roger Mehl has written, contrasting traditional science and modern technology:

'Particular societies owe their existence to the great diversity of technology and to the beliefs which support and reinforce it. Although science has been universal for centuries, the awareness of this universality was the possession of a few élites, which, moreover, were concentrated in a very limited part of the world. Technology, on the contrary, has given birth to the means of its own universalisation. By creating extremely rapid modes of transportation and communication, by giving birth to techniques of information that permit every man always to be the

[30] People are 'free' to move in accordance with the 'demands' of the economy, that is, rather than free to move where they will.

contemporary of his fellow men, technology has opened the paths of penetration through the diversity of cultures.'[31]

Such a development is incompatible with the continuing life of religious traditions whose diversity has in large part been made possible by the diversity of experience of discrete groups of people within society. The experiences which have become universal throughout what used to be called Christendom, such as exposure to the same newsreel films of men on the moon, are doubly universal since they are no longer mediated through traditional religious communities, each of which might have provided its own interpretation. Hence the unique experiences which gave life to correspondingly unique traditions of religious symbols are undermined by experiences which are increasingly universal. The process is halted only where a religious group, by forbidding the use of such things as television and 'heathen' newspapers, is able to preserve that interpretation of experience which is mediated through itself. At the same time as religious traditions thus become less compellingly real they also move closer together, since widespread contact is unavoidable. As Moberg has said:

'As the world "shrinks" through improved transportation, religious organisations are brought closer to one another, and co-operation is thrust upon them. The ecumenical movement can be explained partly as an outgrowth of the same forces that brought the United Nations into being.'[32]

This explanation is very incomplete, of course, but the general context of technology in the West is essential to an understanding of how a plurality of disembodied religious traditions has come into existence. Disembodiment is entailed in the much wider process of modernisation.

Modernisation, which is a shorthand term for the social effects of scientific and technical innovations, has had two independent consequences for the religious traditions of the West. By breaking

---

[31] MEHL, op. cit., p. 196; for the effect on traditional ethics, see ROBERT A. NISBET, 'The impact of technology on ethical decision-making' in ROBERT LEE and MARTIN E. MARTY, eds., *Religion and Social Conflict* (New York, Oxford University Press 1964).

[32] MOBERG, op. cit., p. 260.

down established social groups it has resulted both in the decline of the real credibility of discrete traditions of religious symbolism, and also in the blurring of the traditional boundaries between religio-social groups. The first result may be termed secularisation, and the second ecumenism; but they are independent results and neither can be adduced as the cause of the other. Ecumenism develops when a variety of religions cease to be distinctively credible and, as Berger said, there would have been a 'crisis in credibility brought on by pluralism as a social-structural phenomenon, quite apart from its linkage with the "carriers" of secularisation'.[33] Only by using the expression 'secularisation' to mean one aspect of the process of modernisation, rather than as a description of some of its effects, can it be accorded causal status. Whether or not ecumenism and secularisation, in this limited sense, are aspects of the final decline in the viability of religious symbolism *per se*, which would be true secularisation, is an empirical question. To answer that question would lead us back to an examination of what should count as specifically *religious* symbolism. The problem of what religion really is constitutes the principal focus of interest for the social scientific study of religion and every specific problem in the analysis of religion leads back to it in the end.

[33] PETER L. BERGER, *The Social Reality of Religion* (London, Faber and Faber 1969), p. 150.

PART THREE

BIOGRAPHICAL NOTE

JOHN KENT *is a Methodist Minister who has taught history at Emmanuel College, Cambridge and at Methodist theological colleges in Leeds, Cambridge and Manchester. He moved to the Bristol University Theology and Religious Studies Department in 1965, and was made Reader in Theology in 1969. His most recent publications are 'The Study of Modern Ecclesiastical History since 1930', in* The Pelican Guide to Modern Theology, *Vol. 2 (1969), 'Models of the British Nonconformist Ministry' in the 9th Downside Symposium, ed. N. Lash and J. Rhymer (1970). 'Feelings and Festivals', a study of 19th century urban working-class religion, will appear in* The Victorian City, *ed. H. J. Dyos and Michael Wolff (Routledge 1973).*

10 Old-Fashioned Diplomacy

JOHN KENT

THE RADICAL PROTESTANT, IN WHAT MIGHT BE CALLED his para-ecumenical position, doubts the value of traditional ideas of 'membership' and perhaps exaggerates the value of what is often described as 'open communion'. He doubts the value of membership on the ground of a sociological interpretation of existing ecclesiastical institutions, but advocates an 'unfenced' table or altar because he does not think that the religious institutions that we know possess the authority to deny admission to the eucharist to those who come in peace. His position is worth recalling at this stage in the history of ecumenism, for there is a tendency at the moment in some quarters to feel that what has divided Protestantism and Roman Catholicism belongs to the past in every sense and that all the members of both groups can now be combined quite swiftly into a single institution which, if present proposals are any guide, would be based on the more centralising attitudes to belief and practice to be found on both the former sides.[1] In fact, the radical Protestant – and I am not competent to say whether he has a Catholic equivalent – remains unconvinced that either the 'Biblical Theology' beloved of the

[1] Discussion implied that 'protestant' was no longer a useful adjective. However, some disclaiming word is needed by those Christians who cannot accept that a Church can pronounce infallibly on matters of faith and morals, whether the 'Church' is understood in terms of the Papacy, an episcopal group, or some wider historical process which 'develops' dogma, or makes law.

World Council of Churches, or the second Vatican Council's movement towards ecclesiastical government by a collegiate episcopate, hold out much hope of the kind of Christian renewal which would be needed to restore Christianity to a dominant place in even European culture.

What he is reacting against, in any case, is belief in the existence of an *ecclesia* which is, simultaneously, divinely and historically established, and which therefore claims to possess through the indwelling power of the Spirit the authority both to define the limits of belief and to admit and expel members. The persistence of this view in the twentieth century has been remarkable. One of the most cogent statements of it in the earlier part of the century is to be found in *Divine Transcendence* (1911), by the High Anglican writer, J. R. Illingworth.[2] He wrote:

'Consider what the Christian position, meaning thereby the position of the Christian Church, really is. It is . . . that the Church did not originate in a book, but in a Person, and consists, and has always consisted of living persons, bound together in an organised ministry, a sacramental system and a creed. The New Testament contains the record of its origin; but the record is not the origin, any more than the Commentaries of Caesar are the battles of Caesar. In each case the record presupposes the life. But in the case of the Church that life is continuous. The Church of today, here and now, is quick with the same vitality as the Church of the first century; and this is due, we believe, to the indwelling presence of the selfsame Spirit, by which the first generation of Christians was inspired . . . and this life is the outcome of the selfsame belief in the Incarnation and the Atonement which reproduces the selfsame life at the present day. . . . And this consideration brings us back from the book to the life. The

---

2 Illingworth wrote in the course of a controversy about the authority of the historical creeds. It is germane to our subject here that the radical climax of this controversy was *Miracles in the New Testament* (1911), by J. M. THOMPSON, then an ordained Anglican Fellow of Magdalen College, Oxford, but who, under the pressure which his specific rejection of the historicity of the Virgin Birth produced, withdrew and made a second career as a historian of the French Revolution. I have the impression that at least since the Deist controversy of the early 18th century public denial of the doctrine of the Virgin Birth has been the limit at which radical theologians have found themselves compelled either to withdraw the statement or themselves. Yet the Archbishops' Report on Doctrine did not endorse this attitude; cf. p. 238 et seq.

book is not the origin of the life but the record of its origin. And the life is being lived in the midst of us today. How, then, is it originated and sustained? Essentially, as we have seen, by the indwelling presence of the Holy Spirit. But the Spirit uses human agency as the medium of His communication – the living voice of the preacher, the living ministry of the sacraments, the living sympathy of fellow Christians, the support and stimulus of common worship, the solemn recitation of the common creed. All these things react upon the spirit within us, and bring it into concrete touch with the life that has come down to us from apostolic times. For *omne vivum ex vivo.* . . . The synoptic gospels are an important factor in the transmission of this life; but the gospels as utilised, as vivified, and *a fortiori* as interpreted by the Church. . . . And however much the Gospels may be read by themselves, for their intrinsic spiritual worth, they cannot be the same when so treated, as when interpreted in accordance with the immemorial creeds of the Church'.[3]

Criticism of the gospels could not, in Illingworth's view, affect their authority, since they served primarily as witnesses to a continuous tradition of belief and practice which began without them and was sustained not so much by them as by the beneficent activity of the Holy Spirit. This activity took place within a Church, of which he also said: 'Jesus Christ not only claimed spiritual authority over man, in virtue of His Mission from the Father, the source of all authority; but he also left behind him a society, to perpetuate the claim. And the corollaries of this fact that we would emphasise are . . . that there still exists a religious authority in the Christian episcopate and its attendant priesthood which is identical with that of old, and wholly unaffected, as authority, by the advances of criticism or the fluctuations of popular prejudice.'[4]

Illingworth's emphasis on the episcopate, typical of his local tradition and period, should not mislead one: what matters is not succession through an 'historic episcopate' but the identification – common to Anglican and non-Anglican authors who do not regard

---

[3] ILLINGWORTH, *Divine Transcendence*, pp. 186–93. It would be too unfair, given that Illingworth obviously composed these passages at a high level of abstraction, to make much of the word 'immemorial', but the choice of adjectives is illuminating, and the creeds, of course, are nothing of the kind.

[4] Ibid., p. 111.

the episcopate itself as of the *esse* of the *ecclesia* – of presently existing religious institutions with the theological myth of a divine-human Church, part Spirit, part congregation of the saints, an identification which replaces the concept of 'membership' as Christian discipleship with a far more mysterious image of 'participation in the Body of Christ'. The image of discipleship may be only loosely united with the Eucharist, but the second image brings the ideas of membership and eucharist tightly together, as in the Anglican – Roman Catholic *Agreed Statement on Eucharistic Doctrine*, where we find, for example:

'The real presence of Christ's body and blood can, however, only be understood within the context of the redemptive activity whereby he gives himself, and in himself reconciliation, peace and life, to his own. On the one hand, the eucharistic gift springs out of the paschal mystery of Christ's death and resurrection, in which God's saving purpose has already been definitively realised. On the other hand, its purpose is to transmit the life of the crucified and risen Christ to his body, the Church, so that its members may be more united with Christ and one another.'[5]

In other words, the claims of those who regard themselves as the present representatives of this allegedly continuous tradition, to have a divine as well as human authority to maintain the Creeds of the Church unaltered and to judge the ethical demands of the faith upon society and the individual, really depend upon a prior act of faith, indemonstrable, as the radical would say, at the historical level. According to this act of faith, the primitive community was guided by the Holy Spirit to set up sufficient means of contact with the life of Jesus (through the sacraments, more especially), to write down an adequate, because revealed, account of the community's origin and faith (in the Gospels and Creeds), and to work out means for handing on these legacies unchanged (through the episcopate acting in reliance on the Spirit, but also through wider, less purely administrative channels). It is important to the radical that neither more than two centuries of unbroken Biblical Criticism, nor the steadily accumulating knowledge of the history of the institutional Church – whether in 'western' situations or in the 'overseas' mission-fields – nor theological criticism, has seriously weakened this

---

[5] *An Agreed Statement on Eucharistic Doctrine* (7 September 1971), III, 6.

faith-attitude in the power-centres of the institutionalised Churches. But it is not always clear that those who make this act of faith recognise it for what it is.

The *Agreed Statement on the Eucharist* (1971), for example, begins by saying that 'our intention has been to seek a deeper understanding of the reality of the eucharist which is consonant with biblical teaching and with the tradition of our common inheritance'.[6] That is, the consensus achieved was to be offered as the essence, doctrinally speaking, of what the two bodies had always believed under the guidance of the Holy Spirit. What is being asserted here is that we know (because it has been revealed, in the last resort) the only way in which the development of doctrine can take place legitimately. The Anglican-Methodist *Conversations* (1963), for example, stated that:

'while the problem of development under the guidance of the Holy Spirit cannot be shirked, it nevertheless can be laid down in principle:
(a) that the Holy Spirit will not contradict the mind and will of Christ as known to us through the New Testament;
(b) that development must be within and loyal to the given;
(c) that the purpose of any development, as of the originally given, will be to offer and foster life, according to, and by, the Gospel.'[7]

What goes wrong with this statement, which was only intended to repeat text-book propositions, is that (c) the offering and fostering of life, may well clash with (b), 'that development must be within and loyal to the given', unless the authority which claims to be guided has *always* been right in defining what the given actually was. And this, of course, involves the strictly conservative point of view, that we do know in simple propositional form what Christianity is, and that we know this not only in the broadest sense, as when some

[6] Ibid., para. 1. This is not quoted from the Introduction signed only by the two co-chairmen, but from the first paragraph of the Statement proper, which is therefore attributable to all the signatories, and distinguished only by the figure 1.

[7] *Conversations*, 1963, p. 21. The various reports of these negotiations have not been clearly distinguished from one another on the title-page: it is simplest to distinguish them by their date of publication. In these Reports the sections on 'Scripture and Tradition' seem to use 'tradition' as a synonym for legitimate development: tradition is what has been *added* after being tested by the scriptural norm; as with development, the idea that traditions which have been tested and added may at a later stage be dropped, is not raised: development means addition, not subtraction, and this is the Protestant version of a doctrine of the infallibility of the historical Church.

primitive affirmation such as 'Jesus is Lord' is regarded as expressing the core of the given, but also in detail, the kind of detail which was invoked in another paragraph of the 1963 report of the Anglican-Methodist *Conversations*:

'What is *given* in Order includes worship, word, sacraments, ministry, pastoral care, discipline of members, and participation of members in regulating the common life. These are the gifts of the one Spirit and should operate harmoniously. It is true that the New Testament provides no fixed and self-evident pattern in which all these cohere, but some of the *given* elements help to shape other elements in Order. For example, the sacrament of Holy Communion involves the saying of certain words and the performing of certain actions, and requires rules as to who shall say and perform them and who shall be admitted to it.'[8]

When one considers the continuous crisis through which both western religion and western Christianity in particular have been passing since at least the late seventeenth century[9] this sort of certainty looks unimpressive. The undisclosed act of faith becomes in the long run the assertion that existing denominations have divine authority to require, as conditions of membership, prior assent, and continuing *public* assent, to a mass of theological propositions; that they have the right to control both the admission of their own members to the Eucharist (sometimes denying it on purely ethical grounds), the admission of the members of other bodies to what becomes 'their' Eucharist, and the freedom of their own members to communicate at the celebrations of other bodies.[10]

From the point of view of the radical Protestant it becomes clear just how far this claim may conflict with his own position when he examines documents like the 1968 Anglican-Methodist Report, *The Scheme*. In the Methodist Church there had gradually arisen a situation of almost totally open communion: if this lacked definite

---

[8] *Conversations*, 1963, p. 21.

[9] Space forbids discussion of this, but the importance of the seventeenth century in the development of modern society is now generally recognised. For the effect of the process of theological change on doctrinal statements see especially, VAN HARVEY, *The Historian and the Believer*, 1968, Harvey's concept of the changing possibilities of belief seems relevant to the authority which the believer is obliged to grant the institution.

[10] I have saved space by not particularising here: cf. Appendix A for the situation as it is in England today.

theological foundation it also seems to have gone on for many years without producing the kind of 'scandal' which orthodoxy always fears from such freedom. The Report described it in these terms:

'it is now a widespread practice to invite to Holy Communion not only the members of the Methodist Church and members of other Churches, but "all those who love the Lord Jesus Christ". The invitation to participate is construed in terms of the call to all those who truly and earnestly repent of their sins, in the order of the service itself. The practice of issuing this invitation is highly valued by many Methodists, as a witness to the universality of the Gospel and the readiness of the Lord Jesus Christ to receive repentant sinners.'[11]

If the Anglican and Methodist Churches came together this practice, which has never been given official sanction, would clash with the situation in the Church of England. Here again, it is simplest to let the Report speak for itself:

'The rubric at the end of the Order of Confirmation in the Book of Common Prayer states: "And there shall none be admitted to the Holy Communion, until such time as he be confirmed, or be ready and desirous to be confirmed." There is diversity of interpretation of this rubric within the Church of England. In some parishes it is held not to exclude a general invitation to communicant members of other Churches to receive Communion in the Church of England. The Resolutions of the Upper Houses of Convocation in 1933 appear to have regarded the rubric as exclusive. These Resolutions provided for exceptions to the rule in the case of colleges and schools, gatherings designed to promote Christian unity, and members of other Churches cut off for a period from the ministrations of their own Church. They are generally taken as the standard of practice. No one who presents himself is likely to be repelled from the Table but if someone who is not confirmed wishes to present himself regularly, though he is not prevented by distance from communicating in a Church of his own communion, he will be encouraged to seek confirmation.'[12]

---

[11] *Report of the Anglican-Methodist Unity Commission*, 1968, p. 64.

[12] Ibid. See also the Anglican position in Appendix A, but changes in the rules do not affect the clash as far as 'open' communion is concerned. The rule book gives the Church the power to decide who communicates; the open system leaves the decision to the individual and God, not a popular combination in modern Protestant theology.

Anglican standards, in other words, while cautious about 'un-churching' other Churches, and anxious to avoid any one's being refused communion at the rite itself, do not envisage open communion – and indeed, never have. There is nothing surprising in all this: what is more interesting for the purposes of the argument here is the solution proposed in the Anglican-Methodist Scheme:

'These divergent practices can be reconciled when the two Churches are in communion with each other, if (a) Methodist ministers invite to Holy Communion those who are members of the Methodist Church or of any Church with which the Methodist Church is in communion, and those who love the Lord Jesus Christ *and who, having been baptised,* wish to show by their coming to the Lord's Table their repentance and their desire to be prepared for reception into full membership of the Church or confirmation; and (b) the Church of England recognises this practice as legitimate. In this way the dual concern for the Sacrament as a sign both of incorporation into the Body of Christ, and of God's universal love for sinners, will be recognised and expressed.'[13]

One need not do more than mention the obvious criticism that the compromise proposed here does not recognise or express the idea of universality, because the formula to be used would limit the intention with which the open invitation had previously been given. What matters to the radical is rather that in this way the comparative openness of the Methodist Eucharist, an openness which had had no harmful consequences as far as one knows, simply disappears under the pressure of those who *know*, because it is given, or is implied with absolute certainty by what is given, that there can be no sense of the phrases 'Christian membership', 'membership in Christ', or 'the Body of Christ', which does not include either membership or the intention of seeking membership in one of the visible historical institutions which identify with themselves in their corporate existence whatever they understand the New Testament to say about the society of Christians, and which therefore set up dogmatic tests of fitness for admission. This does not seem an advance. If one looks at the history of the Christian Churches one sees that all attempts to restrict membership to those prepared to

[13] Ibid., p. 64.

affirm particular orthodoxies have always failed in the long run. Beyond Rome, Canterbury and the various centres of the Orthodox Churches, outside the Baptist, Lutheran and Methodist Churches which are still far from united with the communions of the first group, remain countless European, American, African and other bodies which have redefined membership to please themselves.[14] Heredity and environment secure much conformity, but there are sects even in Italy. The Christian passion for definition, doctrinal purity, and exclusion has not prevented institutional disunity and separate memberships; not all these groups will be reunited by an ecumenical movement whose impulse is to eliminate 'open communion' whenever it stumbles upon it. . . . The identification of the kind of unity which is represented by membership of an historical Christian institution with the kind of unity which is achieved by sharing in the eucharist has not produced the peaceful fruit which might have justified it.[15]

To survive historically, the theory that the Church lives under the continuous guidance of the Holy Spirit who guarantees the kind of theological development allowed for by such documents as the Anglican-Methodist series, required some machinery: therefore at intervals the Church would make a formal, institutionalised plea for divine guidance. The resulting Councils were seen as clarifying that which had already been revealed and identifying and dismissing improper, heretical variations on tradition. It was inconceivable that such meetings (for they were special meetings with a distinct purpose rather than permanent channels of decision in constant use) should discover that the Church had taught what was now recognisable as error

[14] Dr Sharpe's paper on Christianity and caste in India illustrates the price which has often been paid for treating western definitions of the conditions of membership as though they were so certainly derived from the 'given' that they must hold absolutely in any conditions; the same pattern is familiar to any one who has studied the history of the Christian missions in Africa. For a bibliography of this subject, see the present writer's contribution to *The Pelican Guide to Modern Theology*, Vol. 2 (1969), with A. H. Couratin and Jean Daniélou.

[15] Professor Wiles's paper on the Primitive Church illustrates how from the beginning the eucharist played a divisive as well as a uniting role; how Christians of the allegedly 'undivided Church' already regarded themselves as entitled to refuse to communicate with others on doctrinal grounds: to me, the first five centuries present an unedifying spectacle of multiple division in which everyone finally lost hold of the essential idea of a Christian discipleship which men could share despite their disagreements.

in the central areas of doctrine such as the doctrines of the Trinity, Incarnation, Atonement, etc. Nor was it supposed that such meetings could introduce new teaching which could not be related logically to what had always been taught. 'Development', that is, was taken to mean logical addition, never subtraction. In the case of the Roman Catholic Church, Möhler and Newman only added to this position the possibility of taking 'logical addition' in a less strict sense. The offence of the more radical Catholic Modernists, Loisy and Tyrrell for instance, was that they wanted to dispense with certain articles of belief, whereas orthodox schemes of development had only envisaged the problem of how to prevent improper additions to what the Church officially taught.

The official attitude of the Church of England is less certain, but the far from well-known *Doctrine in the Church of England* (1938)[16] did open a door, if not to the rejection of what had been taught in the past, at any rate to the admission in the case of some doctrines of radical alternative positions, as in its note on the doctrine of the Virgin Birth:

'Many of us hold . . . that belief in the Word made flesh is integrally bound up with belief in the Virgin Birth, and that this will be increasingly recognised. There are, however, some among us who hold that a full belief in the historical Incarnation is more consistent with the supposition that our Lord's birth took place under the normal conditions of human generation. In their minds the notion of the Virgin Birth tends to mar the completeness of the belief that in the Incarnation God revealed Himself at every point in and through human nature. We are agreed that belief in our Lord's birth from a Virgin has been in the history of the Church intimately associated with its faith in the Incarnation of the Son of God. Further, we recognise that the work of scholars upon the New Testament has created a new setting of which theologians in their treatment of this article are obliged to take account. We also recognise that both the views outlined above are held by members of the Church, as of the

---

[16] Begun in 1922, this report, originally thought of as offering solutions to the uncertainties created by Liberal Protestantism, did not appear until 1938, by which time the Liberal theology had fallen out of favour and the Report, influenced by some very level-headed Anglican divines, was too tolerant towards doctrinal liberalism for contemporary taste. The World War then intervened.

Commission, who fully accept the reality of our Lord's Incarnation, which is the central truth of the Christian faith.'[17]

This is a careful passage, which protects the doctrine of the Divinity of Christ but tolerates what amounts to the denial of the doctrine of the Virgin Birth as traditionally understood. The calm admission that there were those in the Church of England and in the Commission who believed in the Incarnation without believing in the traditional view of the Virgin Birth brings us back again to the question of membership, for *Doctrine in the Church of England* did not suggest that this position was either un-Anglican or unorthodox: the Commission's way of putting the whole issue implied, I think, a preference for the traditional view, but did not imply that one taking the liberal line ought either to re-examine his position, or question his loyalty to the Church of England, or, in the last resort, withdraw from membership. When one combined this note with the Commission's conclusions on other doctrines[18] one is someway towards the possibility of doctrinal plurality, though by no means the whole way. In so far as the Commission worked by cautious addition to what members of the Anglican Church might believe, the approach was traditional, and the Commission did not suggest that Anglicans should actually stop believing anything which they had always believed in the past: 'there must be room in the Church both for those who believe that some will actually be lost, and also for those who hold that the Love of God will at last win penitence and answering love from every soul that it has created',[19] was the characteristic verdict on the subject of Hell and damnation.

Even this method could have drastic results, however, as when, for example, the Commission, having said that 'we are agreed in asserting that man, as known to history, both now and throughout the ages,

---

[17] *Doctrine in the Church of England* (1938), pp. 82–3.

[18] The Report needs to be read as a whole. On miracles, the Atonement, the Trinity, the Commission was not very flexible; on the Virgin Birth, and on the whole problem of Sin (cf. the passages cited above), much wider liberty was offered; as to angels and demons, the Commission, having said that many of its members believed in them, concluded: 'nevertheless, the Commission desires to record its conviction that it is legitimate for a Christian either to suspend judgement on the point, or alternately, to interpret the language, whether of Scripture or of the Church's Liturgy, with regard to angels and demons in a purely symbolical sense' (p. 47).

[19] Ibid., p. 219.

has been under the influence of a bias towards evil',[20] then went on to list at least six alternative interpretations of this fact, none of which, it said, should be regarded as illegitimate in the Anglican Church, and the first of which – 'some hold this influence of social environment upon each individual is a sufficient explanation'[21] – was radically opposed to the later view that 'there is a transcendental solidarity of the human race in evil which creates or determines a proneness to sin in each individual'.[22] Anglicans, in fact, were left to choose between varieties of interpretation, though the choice could not be called entirely free because the Commission did not list as permissible for Anglicans all radical alternatives to orthodoxy; the result was a limited plurality, rather plurality as such.

The possibility of such wide divergences being tolerated officially raises the issue of the guidance of the Holy Spirit once again. Was the Commission being guided towards plurality by the Holy Spirit, or was it simply failing to defend orthodoxy? The actual form of the Report – perhaps in the end the most important thing about it – would lead one to answer this question by saying: 'Some of us see in this move towards a greater freedom in the understanding of Christian doctrine a leading of the Spirit; others, on the other hand. . . .' At any rate, the Report was not rejected officially by the Church of England, and in as much as it still sets a standard of belief for those who belong to that Church, it raises a further question about membership: how far is it proper to require of those who wish to become members of a Church acceptance of more detailed and often more traditional views of theology than are required for the retention of membership once it has been obtained? It was really to the second of these situations that the 1938 Report originally addressed itself.

In the case of the Roman Church the growth of the theory of Papal Infallibility suggests a certain dissatisfaction with the system of formal and collective appeals for guidance by the Spirit, but it is significant that infallibility should not have been made *de fide* until

---

[20] Ibid., p. 62. It is interesting that although the Commission was by no means anti-liberal it ignored or contradicted the views of F. R. Tennant on this and similar topics; Tennant said that the supposition of a bias towards evil was no more rational than that of a bias towards good: 'The hypothesis of a bias is purely gratuitous', *Origin and Propagation of Sin*, 2nd ed., 1906, pp. xxviii–xxix.

[21] Ibid., p. 62.

[22] Ibid., p. 63.

as late as 1870, and Hans Küng's comment, in *The Church*, written after the second Vatican Council had taken place, is not only moving but also goes to the heart of the idea of divine guidance through institutions: if 1870 had not already defined infallibility, he asked, would the Second Vatican Council have done so? – leaving the clear impression that in his own opinion the definition would not have figured on the later agenda. Roman institutions are deeply committed, however, to the model of theological continuity. In his more recent book, *Infallible?* (1971), Küng illustrated this from the case of contraception. The weight of the conservative arguments against a change in the official attitude to the subject was, he said, that 'the moral impermissibility of contraception had been taken for granted for centuries, and then, against resistance in our century up to the time of the Second Vatican Council (and the resulting confusion) had been specifically taught by bishops everywhere in the world, acting in moral unity and by common consent, as Catholic morality to be observed on pain of eternal damnation. From the point of view of the ordinary *magisterium* of the Pope and the bishops, it was therefore *de facto* an infallible moral truth, even though it had not been defined as such. This argument, after the obvious breakdown of the developmental theory, was bound ultimately to prevail with the Pope. He must have said to himself, rightly from this point of view, that he could not be expected to abandon as error a moral truth constantly and unanimously taught by the *magisterium ordinarium* and therefore in practice infallible'.[23]

A further quotation from Professor Küng's book will illuminate his reference to the failure of the developmental theory. He said that 'the theory of the development of dogma abundantly used and abused in Catholic theology since the nineteenth century – under the influence of Newman and the Catholic Tübingen school, especially Johann Adam Möhler – did not apply here. If the progressive theologians had been able to present Paul VI with a formula enabling a positive teaching today to seem merely to be a 'development' of the negative teaching of Pius XI in 1930, enabling him, that is to say, to state more plainly (explicitly) what Pius XI had said unclearly (implicitly), we do not for a moment doubt that Paul would have

[23] *Infallible?* An Enquiry, by Hans Küng, German ed. 1970, English ed. 1971, pp. 48–9.

decided in favour of birth control. For the continuity of Catholic teaching, and that of the last three Popes in particular, would have been maintained. No error would have had had to be admitted, but only incompleteness, provisionality or something of that sort. . . . But this obviously could not be done . . . it would be impossible to persuade anyone that a sanctioning of birth control by Paul VI in 1968 was implicitly if imperceptibly contained in the ban on it imposed by Pius XI in 1930. . . .'[24]

Contraception was a crucial issue because the change demanded involved the reversal of what had been ruled in the past. Nineteenth century theories of development had been based on the assumption that doctrinal changes would fit together; even if they did not do so mechanically, like so many bricks of the same kind, they would do so organically, as parts of the same body; the pattern of the bricks, the form of the body, was determined by the Holy Spirit. The Modernist movement expressed the protest of those who doubted whether revelation existed in this way as a system, organic or inorganic, to be apprehended and taught and made the basis for far-reaching ethical absolutes. This is why George Tyrrell's later writings abound in vague references to the Spirit of Christ, which he does not want to define or limit overmuch in terms of the Gospels themselves.[25]

It is significant of the slow way in which these situations develop that Hans Küng should have gone back to the New Testament sources for ecclesiology after the Second Vatican Council in the hope that they would provide an authoritative settlement of problems of theory and structure. Once the continuity of a traditional interpretation has been broken, however, the appeal to the New Testament is no more than an appeal to a particular exegete and those whom he can persuade to agree with him. In effect, Küng's return to the New Testament also throws a different light on Illingworth's assertion that New Testament criticism could not shake the authority of either the *ecclesia* or the New Testament itself. Küng made his appeal because his confidence in the continuity theory of doctrine had collapsed; Illingworth did not foresee this as a likely situation within the Christian society itself. When Küng went back to the primary documents – only to find that they left him with little

[24] Ibid., p. 45.
[25] Especially *Christianity at the Crossroads* (1909).

demonstrable relationship between the primitive and the twentieth century Church – it was not criticism in Illingworth's sense, a destructive force which cast doubt on holy knowledge, which actually proved to be his difficulty, but the material evidence, the given itself, which he now encountered in all its ambiguity. Without the light thrown and the order imposed by a traditional way of interpretation the New Testament gave him no certain guide to the nature and structure of the Church.

And this state of affairs entitles one to ask, as a Protestant radical, what authority the present Christian bodies have beyond that common to all voluntary societies, to lay down absolute rules about ethical behaviour, conditions of membership. It is interesting here to look at another source, the volume on intercommunion which Donald Baillie and John Marsh edited for the World Faith and Order Conference at Lund in 1952.[26] There Leonard Hodgson, the Anglican theologian, took virtually the same position as had been defended by Illingworth before the First World War.[27] More interesting was the advocacy of open communion by A. T. DeGroot, of the American Disciples of Christ. He wrote:

'If the Church is a "living congregation", and the Lord's Supper is its corporate act of communion, then a proper handling of intercommunion among the Churches waits upon a conscious acknowledgement by each Church of the Christian status of the *individuals* in the Churches, who, through the promptings of the Holy Spirit, seek Holy Communion, rather than waiting upon legal approval of the denominations involved. The placing of the privilege for

---

[26] *Intercommunion*, 1952, being the report of a commission set up by the Continuation Committee of the World Faith and Order Conference.

[27] Ibid., pp. 255–68. The essay was a good example of the view that orders are the primary issue, a view from which the Lund Conference could find no escape. Against this one has to set Thomas Torrance's view: 'The actual ordering of the Church partakes of the form and fashion of this passing world, and as such it can never be identified in its historical structure with the essential form of the Church or be allowed to anticipate the order yet to be fully disclosed in the *eschaton*. It can only point beyond itself. The Church that is truly ordered will possess its orders as if it possessed them not, coveting earnestly the more excellent way which abides for ever, the way of love, when all orders, however necessary and sacramental they are within history, will pass away . . .' (ibid., p. 345). But Torrance was a Presbyterian, which was enough to discount the force of the passage, which is reminiscent of Harnack's attitude to the structure of the visible Church in *The Essence of Christianity* (1900).

communion, and of responsibility for participating in this essentially personal act, has been set by the Disciples of Christ (as a Christian body) where they believe it belongs – in the conscience of the Christian himself. . . . The manner in which this acknowledgement of the full communion status of all who claim it is administered by the Disciples of Christ, is to place the responsibility for *spreading* the Lord's Table upon the organised Church, but to place the responsibility for sharing in the feast on the individual Christian. . . .'[28]

In retrospect it is clear that at Lund in 1952 Protestant ecumenism ought to have broken through to decisive action: for various reasons, which cannot be discussed here, nothing was done. Read twenty years later, the impassioned words of Thomas Torrance – 'intercommunion should come early in the approach of the Churches towards full unity in the ecumenical fellowship, for that unity can never be reached as long as the separated Churches refuse to give each other the divine medicine for their healing'[29] sound ironical. It is not even clear that in the 1970's we are moving towards a goal that the radical Protestant can accept at all. This brings me back to the problems set by the Agreed Statement on the Eucharist to which reference was made earlier.

The most important point here is to consider what the Anglican-Roman Catholic commission has done in principle. Nothing is to be gained by arguing about the truth or falsity of the interpretation of the rite which the statement contains. The Introduction to the document says that 'our intention was to reach a consensus at the level of faith, so that all might be able to say, within the limits of the Statement: this is the Christian faith of the Eucharist,'[30] to which must be added the passage which I have previously quoted, to the effect that the commission was seeking a deeper understanding of the reality of the eucharist which would be consonant with biblical teaching and with the tradition of the common inheritance of the two Churches. The phrase, 'within the limits of the Statement' is

[28] Ibid., p. 173, 'Intercommunion in the the Non-clerical Tradition'. The Disciples of Christ originated in the U.S.A. in 1811 through Alexander Campbell, and became a completely separate body in 1827. These churches practise believers' baptism, have a congregational type of church order, and celebrate the Lord's Supper every Sunday; the total membership, almost all in America, exceeds one million.

[29] TORRANCE, T., op. cit., p. 349, in an essay called 'Eschatology and the Eucharist'.

[30] This comes from the Introduction to the statement.

ambiguous: it looks as though it means that the parties concerned might *add* to the statement what they additionally believed about the eucharist; certainly, it appears to declare that what is said in the Statement forms part of any complete version of the Christian faith of the eucharist. From which one concludes that if one does not agree with the consensus here expressed – and I mean that one might reject the proposition, made more than once in the Statement, and fundamental to its meaning, that the bread and the wine *become* (the word is used more than once) the body and blood of Christ – one is rejecting part, implicitly the greater part, of the *Christian* faith of the Eucharist. This aspect of the matter does not seem to have struck the commission because its members were absorbed in what they regarded as their ecumenical purpose, and official unity between Canterbury and Rome would seem to require some consensus of this kind, if there was to be an agreed statement on eucharistic doctrine at all. Which leaves one a little bewildered as to the position of the Anglican members of the commission, for *Doctrine in the Church of England* (1938) not only devoted much careful attention to the doctrine of the sacraments, but printed two special memoranda, one called 'The Doctrine of the Real Presence', the other simply 'Receptionism', with the comment that 'the memoranda are not offered as expressing views held by the whole Commission, nor as covering all varieties of interpretation, but the Commission is glad to present them with its Report *as expressing types of theology admissible in the Church of England*. . . .'[31] It is not clear whether the *Agreed Statement* was intended to rule out Receptionism (or Virtualism) altogether, but it is quite clear that only one doctrinal interpretation of the rite is mentioned.[32]

Now if one is less interested in unity than in doctrinal freedom (on the ground that the first has never survived long without the second),

[31] Cf. *Doctrine in the Church of England*, p. 171. The memoranda follow between pages 172–82.

[32] I don't think that this is an unreasonable statement. The note on the term 'transubstantiation' makes the point most clearly: 'The word . . . is commonly used in the Roman Catholic Church to indicate that God acting in the eucharist effects a change in the inner reality of the elements. The term should be seen as affirming the *fact* of Christ's presence and of the mysterious and radical change which takes place. In contemporary Roman Catholic theology it is not understood as explaining *how* the change takes place.' This summarises the teaching of the whole document.

or, to put it another way, if one doubts whether the Christian Church itself can survive if it abandons the problem of plurality of meaning, then one is not going to become very excited about the degree of unanimity which emerged from the Commission. No doubt some members of the Commission had reservations about 'become', no doubt some held that the word had no possible definition in this context and so remained in the last resort unobjectionable; others may have thought that what was being considered was liturgical rather than doctrinal, and that in liturgy ambiguity is both necessary and praiseworthy, a point to which I shall return in a moment. It remains that the *Agreed Statement* rules out plurality of interpretation beyond a very narrow limit, commits the 'Christian faith of the Eucharist' to a particular tradition – recognisably Anglican as well as Roman Catholic. There is here a specific image of the Church as the company of the redeemed who are spiritually fed in the Eucharist – 'its purpose is to transmit the life of the crucified and risen Christ to his body, the Church, so that its members may be more fully united with Christ and with one another.'[33] This is familiar but particular. Where *Doctrine in the Church of England* sought to include, this statement tends to exclude by implication.

This is evident if one returns to the question of liturgy. If a united liturgy were composed which made it impossible for people to communicate if they did not accept the doctrine of the real presence of Christ in the eucharist which is expounded in the joint statement, then they would either have to withdraw and set up their own celebration – and the Church no longer has the support of the civil power in its efforts to prevent this – in which case the ecumenical end would not have been achieved; or they would be obliged to communicate in terms of a personal interpretation which involved simply not listening to the interpretation with which the Church-as-institution had surrounded the central action, the few words taken from the biblical narratives. This latter action would not be dishonest, unless one is going to assert that the authority of the ecclesia in such matters is so absolute that even silent indifference is mortal sin. After all, revised liturgies differ totally from antique, unretouched liturgies. The ancient liturgy has, in the twentieth century, no strict meaning at all; there is a patina; there remains a consequent freedom of interpretation;

[33] *Agreed Statement*, III.6.

the words of the liturgy are background music recorded deep in the past to be replayed in a perpetually recreated present. Once the liturgy is revised, however, the situation changes. This is not affected by keeping reminiscences of traditional phrase and form in the new work. A revised liturgy can only mean what it appears to mean; a revision therefore requires ambiguity if it is to survive. A revision which imposes a single understanding of the rite becomes a political rather than a liturgical matter. No Church has so far surrounded the repetition of the Lord's Prayer with a cocoon of comment, so that only those who can accept the gloss can repeat the words – though one can see the shadow of this possibility when in some Protestant services one is invited to join in 'The Family Prayer'. Personally, I do not find this title helpful; moreover, the change of label implies that the prayer is not so much the Lord's as the Church's. This may be in line with the modern tendency to make everything in Christianity revolve around the concept of the Church; liturgically, however, the problem of meaning should be left to the individual.

As for the truth or falsity of the doctrine which is contained in the *Agreed Statement*, let me repeat that those who are committed to a pluralist position are bound to tolerate this as one possible interpretation of the eucharistic narrative. I do not think that one can be obliged to do more than this intellectually, because there is no obvious way of testing the correctness of the various eucharistic theologies which have been proposed in the past, and the pluralist is himself no longer convinced that one can solve this kind of difficulty by appealing to 'tradition'. At the same time, the pluralist feels that he is entitled, when statements of this kind are drawn up, to assume that they will contain more than one interpretation of the past history of the doctrine under review. It is clear, even from as recent a survey as that attempted by the Anglican committee in 1938, that the doctrine of the Real Presence cannot be put forward as *the* Anglican doctrine of the eucharist – that one has to make room for those who have held positions fairly well identified as 'virtualist' or 'receptionist'. Nor is it enough to say that one may expect a future ecclesiastical assembly to vote that this is *now* the agreed doctrine of the uniting Churches: the modern mind no longer accepts such political methods as valid ways of deciding doctrinal issues – the first Vatican Council stands as a perpetual warning of the danger of making theology by majority votes, whether of bishops or of the whole body of the ecclesia by implication. Nor is the pluralist impressed by the argument that some sort of 'development' is going to lead the ecclesia to discover that this doctrine is the 'true' one: the 'organic' metaphor is not conclusive, so that the pluralist may well hold that no coherent idea of development has survived from the moment when it was first realised that change could mean not only addition, but repudiation, of doctrine.

The approach of the Anglican-Roman Catholic commission to the problems of union, intercommunion and membership is therefore mistaken. The Statement is the result of an effort to arrive at an agreed doctrine of the eucharist, whereas it should be clear from the history of the doctrine that no such agreement is possible at the religious, as distinct from what I have called the political, level. As far as the doctrine of the eucharist is concerned, one feels that the only fruitful way of solving the problem of union is by agreement to tolerate, in whatever kind of ecclesia is envisaged, at least the plurality of Christian interpretations of the rite which have been produced by Christian society in the past. We must unite our disagreements, instead of producing formulae which will allegedly reduce them to agreement. If a man comes in peace, asking for admission to the Lord's Table, the local ecclesia (for it will be the *local ecclesia* that is really involved), seems to me to have no demonstrable divine authority to refuse him admission. Habit and history have persuaded us that a case has to be made for intercommunion: in practice, the problem is to make a case against it. As A. L. Lilley wrote to Maud Petre, 'the closed mind and the closed heart are the only things which are absolutely fatal to religion'.

BIOGRAPHICAL NOTE

ROBERT MURRAY *was born in Peking in 1925, where his father was a missionary. He became a Catholic in 1948 and joined the Jesuits in 1949. He has been a lecturer in the theology of the Church and in various scriptural subjects at Heythrop College since 1963 and shared in the College's recent move to London. Apart from contributions to various symposia and journals, he has written* Behold the Lamb of God, *and* Newman on the Inspiration of Scripture (*in collaboration with J. D. Holmes*).

11 *Tradition as Criterion of Unity*

ROBERT MURRAY S.J.

WITHIN THE GENERAL PURPOSE OF THIS BOOK, WHICH IS TO discuss the theological criteria governing the possibility of inter-communion between Christians who inherit separated traditions, it is the particular aim of the present paper, if possible, to go back behind our various studies of criteria and to attempt a more global and comprehensive look at the picture of that historic believing community which is somehow identified and defined by its response to the God of Abraham, Moses and Jesus. It may seem intolerably bold to say 'community' in the singular, but this expression characterises the level at which I am trying to think and speak: a level at which either we allow such a term in the singular or we must say that the unity and identity which Jews, Christians and Moslems all ascribe to their God is illusory, a matter of words but not of fact. The latter position is that of Marcion, the second-century heretic who will feature much in the following pages, for he polarised more fundamental questions more acutely for Christianity than any other thinker in Christian history, and left poisoned stings in the Christian body which have never been entirely neutralised. I trust we agree that we cannot accept this second alternative, which denies a unity in human apprehensions of the one God, and therefore that we do accept the first alternative, that in some very basic and general sense there is a community of faith in that one God. It is about this vast and almost infinitely diversified community that I wish to speak; but (since our terms of reference primarily concern intercommunion between Christian Churches) we must necessarily leave Islam aside, except for occasional reminders that the identity of our God remains a challenge to us to rediscover our basic unity in faith with Moslems. (I do not wish to exclude other religions from my viewpoint, but this is not the time or place to consider them.) As for the relationship between Christianity and Judaism, while evidently we cannot concentrate on it (especially as Judaism has, as Dr Jacobs has reminded us, its own complex and painful diversity), I become increasingly convinced that we cannot leave out of account the fundamental unity of Israel and the Church, and that ecumenical sums done without Judaism will never add up. Consequently this aspect of our ecumenical problem will come in far more often in the following pages than some Christians may see the need for.

I speak, then, of a historic community of man identified by belief in the same one God, and I speak, also in the singular, of that community's faith, both its living experience and its patrimony inherited from former believers who have experienced, worshipped, spoken and written. For this patrimony, in so far as it can be spoken of in the singular, I shall use 'Tradition', with a capital 'T', meaning the word in the broadest sense, as I shall explain below.

It is, perhaps, a risky theological undertaking, to propose to move from a standpoint of clearer analysis and definition, such as that so usefully adopted by Dr Lash, to one which eschews (indeed, prohibits) clear definition and even adopts imagery of the kind which precedes theological elucidation. But this is what I mean to attempt, for reasons both theological and practical. My theological reason is a profound conviction that many theological problems, and particularly those which are our present concern, will never be rightly identified till they are once again located in their proper native sphere of symbolic expression which reveals itself pregnant with deep insight but which often allows of more than one authentic interpretation. My practical reason is that we have no Eastern Orthodox speaker in this Symposium, a lack which, if it cannot be supplied, it is essential that we should not leave out of account. It would be to crown my boldnesses with one beyond justification if I were to claim to speak for the Orthodox Church; my Orthodox friends could too easily point out the matters in which I do not represent them. But in the view of Tradition (in the broad sense) to be expressed here I trust that the Orthodox will recognise a position not substantially different from that expressed by representative Orthodox theologians;[1] if my conclusions go beyond what they can permit, I hope that the present paper will nevertheless offer them acceptable grounds for dialogue.

The Meaning of Tradition

It is not necessary here to rehearse in detail the various ways in which we use the word 'tradition' theologically. Not to mention vast works like Congar's Tradition and Traditions,[2] it is enough to refer to a summary account such as Vatican II gives us in Dei Verbum (on Revelation, hereafter DV) 7–10. As said already, the sense on which I wish to concentrate is the broadest one, which includes in its reference all the activities by which the believing community responds to God's self-communication and hands on the record of revelation and response. At this level 'Tradition' is one of a group of words of central theological importance, others of which are 'Revelation', 'Mystery', 'Covenant', 'Gospel', 'Witness', 'Scripture' and 'the Faith'. All of them, coming to us from the cultural world of the biblical believing community, reflect that community's conviction that it has religious notions which are not merely of man's making, but are due to interventions by the personal God who made man and man's mind, and who can and does communicate with man. To affirm this is to have

---

[1] See e.g. P. EVDOKIMOV, L'Orthodoxie (Neuchâtel-Paris 1959), pp. 187–97; N. ARSENIEV, 'The Teaching of the Orthodox Church on the Relation between Scripture and Tradition', ECQ VII (1947), pp. 16–26; T. WARE, The Orthodox Church (Penguin Books, Harmondsworth 1963) pp. 203–5. For further bibliography see V. KESICH, 'Criticism, the Gospel and the Church', St Vladimir's Seminary Bulletin 10 (1966), pp. 134–62, especially pp. 155–7 (this article's scope is not that of our present question, but it is a valuable Orthodox comment on problems of Biblical criticism which are closely relevant to the theology of Tradition); I. BRIA, 'Sfînta Scriptura şi Tradiţia: consideraţii generale', Ortodoxia (Bucharest), Series 11, XXII (1970), pp. 384–405, bibliography on pp. 401–2. I draw attention to Romania because, since the deaths of Evdokimov and Afanasiev in Paris, and theological thought in Greece being largely stifled, the most vital centre of Orthodox theology (outside a small circle in the U.S.A.) is in Romania, where also is probably the greatest living Orthodox theologian, Dumitru Staniloae.

[2] ET 1966 London (original, La Tradition et les Traditions, Paris 1960, 1963).

come to conscious faith, and thereby to be able to use 'faith words' like 'revelation' and 'mystery', which connote God's communicating to man an awareness of God's being and a power to interpret events and things as expressing God's purposes. 'Covenant' expresses the community's belief that God desires and commands a relationship of commitment to himself and between fellow-members of the community. 'Gospel' connotes the explosive joy which makes the community desire to share and spread its faith by 'Witness', the act of attesting the Gospel by affirming one's personal commitment. As records of the community's covenantal commitment and history, and personal statements of response and witness, came to be written, a process of evaluation in the community led to its according to certain documents a special and normative status connoted by the word 'Scripture'. Finally the totality of the community's consciousness of revelation and response can be referred to as 'the Faith', connoting what is believed, or as 'Tradition', connoting the continuity of the Faith in successive generations. 'Tradition' can, of course, be used in limited senses at lower levels than this global sense. At one level 'tradition' has been contrasted with Scripture, often (in the century or so before Vatican II) by a crude and quantitative way of thinking which distorted a passage in the Tridentine decree 'on Scripture and traditions', forgetting that the underlying subject of the key sentence is 'Gospel' in the global sense (DS 1501). *Dei Verbum* has clarified this confusion (DV 9–10) but it could still be made clearer (as the Orthodox authors cited above make it) that 'Tradition' in the broad sense *includes* Scripture, for it was there before Moses and the Prophets, and again before the apostolic writers wrote.[3] 'Scripture' connotes essential moments in the historic progress of 'Tradition', moments which the community regards as normative and always asks God to renew for successive generations by the action of his Spirit, the same Spirit to whose action the community ascribes the original experiences which gave rise to 'Scripture'). Scripture is indeed uniquely normative, but precisely because the total Tradition of faith is normative. It is this normativeness which allows

[3] The continuing need for this clarification is shown by the way so good a theologian as Hans Küng (doubtless through long association with friends like Ernst Käsemann) swallows the dated Lutheran formula which calls Scripture *norma normans non normata* in his *Infallible? An Enquiry* (London 1971), p. 62. On this see the penetrating criticisms by GREGORY BAUM in *The Ecumenist*, 9 (1971), pp. 33–48 and 71–7.

us to consider Tradition as a criterion for questions of right belief and action, such as our present question about mutual acknowledgement by Christians and its eucharistic expression. In saying 'normative', however, I do not mean that either Tradition, or the words of Scripture, or dogmas of the Church, can always yield a precise and single answer to a question. What they teach us may well be that we must live with alternatives, none of which we are entitled to exclude.

To emphasise what has just been said I intend now to take flight into the even greater imprecision of poetic imagery, as Plato sometimes abandons dialectical argument for a *mythos*. Sometimes, when speaking on the present theme, I keep this 'prose poem' to the end for a peroration to bring the house down; but it is more honest, perhaps, to reveal earlier on how impenitently pictorial is the mental framework within which the present argument is actually conceived.[4]

My inspiration is the vision which was given first to Ezekiel (47: 1–12), glimpsed by Zechariah (14: 8) and perhaps the author of Ps. 46, and finally recalled by the prophet John on the last page of our New Testament (Rev. 22: 1–2): the vision of the water of life issuing from the temple and forming a great river flowing towards the east and throughout the world, flanked by trees of healing and sweetening the waters of the bitter sea. This river can have many meanings, but St John directs us to refer biblical water imagery especially to the Holy Spirit (John 7: 37–9). The gifts of the Spirit are manifold and his work of 'irrigation' may be understood in various senses; I propose to concentrate on the gift of knowledge of God. 'With thee', says the Psalmist to the Father, 'is the Fountain of Life' (the Holy Spirit), 'and in thy Light (Christ) we see light' (Ps. 36: 9). The river rises from the springs of the Spirit in the heart of God, and its waters are the gift of divine revelation to man. The flow of the river is man's understanding of the true God since the first man responded to him. This understanding is given to each believer for

---

[4] My allegory is perhaps nearest to Ben Sira's verses on Wisdom (Ecclus 24: 23–31), though he does not depend on the Ezekiel tradition but represents another part of the wider literary tradition connected with the rivers of paradise (Gen. 2: 10–14), which Rupert of Deutz, the greatest medieval allegorical commentator, refers to the grace of the Holy Spirit and the inspiration of Scripture (*De Trinitate et Operibus eius*, In Gen. 11, 28–9, PL 167, 273–6); cf. also King Alfred's Epilogue to his translation of St Gregory's *Regula Pastoralis*, though I was not conscious of this.

himself, but it also forms a tradition of belief, worship, witness and way of life. There is a living continuity between the higher waters of the river, the time of ancient Israel, and the lower reaches, the time of the Church; and from as far back as we know the water flowed in several streams. But some of these streams have grown far apart. Human weakness and corruption, affecting both understanding and behaviour, have polluted the river, clogged and silted up its channels and made it find new and separated courses (some of which have dried up, while others have accommodated themselves to new land-scapes); nevertheless there remains a real basic identity of water between the separated streams of Judaism, Christianity in its various forms, and Islam. (I do not mean to deny that other streams also carry the true waters of life, but my present scope is all too vast even if I stop at Islam.)

Now this river has the strange property that its water does not all come to it by flowing visibly from the ancient source. It is as though the source were also sending forth a stream which flows hidden beneath the visible river, and every now and then bursts up through the bed of the river, creating a new fountain which freshens and purifies the age-old waters. These fountains are the charismatic experience of believers and prophets, first in the old dispensation and then in the new; the most notable among them form a group whose waters we call 'Scripture'. In the midst of the river is the supreme fountain, the experience of Christ, from whose heart the water of the Spirit flows in such abundance and so sweetly that it is as though Christ were the new source of the river, and yet the river and the water were there before his historic life (and indeed, as the Eternal Word, he was also there when the spring first rose). Since the fountain of Christ the streams have again become divided and polluted, though new fountains always break out again. Some streams become so cut off from others that those who live by them may imagine that their stream is the only one, and yet it is not. Streams can join up again, especially when a fountain bursts out in one stream so abundantly that it overflows what was a hindering spit of land between one stream and the next. The river flows out into the sea, or rather will become the sea, when 'the earth shall be filled with the knowledge of God as the waters cover the sea' (Isa. 11:9). Till then, however, the river is not, as far as we know, the whole world (though we do not know where the underground streams do not flow). It has banks which contain the channel of the water and there are deserts where the water once flowed but has dried up. My allegory does not express a delusively optimistic universalism. Tradition has limits within which authenticity is recognised; the water of the river, at any point in any stream, can be tested by that of the fountains, and some water can and must be declared undrinkable till it is purified. The strength of the figure is in the continuity of the water upstream and downstream and its fundamental identity in the various streams in which it flows. It is to this variety, meaning the pluralism of authentic Tradition, that we must now turn.

Tradition is Essentially Manifold

Before developing this theme let me emphasise that I totally reject all flabby indifferentism, and am fully aware of, and concerned to maintain, the limits of pluralism and the need to declare certain positions unacceptable; this will occupy us in the next section, and then we can move towards a discussion of the criteria for acknowledging what positions are acceptable, and for expressing such acknowledgement in eucharistic communion. But it is dangerous to consider the limits of what can be acknowledged before we have really faced the essential pluralism of authentic Tradition. This entire paper is written in the profound conviction that, like the love of Christ, the Faith 'constrains us'; we may not pick and choose. And a crucial feature of the data given us by God is pluralism. We *may* not reduce this to univocal expressions or to a 'monolithic' unity. There is something in man that drives us on to simplification and unification, and we may appeal to the unity of truth and of God himself as our justification; but that drive is part of 'the flesh' which needs healing, not the pure voice of the Spirit.

It should not be necessary to prove the manifold nature of authentic Tradition, but it may be helpful to survey the range of its variety and suggest where we should look for the reasons why things are so and must be so: why pluralism in man's religious apprehensions is neither a disastrous wound blasphemously inflicted on the unity of truth, nor a necessary evil due to the fall, but is simply given, by the dispensation of the One God in his infinite wisdom, who looked on the multiplicity of his creation 'and behold it was very good' (Gen. 1:31), and thereupon he rested in joy.

Some aspects of the variety of authentic Tradition may seem no matter for theological anxiety. It is evident that the Bible contains both prose and poetry, factual narrative and parable, praise of God and musings over human folly, sober instructions for organisation and worship and violently coloured eschatological symbolism. But the fact is that this diversity has again and again been misinterpreted by that refusal to allow diverse modes of truth in the Bible which we call fundamentalism. Wherever the diversity of genres and styles in the Bible is ignored, it is unlikely that its deeper and truly theological pluralism is going to be recognised and accepted. But pluralism is there, with different elements coexisting in a tension which still maintains, as complementary strands of the whole, points of view that were once, perhaps, in real conflict. Though the passages hostile to sacrifice in Amos, Hosea and Jeremiah must not be exaggerated out of their total contexts, they do seem to relativise the value of a cult system which for the priestly writers must have been much nearer absolute; even if some scholars have pictured too much opposition between prophetic and institutional religion in the Old Testament, it can hardly be denied that there are elements in radical tension with each other. Again, the community which eventually recognised as 'Scripture' a collection of books reflecting about a millennium and a half of experience and Tradition, chose to 'canonise' books from various periods which, if not reflecting a simultaneous tension, are all but incompatible in their approach to pretty fundamental matters. It is not clear, to say the least, whether the chronicler of the Maccabean martyrs with his passionate faith in the afterlife, could have found much value in the weary this-worldly pessimism of Qoheleth, yet we may see that it enhances the universality of Scripture that it should include the latter.

Theological pluralism in the New Testament may not strike every eye so clearly as in the Old. The devout reader of the gospels is predisposed to harmonise them, and to view the Synoptic presentations of Jesus through a Johannine lens which masks their differences. Even the greatest contrasts between the New Testament books may seem less striking than the new faith which they all express. The explicit contradiction between James and Galatians can perhaps be explained harmoniously. But a deeper divergence remains between James's pacific profession of the Torah fulfilled in Christ and the passionate plea of Paul in Galatians and Romans that the basis of faith has been radically changed. There is a tension here which, within a few decades, the early Church was to be unable to maintain in harmony. As in the Old Testament, so in the New, some attempts to analyse the tensions (especially on Hegelian lines) have been unsound and exaggerated, but there can be no doubt that the polarity between Christianity maintaining its Jewish framework and Christianity declaring that framework unnecessary is present almost everywhere, as an immediate source of tremendous psychological energy and a potential source of destructive power. It is this polarity in Paul's own mind which creates the experience expressed in Romans; the destructive power was to reveal itself in Marcion's attack on the Judaeo-Christian synthesis. But the Christianity which survived Marcion was still powered by this vital polarity, for it was nothing other than the fundamental polarity in the Old Testament, re-awakened in reaction to Jesus, as what Jean-Louis Leuba has characterised as ' l'institution et l'évènemont'. His profoundly perceptive book with this title[5] was published some ten years before Pope John's initiative inspired a new kind of theological dialogue between Catholics and Protestants. Avoiding the Hegelianism of the Tübingen schematisers, Leuba shows how in the New Testament, both at the level of Christology and at that of ecclesiology, there is an essential, original and irreducible duality of ideas: those coming from the continuity of God's people, with its faith and its need to express that faith in institutions, and those coming from the new and unexpected event of God's intervention, pouring out unpredictable charisms. Some titles of Jesus connote the former, some the latter; the Twelve symbolise the former, Paul and his churches the latter. But the two elements are essentially complementary; the New Testament and the Church were born of their fruitful interplay. Only on his last page does Leuba hint at the ecumenical implications for the mutual understanding of Catholicism, which in 1950 still seemed so monolithically institutionalised, and Protestantism, which liked to think it had an unchallengeable corner in charisms.

This essential tension in Christianity arises historically out of its

[5] Neuchâtel-Paris, 1950; ET, *New Testament Pattern* (London, 1953).

relationship to Judaism. It is not the only vital and fruitful tension, but perhaps it is the most fundamental one. Of course, it is not peculiar to Christianity, for Judaism has inherited its own forms of the tension, and the plurality of sects or churches in both forms of the ancient faith is still accountable for, to a remarkable degree, by different attempts at practical solutions of the problems of living with the tension. 'Human kind cannot bear very much reality', says T. S. Eliot; human kind tries to simplify patterns. Some simplifications are good, for example the elimination of bureaucratic nonsense; but if someone tries to eliminate one pole of the vital tension because he thinks he can identify himself with the other, he is destroying or at least tragically maiming the Faith. This, we shall see, is the point at which heresy (the option for one pole against the other) becomes an unbearable threat to the community's health. Unfortunately history has shown repeatedly that people cry 'heresy' not only when this threat really arises, but also when they are faced by the tensions of authentic pluralism.

Conversely, the wound of the breach between Gentile Christianity and Judaism is usually thought of in terms of heresy only in the extreme case of Marcionism, whereas in many Christian traditions the wound has remained a festering sore, and has sometimes proved mortal to Christian faith. To return to the figure of the river, the water of Jewish and Christian faith is still essentially one and the water that flows with supreme abundance from the 'fountain' of Jesus is not different in kind. Christians judge at their peril that they alone drink of his water; many Jews instinctively savour and love its taste, and the Jewish contribution to New Testament studies is a special treasure for those Christians who can find it.

Of theological pluralism in Christianity since the primitive period it is enough to speak briefly. The early centuries saw the diversity of cultural traditions reflected in a variety of liturgical forms and to some extent of church structure, which does not seem to have caused anxiety to church leaders even at the times when unity was most severely threatened. Thus St Augustine's preoccupations about unity in faith did not stop him delighting in the variegated raiment of the 'Queen' in Ps. 45:9,[6] while St Gregory the Great a century later gives his disciple St Augustine great freedom in adapting

---

[6] In Ps. 44 (45): 9, PL 36, 509; cf. Ep. 54, 1-3, PL 33, 200-1.

church usages to his new converts.[7] This sort of diversity is not, of course, what we mean by theological pluralism, but it inevitably fosters it, both because, however much the local churches intend to maintain the same faith, the partial difference in connotation of the words chosen in various languages for the key theological concepts gradually leads to variations in theological understanding, and because different local churches have to react to different pressures and dangers.

Differentiation due to these causes accounts, I think, for all the divergences between the Eastern and Western streams in the original 'Great Church', the streams which are conventionally designated respectively the Orthodox Church and the Catholic Church. At different times and in reaction to differing pressures and concerns, representatives of one side or the other have shown great variety in their evaluations of the relationship of East and West since normal communion has been broken. 'Hard-liners' on either side have declared the other side to have left the one true Church and even to be in heresy. Yet evidence for mutual acknowledgement on a basis of lawful pluralism has seldom been lacking. After all, the Orthodox claim to have simply stood by the earlier ecclesiology of a communion of self-governing Churches adapted to the genius of different nations. However ambiguous the union of Florence was, it was in effect a mutual recognition on the basis of theological pluralism.[8] Official Catholic attitudes have, of course, reflected the centralising and 'subordinationist' ecclesiology of the papacy since the early middle ages, but since Pope John and Vatican II there has been an enormous change, expressed at conciliar level by the forthright acceptance of theological pluralism between East and West in the Decree on Ecumenism, 17. It may be that a good number of the bishops who voted for that decree could not really see their way beyond pluralism in language and rites, but the decisively influential speeches of Cardinal Léger and Bishop Elchinger show full appreciation of theological pluralism in the full sense, precisely because of the richness of divine truth and the limited viewpoint of any actual group of human beings.[9]

[7] Ep. XI, 64, PL 77, 1186a–1187a; cf. Ep. I, 43, ibid., 497c.

[8] Cf. J. GILL, *Personalities of the Council of Florence* (Oxford 1964), pp. 233–53, 'Greeks and Latins in a Common Council'.

[9] *Council Speeches of Vatican II*, ed. Y. CONGAR, H. KÜNG and D. O'HANLON (London 1964), pp. 143–9.

It can hardly be doubted that the modern Orthodox theology of *Sobornost'*, which connotes the communion and conciliar interrelation of autonomous Churches with their own expressions of the one Faith, had exerted a great influence on Catholic ecclesiology through the theologians connected with Chevetogne and the French Dominican *Centre Istina*.[10] Likewise the Orthodox category of *theologoumena*, or matters of faith which may be important but are not suitable for imposition as dogmas, had become familiar to Catholic theologians reared on a less flexible set of theological categories, and Paul Evdokimov anticipated Pope John in using with approval the old formula *in dubiis libertas*.[11]

So far I have kept to the divided streams of the old 'Great Church'. But in ecumenism today we are having more and more to face the question whether, in view of the fundamental and authentic elements which a far wider range of Christians share, the Council's paragraph about different theological viewpoints being complementary rather than mutually exclusive *can* be limited to the context of the historic Orthodox and Catholic Churches. This is one of those features of Vatican II which make one feel that the Council planted some delayed-action bombs in traditional Catholicism. (Another example is the account of Catholic ministry given in terms far wider than the medieval definition in terms of eucharistic sacrifice, which, together with the recognition of 'ecclesial character' beyond the traditional limits, is radically affecting the evaluation of orders in other Churches.) A disturbed conservative author has attacked movements he fears under the title 'The Trojan Horse in the City of God';[12] but I wonder whether his Trojan horse is not really the uncomfortable fact that authentic Tradition is pluralistic and must be so. If heresy is stalking abroad in the Christian Churches (and without doubt it is), the solution cannot be to try to destroy pluralism.

---

[10] Cf. Y. CONGAR, *Jalons pour une théologie du laicat* (Paris 1953), a passage most regrettably omitted in the ET (*Lay People in the Church*); *Tradition and Traditions*, pp. 104–6, with bibliography.

[11] Cf. P. EVDOKIMOV, *L'Orthodoxie*, pp. 193–4; JEAN LECLER, S. J., 'A propos d'une maxime citée par le Pape Jean XXIII, In necessariis unitas, in dubiis libertas, in omnibus caritas', *Recherches de Sc. Rel.*, 49 (1961), pp. 549–60. Lecler shows that the maxim is not (as is often thought) from St Augustine but from the Protestant Peter Meiderlin (1628), the second phrase being originally 'in non necessariis libertas'.

[12] D. VON HILDEBRAND, *The Trojan Horse in the City of God* (Chicago 1967).

It is simply 'given', and by now perhaps we can more easily see why. The polarities in Scripture, the duality of 'institution' and 'event' are rooted in man's nature composed of body and spirit; the pluralism of religious expressions is due to the diversity of mankind, responding to the multiplicity of the Spirit's gifts. Some of man's responses have rung with a clearer resonance, others have been more impaired by the 'flesh'; but if the range of expressions and moods in Scripture itself is taken as an indication, we ought to trust that God accepts a considerable variety of human responses. 'Truly I perceive that God shows no partiality, but in every nation any one who fears him and does what is right is acceptable to him' (Acts 10: 34-5).

The Limits of Acceptability

The more, however, we stress the pluralism of Tradition and the need to maintain certain vital polarities, the more urgently the question arises whether acceptable pluralism has limits, or what type of position or tendency cannot be welcomed in the believing community. To use the traditional word, what is heresy? Our conclusions in this section cannot yield clear answers to the questions we face about the criteria for allowing intercommunion, but we may hope to clarify at least some of the criteria which seem to have led Christians to forbid it.

The Greek word *hairesis* (option) has, of course, one innocent sense, as denoting a movement which one chooses to follow. Thus Josephus uses it of the Essenes, and St Luke in *Acts* of the Pharisees, the Sadducees and the Christians. In this usage the word *hairesis* is not antithetical to any idea of orthodoxy, but presupposes a certain recognition that several options are possible. It may be that, when we try to evaluate movements in the earliest period of Christianity, it is useful to bear this point of view in mind.

The question of the position of 'heresy' in the early Church has just been brought to the foreground for English readers by the belated publication in translation of Walter Bauer's *Orthodoxy and Heresy in Earliest Christianity*,[13] an attempt by a fine scholar to stand the conventional picture of the early Church on its head, which has

[13] London 1972. The translation of the title is the only possible one, though 'Orthodoxy' and 'Heresy' fail to catch all the ironic nuances of 'Rechtgläubigkeit' and 'Ketzerei'.

haunted the historians since the original appeared in 1934. The picture Bauer presented (no doubt with too much imagination and too much argument from silence) was of an originally very fluid situation in many parts of the early Christian world, where (in Bauer's terms) in the beginning was 'heresy'; 'orthodoxy', for Bauer essentially a Roman conception, only made its way gradually in many parts of the East. I have long tended to agree with Bauer's picture of fluidity in Edessa, for example, but not with his labels. In the second German edition which is now presented in English, Georg Strecker, in a valuable additional essay 'On the Problem of Jewish Christianity' argues rightly that the latter is what Bauer was really talking about, a phenomenon which was essentially varied and loosely-knit, like Judaism itself, and which could not easily clarify its positions in the way that came more natural to the world of Greco-Roman thought. 'Orthodoxy', I believe, is a concept which we can rightly believe was implicit earlier, but which only really emerged gradually as a criterion; what kind of a criterion it is, we shall discuss in the next section. Though I believe that in the earliest Judaeo-Christianity there were indeed elements which were not worthy to survive, I would agree strongly with Gilles Quispel that, in speaking of this period historically, 'heresy' is not a serviceable category.[14] To speak of 'heresy' preceding 'orthodoxy' is to confuse historical with theological categories, whereas what we see in early Christianity is a fluid pluralism tolerating great variety in relation to Jewish practice and to the new developments (charismatic and structural) arising among Gentile converts, a whole world of Jewish and Christian communities coexisting with, and potentially subject to, other religious, philosophical and magical influences. Major threats arose, in the various forms of gnosticism and above all in Marcionism, which swept the Near East with a success which cannot be explained unless, as Bauer says, many were ready for this ruthlessly monolithic and passionately ascetic attempt to purge Christianity of all its Jewish past and of its humanity. In Christianity's battle for identity, no doubt the concept of orthodoxy became clearer, but it was essentially an appeal to the wholeness of the Gospel, of the broad Tradition. It may be that Rome (greatly assisted by non-Romans like Ignatius, Justin and Irenaeus)

---

[14] 'The Syrian Thomas and the Syrian Macarius', *Vigiliae Christianae*, 18 (1964), p. 234; *Makarius, das Thomasevangelium und das Lied von der Perle* (Leiden 1967), p. 4.

played a crucial part, but Bauer has surely magnified Rome's role in the same curiously over-dramatic, almost masochistic, way as Harnack had shown before him. Surely the respective identification of heresy and orthodoxy (that is, the indigestible and the healthy in the life of the Christian community) could never have taken place at all unless the 'waters of the river' somehow brought the ability to test their taste (especially against the taste of the 'fountains'). This ability is, surely, to be connected with the interior understanding and power of discernment promised as a gift of the Spirit, under the New Covenant,[15] and appealed to, as a shared experience, in such passages as 1 Cor. 2 and 1 John 2. The basis on which such experience could be true and not illusory can only be that real experience of the one true God was available to a plurality of people so that they could agree that they were all talking of the same God and of real experience of faith in him. On this basis they could discuss what could be satisfactory alternative forms of experience and satisfactory expressions of faith, and what could not. Such discussion in the early Church was piecemeal and gradual for many reasons; the primitive fellowship doubtless had strong motives for mutual trust and toleration which only yielded, with a speed varying in various areas and under various influences, to the sad reality that things were being said and done which could not be agreed on as satisfactory alternatives.

What I want to stress is that positive conviction came first, a conviction born of a great Tradition and fed by personal experience. This conviction is expressible in various ways according to the manifold character of authentic Tradition, and the positive nature of the conviction entails a power of evaluating alternatives. I am speaking, of course, about that 'faculty' of the Church which has come to be discussed under the heading of 'infallibility', an unfortunate word which breeds misunderstandings like maggots. The recent attempt by Hans Küng to elucidate it[16] seems to me, despite a basically constructive intention, to fail to do justice to the features of authentic Tradition and the positive powers of expression and evaluation which I have just mentioned. In my review of Küng's book[17] I take as typical of this primitive conviction the expression in the Pastorals,

---

[15] Jer. 31: 31–4; Ezek. 36: 25–8; Isa. 54: 13; 59: 21.
[16] *Infallible?* (London 1971), ET of *Unfehlbar?* (Einsiedeln 1970).
[17] *The Heythrop Journal*, XIII (1972), pp. 211–14.

Pistos ho logos, 'it is a trustworthy saying';[18] if the Church is the Church of Jesus Christ it *must* be able, by some means or other and on occasion, to say *pistos ho logos*, and also, on occasion, 'We are sorry, but your *logos* does not seem *pistos* to us'. The former is exemplified by the gradual recognition of what was worthy to be called 'Scripture'[19] and by the adoption of 'doxological' formulas, as Dr Lash has so well elucidated their character; the latter is exemplified by the Church's reaction to 'indigestible elements', for which the word 'heresy', used now in an ideological and not merely sociological sense, soon came to be reserved. The fact that reactions by churchmen have often shown all-too-human qualities of anger, untruthfulness and fear of even lawful pluralism does not change the basic situation, that conviction about the Faith entails the power to declare what is incompatible with the Faith. Recognition of this incompatibility is one of the things that have led to breaches in communion. Even if we are drawn today towards the view that inherited separations in communion often no longer reflect real divisions in understanding the Faith, we must still examine the principles on which the Church seems to have worked; once again, what is heresy?

Of course, one is immediately deafened by the replies from all sides, and the immediate bibliography which lies to hand would suffice to provide material for a safe barricade. My reflections owe more to historical studies like Norman Cohn's *The Pursuit of the Millennium*[20] than to anyone writing about the state of Christianity today; studies in the early Church remain crucial on this subject, on which, besides the scholars mentioned above, Helmut Koester has thrown more light than most.[21] Here I propose to offer for discussion the rough classification which I am provisionally inclined to make of the kind of things the believing community has found indigestible (or at least a cause of bad dreams). It will correspond to some extent to the things which the Catholic and Orthodox Church have declared

---

[18] 1 Tim. 1: 15; 3: 1; 4: 9; 2 Tim. 2: 11; Tit. 3: 8; cf. Apoc. 21: 5; 22: 6.

[19] Cf. R. MURRAY, 'How did the Church determine the Canon of Scripture?' in HJ XI (1970), pp. 115–26.

[20] London 1957; 3rd edition, Paladin Books, 1970.

[21] See, e.g. 'The Theological Aspects of Primitive Christian Heresy' in *The Future of our Religious Past: Essays in Honour of Rudolf Bultmann*, ed. J. M. Robinson (London 1971).

heretical, but also, to some extent, to the things that have caused trouble and division in Judaism, Islam and some Protestant Churches.

I think we may classify 'heresies' or heretical tendencies broadly as those which have disturbed the community by a zeal that was felt to drive some point too hard or too far, and those which have been felt to fall short of, or to fail to keep up with, the community's understanding of Revelation and Tradition. I shall refer to these two main tendencies respectively in terms of 'excess' and 'defect', and shall try to list under each certain typical ways of thinking and acting. But first some essential qualifications are necessary, which must be remembered throughout. 'Heresies of excess' may mostly arise from enthusiastic zeal, but I do not mean to suggest that 'heresies of defect' are deficient in zeal; often just the opposite. Further, I am not simply trying to classify actual 'heresies' and find a pigeon-hole for each. Several historic 'heresies' have features simultaneously of 'excess' and 'defect'. The characteristics of each main class mentioned below seem to me the main things that have proved unacceptable or unsatisfactory, but such tendencies are probably never found alone; I may have missed others of comparable significance, and of course the 'heretical' tendencies have usually formed part of a synthesis including many features entirely acceptable to the main Tradition. Lastly, some tendencies to be mentioned do not necessarily ever come to such a pitch of excess or defect as to be designated 'heresy', and in drawing attention to examples within main-stream Tradition I wish to disavow any presumption of sitting in judgement on anyone who may in fact sympathise with such a tendency. With these provisos, here is my attempt at classification.

1. 'Heresies of Excess'

The seed-bed has usually been ascetical zeal, in reaction against social and religious corruption, and often fanned by eschatological expectations. These phenomena had developed in Judaism before the Christian movement; the Maccabean reforming movement gave rise to various forms of such reaction, including Pharisaism and the extremist sect who settled at Qumran and developed the un-Jewish phenomenon of celibacy. These movements were doubtless the cradle of the apocalyptic literature which flourished from the time of the Maccabees till the end of the first Christian century, when

Judaism rejected such literature for good, perhaps because it had fostered the cause of revolt against Rome with such disastrous results.

Jesus himself is portrayed in the gospels as a zealous reformer, celibate and inviting 'those who can take it' to follow him in this, and a preacher whose whole message is coloured by eschatological urgency. He foretold the disaster of A.D. 70 and the Christian community survived it, but with its relationship to Judaism in greater tension than before, and permanently so; the Church did not follow Judaism in rejecting eschatological excitement, but it had to adapt its outlets. As year after year the hope of Jesus' imminent return was not realised, the eschatological orientation of Christianity remained an incentive to enthusiasm whose natural expression was, as before but ever more explosively, reaction against the 'world'. Another motive for such reaction was the dualism of spirit and matter which had affected some streams in Judaism already before Christianity and which characterised all forms of gnosticism. The New Testament contains dualistic imagery, though its characteristic doctrine about the 'flesh' and the world is that in Christ they are healed and transfigured, not escaped from and destroyed. Already in the New Testament St Paul warns Christians against excess in respect of eschatological expectation, abandonment of marriage, and gnostic speculations.

This sketch has set the scene for the first great explosion in this inflammable situation, which was touched off by Marcion about A.D. 150. In his system every violent element referred to above was released and encouraged. Anti-Judaism and eschatologically-inspired celibacy found their place in a gnostic cosmology under theistic dualism to form a ruthlessly consistent doctrine in which the Creator-God of the Old Testament and his material world were abhorred in favour of a spiritual Christ, teaching a rigorously pruned Gospel interpreted by an anti-Jewish Paul, a gospel of salvation from the flesh, to be attained only by celibate asceticism. This doctrine had a devastating appeal in areas where, as in Syria and Mesopotamia, the Judaeo-Christian communities seem, like the Qumran sect, to have centred round an 'élite' called the 'Covenant', to whom (at least at one time) baptism seems to have been reserved, on their vowing virginity or abstinence from marital sexual intercourse. This system (still echoed in 'orthodox' Syriac writers of the fourth century) encouraged the Marcionites to set up a two-tier, élitist church, a structure which was soon adopted and developed by the even more ruthlessly dualistic movement founded by Mani out of a fusion of sectarian Judaeo-Christian and oriental elements.

With this sketch, though historically it has not gone beyond the third century, I think I have named the main features of 'heresies of excess': anti-Judaism, breaking the vital tension between Christianity and its matrix; selectiveness with regard to Scripture; eschatological and millenarian excitement; hostility to the world, sex and marriage, and an élistist community structure. I will not propose further identifications. It is enough to refer again to Norman Cohn's *The Pursuit of the Millennium*, which shows how movements characterised by these features were almost endemic in European Christianity all through the middle ages, often on a truly terrifying scale. The representatives of the institutional Church often appear as the isolated defenders of the Gospel and of sanity. As for main-stream Christianity itself, it is painfully evident that every one of the features just listed lives on, as what I have called a poisoned sting – some more in Catholicism and Orthodoxy, some more in Protestantism, some in all but in different ways – while the fear of anything like an élitist movement has made main-stream Christianity and its leaders permanently over-suspicious of any movement stressing the charismatic element.

2. 'Heresies of Defect'

This class cannot be described historically, for it has no coherent unity and it may, in fact, be a mistake to suggest such a grouping. Yet it seems that, if we look at a number of the doctrinal positions which main-stream Christianity has felt the need to censure, the reason has been that these positions were felt to do less than justice to essentials of the Faith; to be too human and not to give enough place to the power and mercy of God. I cannot name a single 'seedbed' for the tendencies I have in mind, but perhaps a twofold pattern emerges. One element is the desire to satisfy the claims of human reason and to follow its light as far as possible in looking at the biblical documents, Jesus, the Church and Tradition as a whole. The typical activity which may foster a tendency to the defective in this way is apologetics; its practitioners desire to commend faith as not affronting reason, but they run the risk of undermining the sense of revelation and God's intervention in history, and they may tend towards over-simplification. The traces of this tendency are manifold; it is relevant to several of the classical christological heresies, to all rationalist movements, to modernism and also to the simplistic reaction against it.

The last-named phenomenon, however, also points to the other 'seedbed' to which I wish to draw attention, namely a dogged con-servatism, often with a certain anti-intellectualism and a desire for clear short answers in matters both doctrinal and practical. Helmut Koester finds in the early heresies a widespread pattern of this kind, which he characterises as a 'failure to demythologise' and an 'escape into tradition'.[22] The inability to see that both Scripture and the other documents enshrining important aspects of Tradition involve many kinds of discourse – poetic, legal, doxological or historical (itself a multiple category) – and that all this multiplicity is also subject to historical and cultural variation, gives rise to biblical fundamentalism, doctrinal immobilism and practical and liturgical legalism, features which are closely analogous in Judaism, Christi-anity and Islam, and in many of their varieties. The failure to re-valuate symbolism, in the name of fidelity to tradition, gives a tragic character to many individuals and movements which have come into conflict with the communities in which they arose, and this is true also of some movements which we would place primarily under the 'excess' class. For example, both Donatism and Pelagianism were movements of great ascetical seriousness which created or tended to create 'élitist' churches, but Donatism was essentially a conservative reaction to a pastoral development in Catholicism, while the defeat of Pelagianism is significantly characterised by Peter Brown as a stage in the end of the 'Ancient World' of the early Christian Church.[23]

Of course, all the characteristics referred to in this section flourish in main-stream Christianity, creating tensions of which we are very conscious today as dividing Christians within their own communions and making them often more unhappy about some of their fellow-communicants than they are about like-minded Christians from whom they are separated in ecclesiastical communion.

22 'The Theological Aspects'. . ., p. 83.
23 *Religion and Society in the Age of St Augustine* (London 1972), p. 207.

In conclusion, my two classes of 'excess' and 'defect' may be regarded in terms of (and, indeed, may well have been suggested by) the Pauline antithesis of 'spirit' and 'letter', in the sense that they may seem respectively to emphasise one or the other more. It remains now to see whether we can say something about the criteria which mainstream Christian Tradition has applied when tensions between believers have arisen. Even if practice has been irregular, particularly in the amount of variety which has been felt tolerable, can we find a pattern for the recognition of unity in essentials, which could allow us to suggest a workable criterion for allowing intercommunion even without structural unification?

THE CRITERIA FOR ESSENTIAL UNITY
AND FOR INTERCOMMUNION

The questions about essential or sufficient unity in faith and about the possibility of intercommunion are not identical, though they are evidently closely linked. Not to argue the point at the moment, it is a fact that some of the Churches which are 'stickiest' about insisting on unity in faith do in fact allow cases of intercommunion across the frontiers of normal ecclesiastical communion, so that in principle it cannot be ruled out that they should acknowledge in more cases, and more frequently, that there is a basis of shared faith sufficient to be expressed in eucharistic intercommunion. In what follows I speak primarily of the criteria for full communion, for it is against these that decisions about the possibility of intercommunion as a temporary or occasional stage must be weighed.

It is evident that the criteria for inclusion or exclusion, and the ways of applying them, have varied throughout history, from the 'bloody question' of the proverbial 'shibboleth' test (Judges 12:5-6) to the sweet simplicity of the common Free Church formula 'We cordially invite all those who love the Lord Jesus to join with us at his table'. In between lie all the attempts of traditional Christianity to soften the hard edges of their criteria for recognition: the Orthodox doctrine of 'economy', the Catholic doctrines of *vestigia Ecclesiae* and implicit desire, and finally the far more flexible but still too complex ecumenical ecclesiology of Vatican II. Can we get behind all this variety and complexity and locate the essential criteria?

Since this whole paper is an attempt to stand back and look at the picture as a whole, let us ask ourselves again what the whole question is about. To put it very simply, surely it is about the terms on which Christians who have grown apart ought to be able to accept each other as fellow-guests at Christ's table. First, therefore, and basically, I suggest that we are talking about *Fellow-discipleship of Jesus*. 'You have not chosen me', he said, 'but I have chosen you' (John 15: 16); he is the Master, he makes the rules of discipleship and fellow-discipleship (John 13: 34–35). If fellow-disciples have become strangers they have to be able to recognise each other in order to accept each other. Not seldom this proves easier with total strangers than with our everybody neighbours, as is illustrated by the case of the Chinese Nestorian monk, Rabban Sawma, who visited Europe in 1287–8 and was received in communion with great joy by Pope Nicholas IV, after apparently only the most cursory discussion of credal matters.[24] But to find a true disciple in our close neighbour we may well need criteria that will force us against our own inertia or prejudice. One way or the other, we need criteria. What do they concern?

Fundamentally, three questions: whom do we think we are following, how should this make us behave, and who are we? These questions point towards criteria which, even if each separately is not decisively, when taken together in balance can give a sufficient answer. As regards whom we are following, it is not enough to say 'Jesus' as opposed to someone else, with no rules about understanding him, for Jesus challenges us precisely as Master of disciples, claiming the right to reinterpret what was understood as God's unchangeable revelation and law; Jesus whose death was interpreted by the first disciples as no mere sordid political murder but as the one all-sufficient atonement for human sin; Jesus whom the same disciples said they had witnessed truly risen again; Jesus who, they said, had promised and then given the Holy Spirit to re-create them and to be communicated to others through their witness. When separated disciples in latter days are trying to recognise each other as disciples they must be able to find sufficient basic agreement

---

[24] Cf. E. A. WALLIS BUDGE, *The Monks of Kublai Khan* (London 1928). The credal discussion was with the cardinals during the interregnum, and it is hard to suppose that much mutual understanding was achieved.

about the Master and his claim; in short, one criterion concerns right belief or *orthodoxy*.

The second question concerns behaviour. Since Jesus both acted and taught in the framework of biblical revelation, and urged new emphases on his own authority, it is clear that certain modes of behaviour are shown to us as appropriate, others as inappropriate, to discipleship. To refuse to worship God is contrary to the tradition which Jesus accepted and reaffirmed; to fail a fellow-man in need for the sake of ritual purity is to fail to follow Jesus in one of his most important personal teachings. The difficulty about behaviour as a criterion, as we have seen in our discussions, is that while we all agree that it is centrally important, taken alone it cannot prove either discipleship or apostasy. For the moment, therefore, I refer to the previous discussions about 'orthopoiesis', 'orthopraxy' and ortho-doxy, and pass to the third question, concerning who the disciples are. This relates to the different character (individual, cultural or national) of those who seek mutual recognition as fellow-disciples. Once one has come to understand the variety of attitudes in the New Testament and in the united Church of the past, a variety which was viewed not as impairing discipleship but as enriching it, we can set a value on variety in fellow-discipleship which can enable us to form a criterion of *catholicity*.

These three criteria balance and control each other. Right belief and acceptance of diversity in faithful discipleship balance each other, and both are under constant surveillance by the criterion of behaviour, even though the latter's applicability is irregular; a serious failure in behaviour need not mean that the offender has ceased to be a disciple, though it may mean that special steps must be taken to reconcile him with Christ's Body. Orthodoxy is always under pressure from the human drive towards definition and therefore exclusion, which may offend against the ideals of behaviour and catholicity. Catholicity as a sole ideal can be led by easy-going tolerance towards uncritical inclusiveness.

In the light of history, the last remark inevitably has an ironic ring. The sad truth is that orthodoxy has too generally been made the dominant or sole criterion, and has been understood as a total system, according to the Pharisean principle enunciated by St James: 'If a man keeps the whole law apart from one single point, he is guilty of breaking all of it' (Jas. 2:10). But catholicity has its real claims against orthodoxy, claims forcibly backed up by the more total ideal of orthopraxy. What catholicity ought to remind us is that it is Jesus, not we, who signs on his disciples. St Paul has powerful pages on this theme in 1 Corinthians and Romans. 'Who are you to pass judgement on the servant of another? It is before his own master that he stands or falls. And he will be upheld, for the Master is able to make him stand' (Rom. 14:4).

Here, once again, I want to come back to the relationship of Christianity and Judaism. The definitive breach was a permanent wound to the ideal of catholicity right at the heart of discipleship; for how can we love Jesus without loving his people, the faith he received from them and the way of worship he followed with them? What kind of orthodoxy can it be that battens on hatred of Jesus' people? The words I have just quoted have their context in the problems of coexistence between Jewish and Gentile disciples, a coexistence which continued, however uneasily, for a few generations after Jesus. When it was strained beyond bearable limits by events and shattered by the monstrous ideology of Marcion, the sense of normative orthodoxy, which was gradually emerging out of the primitive mood of trustful discipleship, contented itself with two firm but very modest reactions. One was to insist that the God of the Old Testament and the God of Jesus are the same and that Christianity accepts the Old Testament as inspired by the Spirit of God; the other was to defend the goodness and lawfulness of marriage. (Unfortunately the latter corrective was murmured very quietly, and by spokesmen whose personal enthusiasm was all for celibacy; the realistic attitude to sexuality always maintained by Judaism was expressed in similarly healthy tones in the second-century Judaeo-Christian 'Pseudo-Clementine' romance, and then fell silent in theology practically till our own times.[25])

I have wanted, one last time, to insist that the ideals of catholicity and Christian behaviour must never again be allowed to neglect our brotherhood with Jesus' own people, and that both orthodoxy

---

[25] Cf. *Clementine Homilies* in *Ante-Nicene Christian Library XVII* (Edinburgh 1870), pp. 86–7, 112–13, 187–8, 220–2, 307, 315, and my article 'From Bible to Fathers: Changing Attitudes to Sexuality' in the forthcoming symposium *The Sexual Nature of Man*, ed. P. M. C. Davies.

and orthopraxy have suffered terrible harm from this neglect or worse-than-neglect. But for the rest let us now concentrate on the implications of orthodoxy, for however much it may need to be balanced and controlled by the other criteria, it is evidently central for our understanding of the meaning of discipleship and communion.

In our present context it seems to me, in the light of reflections both historical and doctrinal, that orthodoxy is not to be understood as an undifferentiated system of beliefs, but that it is focused on *Christology*, that is, on the evaluation of Jesus' person and significance. I have suggested that the sense of orthodoxy grew as a kind of precipitate out of the experience of discipleship. The great debates in the fourth and fifth centuries centred on the question how Jesus is related to the Father; it was the agreement reached by the 'Great Church' that Jesus is fully and truly both God and man which gave us the core of what we mean by orthodoxy, and the essential criterion for whether there is enough shared discipleship for people to sit together at Jesus' table.

In saying this I am drawing attention to two ways in which we can develop and apply the idea of orthodoxy. One way is as a system of belief which is in fact a whole way of life, orthopraxy, which will be interested in many more doctrines and practices besides strictly christological beliefs, but nevertheless orthodox Christology remains the centre and controlling principle of the whole system, providing a pattern which is worked out analogically through almost the whole of theology. This is an ideal, inherited from the great age of the Councils and the fathers, but we must face the fact that Christians do not agree on which actual Church is nearest, or anywhere near, the ideal. Be it proudly or humbly, several communions claim to be there or nearest, while many more agree in denying such claims. In this situation the centrality of Christology can help us in the other way; though fuller agreement may fail, surely we can agree that at least here many can meet in sincere mutual acknowledgement of shared discipleship, an acknowledgement which it is not repugnant to think of expressing through provisional intercommunion, even though full communion is not yet possible.

It may be replied that this second way of concentrating on Christology as the essence of orthodoxy means minimising the Faith intolerably. To this I answer, first, that it is suggested not as an ideal but as a realistic response to a situation that ought not to exist and must be healed, because it is repugnant to the idea of discipleship of Jesus that disciples should refuse to sit together at his table. But my second answer goes deeper. If we reflect on orthodox belief in its fuller sense, we shall see that the whole analogical structure implies that orthodoxy in Christology will naturally be reflected in ecclesiology, the theology of grace, of Scripture, of the sacraments, and so on. In Christology we see orthodoxy as a balance between views of Christ as God not really incarnate and as man merely 'adopted' or divinised. There are positions which break the balance or essential tension involved in orthodox faith, while there are others which (today at least) are agreed to be merely verbally divergent from the ideal balance.[26] Not every divergence from classical formulas is intolerable. We see the same in sacramental theology. A Christian who really believes in the Incarnation will have, however inchoately, an incarnational, sacramental, idea of how Christ works in the world. He will almost certainly want to say, in a strong sense, that Christ is really present and active in the Eucharist, though he may have insuperable difficulties with traditional Catholic attempts to 'explain' the Real Presence. Since Trent Catholic church authorities have demanded a standard in formulation of eucharistic doctrine which was perhaps more rigid than the controlling centre of the whole system requires (whereas for members orthodoxy is generally assumed and 'orthopraxy' is the practical rule applied through the penitential discipline).

The above sketch, all too brief though it is, has (I hope) shown how Christology is both the controlling centre of the whole system of orthodoxy and orthopraxy which can be the basis for full communion, and is the essential centre, acceptance of which could, I submit, be an acceptable basis for provisional intercommunion in order to let the experience of shared discipleship grow. In both ways of thinking about orthodoxy, it will be noted, the idea of balance and acceptable pluralism has been actively present. This is due to the constant influence of the criterion of catholicity, which essentially connotes diversity in harmony. An orthodoxy which tries to exist by destroying

---

[26] Cf. Y. CONGAR, 'Dogme christologique et ecclésiologie: vérité et limites d'un parallèle', in *Das Konzil von Chalkedon*, edited by A. E. Grillmeier and H. Bacht (Würzburg 1954), pp. 239–68.

lawful diversity and legitimate tensions cannot, in fact, remain truly orthodox.

But then what a mess we are all in! All these words to try to clarify the situation we are in, and now we see that it is too untidy to clarify. Our criteria can point to positions and behaviour which are not recognisable *at all* as Christian, but it hardly needs criteria to see them. The whole problem is that unorthodoxy, unchristian behaviour and uncatholic intolerance have degrees, and we cannot have such a tight little church that no degree of unholiness shall be able to breathe within its walls, for the fact is that our faults are partly simply the reverse side of inevitable human variations of ideas and behaviour. We all know that we fall short in both, but we hope to find indulgence for our weakness, or (in graver faults) to be given a chance of repentance. But perhaps even our behaviour has not done the worst damage to Christ's once united disciples. Perhaps worst of all has been the uncatholicity of our orthodoxy. Inspection of the christological analogy reveals an uncomfortable fact. Traditional Catholic and Orthodox Christianity have a kind of 'magnetic north' which is not exactly 'true north'; their popular positions are characteristically and habitually on the 'monophysite' side of the ideal balance represented by faith in Jesus as fully and truly both God and man. This characteristic goes together with a constant undertow of conservatism and literalism which, as we saw, is one of the 'seedbeds of heresy'. We have not let catholicity correct our orthodoxy enough, or teach us that essential orthodoxy embraces considerable variety and can tolerate a certain amount of imperfection before we have a right or duty to speak of heresy.[27]

But now the challenge has come, and has been accepted, however cautiously, by Vatican II. The old axiom 'outside the Church no salvation' has been stretched till it cannot spring back into shape. Doctrinal pluralism has been affirmed at least between East and West, and (as was argued above) it is impossible to stop there, if a doctrinal position held by yet other Christians makes its way in the light of Scripture and authentic Tradition. We *are* coming to recognise

---

[27] Cf. Vatican II, *Decree on Ecumenism* 6, which speaks of 'deficiencies in conduct, in church discipline or even in the formulation of doctrine (which must be carefully distinguished from the deposit itself of faith)'; this also has bearing on the whole question of pluralism in doctrinal expression.

authentic discipleship under varied expressions, just as the Catholic Church's former tendency to insist on centralisation and uniformity is yielding to a more truly catholic pluralism, which despite constant setbacks is giving cautious hope to those who hope for a restoration of communion without rigid structural unification.

Our aim must be full communion based on unity in faith, a criterion which in practice can only be applied in the sort of way Nicholas Lash has discussed. But grounds have here been suggested for allowing provisional intercommunion with a wider range of Churches than has as yet been envisaged, at least by Rome. As I understand 'intercommunion', it can only be a relationship between Churches who accept each other as such and desire full communion, but need a period of time in which to get used to each other, so as to discover, over a wide range of shared experience, the reality of their shared faith. Hence my proposal that the criterion of orthodoxy is christological involves a sort of 'double exposure' in applying the criterion; not that there is one criterion (in terms of purely christological formulas) for intercommunion and then a further and more elaborate doctrinal criterion for full communion, but that the doctrinal criterion both necessary and sufficient for full communion is still the christological one, but because of divergences in how Churches 'work out' the central Christian idea, a period of intercommunion should come first, in which the mutually balancing tests of orthodoxy, catholicity and orthopraxy can be experienced as more and more unitive.

I do not suggest that such action is possible beyond where the essential christological basis is shared. Many problems will remain, and in particular our fellowship with the Jews cannot go beyond what they are willing to do with Christians; but there is still much to explore in our shared faith in the same God and the two ways in which we await the Messiah respectively as coming or as returning. But with all who inherit the faith of Abraham we can and should pray together, for this is the way ahead in every part of the total problem of restoring mutual recognition and trust between separated believers and disciples of Jesus. Theological dialogue has its necessary place, but it is only for a few and its fruits affect others too slowly. The shorter and perhaps surer way is by shared prayer. Today, in a spontaneous movement which is growing wider day by day, and which despite human faults strongly suggests the inspiration of God's Spirit, Christians are learning through shared informal prayer to understand each other's responses to God through Christ in the Holy Spirit with an immediacy which can be compared to the discovery by a man and a woman that they are ready to trust each other in the adventure of a totally shared life. This is a bold analogy, but I would press it. I believe that through praying together and revealing to each other our patterns of faith and Christian thinking, we can come comparatively quickly to sufficient certainty that there is essential unity in faith, or even virtually full unity. This is no flight into sentimentality but involves the application of the true criteria; experience can also reveal equally clearly that there is less than sufficient shared faith. The theological evaluation of the present charismatic renewal movement has developed the 'discernment of spirits' at communal as well as individual level, and is producing some of the most important contributions to ecumenical theology.[28]

But – the traditional Catholic will be asking in utter puzzlement – am I going to end with never a word about invalid orders? Is *that* not the reason why we must hold back from intercommunion with some who we may well believe and know to be perfectly splendid Christians?

I cannot, evidently, take up this question at this point in so long a paper. I have alluded to validity of orders as an area in which, whether with knowledge or not, I believe Vatican II has planted a 'delayed action bomb'. It may be that we should stop seeking a theological solution to the validity question and should simply agree on a ceremony of mutual validation and acceptance whose meaning and necessity we would leave to God, acknowledging that we are all squabbling children in his nursery and asking him to do what is necessary for all of us, so that the human need to feel sure of things may be satisfied.

But we may never forget that God does not always wait for human validation, and we Gentiles owe the possibility of our church membership to an occasion when God shattered all the rules about circumcision and baptism, and poured out the gifts of his Spirit on

---

[28] Cf. DONALD L. GELPI, S.J., *Pentecostalism: A Theological Viewpoint* (New York-Paramus-Toronto 1971); less systematic, but better in its survey of past charismatic tradition, is SIMON TUGWELL, O.P., *Did you Receive the Spirit?* (London 1972).

Gentiles who had not got beyond the first generous stirring of the heart. Peter could only stammer 'Can anyone forbid water for baptising these people who have received the Holy Spirit just as we have ?' (Acts 10:47). Perhaps once again, and in our own days, God is going to compel us, by means perhaps not yet known to us, to say, now in relation not to baptism but to our notions of validity, 'Can anyone forbid. . . .?'

PART FOUR

INTRODUCTION

THERE COULD BE NO QUESTION OF A SYMPOSIUM LIKE THIS coming to a single, agreed conclusion, whether at the theoretical or the practical level. That is why it seemed to be reasonable to complete the record of the meetings with two comments, not conclusions, and that one of these, by John Coulson, should be from a Roman Catholic point of view, and the other, by John Kent, should be from a Protestant point of view. This helps to underline the variety of those who took part, and also the fact that intercommunion is still not as widespread as much liberal comment might lead one to expect. These are individual comments and should be read as such: there was no question of a consensus, or of any of the other contributors being committed to what is said in this section.

BIOGRAPHICAL NOTE

JOHN COULSON *is Research Fellow in Theology at Bristol University. He has twice been Chairman of the Downside Symposium Group; and his summing-up is from a layman's point of view. He edited the sixth Downside symposium,* Theology and the University; *the Oxford Newman symposium,* The Rediscovery of Newman *(with A. M. Allchin); Newman's* On consulting the Faithful in Matters of Doctrine; *and* The Saints. *In 1970 he published* Newman and the Common Tradition.

A Roman Catholic Comment

JOHN COULSON

IN THE EVENT, THE ORIGINAL DECISION OF THE SYMPOSIUM
Group to set the discussion of Intercommunion within the broader
context of church membership was justified. Because the two
problems are so closely related, it is essential to grasp how they are
to be distinguished; and the first distinction to be drawn was, therefore, that between communion and intercommunion. The former
expresses that common, confessional membership, by which we
gain our identity as Christians. The character of the eucharist, as it
expresses that unity, is continuous and repetitive. It is the regular,
daily or weekly means of affirming our unity of faith. Intercommunion, on the other hand, is an act of mutual recognition, which
pre-supposes a diversity of membership and belief; and it conceives
the eucharist as the means of bringing about that more perfect unity
we are obliged to seek, and of acknowledging that imperfect communion which already exists. It is a periodical not a continuous act.
Yet each act of intercommunion by weakening the sense of division,
strengthens while it develops a new unity in religion. It is this aspect
of eucharistic doctrine which is now being revived. In practice,
however, fellowship brought about by intercommunion may be
gained at the expense of the loss of fellowship, or of ecclesial coherence,
within one's own communion. What is externally unitive then
appears to be internally divisive. Are these equal alternatives; and,

if so, are the two ways of conceiving the eucharist mutually incompatible?

To conceive the problem thus – as one between equal but incompatible alternatives – may be, however, to refuse to accept the force of social and intellectual change. Circumstances obliged the early Church to identify unity of faith with social unity, as they obliged the Reformers to accept the divisive social and political consequences of deciding to differ in theology. We might be theologically, because historically and sociologically, naive, if we failed to understand that the differences between Christians today are of a different *kind* from those in the early Church. These were between rivals, of whom one must be the master (Wiles, p. 47). Now our beliefs are obliged, politically and socially, to co-exist with each other. But what is also new is the anxiety to grow more closely together. What is its motive? Does it spring from denominational weakness (Towler p. 204)? Some local churches, for example (Clark p. 186; Towler p. 208), are held together only by the buildings they have by custom worshipped in. Or are we being brought to recognise the existence of a new unity in faith, the work of the Spirit, which we fail to recognise at our peril?

Should the latter be the case, it would still be a retrograde step if, while agreeing upon new common formulae of belief, we were enthusiastically to ignore the historical origins and growth of the present plurality, and were, furthermore, to use the achievement of such agreements as the justification for their enforcement. The lesson to be drawn from Dr Swanston's account of the Revisers' Communion is the barren consequence of forcing the issue in advance of what is, in the broad sense, public opinion, and in the technical sense, the consent of the faithful. We gain nothing if we merely unchurch each other to enforce a wider unity, which can be discerned only by an élite of ecumaniacs.

Yet, having said this, we must remember that a plural society speaks with many voices; and that the layman in particular no longer sees his *primary* membership as being that of the local church. He belongs to many over-lapping and discontinuous societies, and no longer to one exclusively. An effect, often under-estimated, of this changed experience of membership is for some differences between members of the same communion to be felt as going deeper than those between friends separated in religion but thinking alike on the political, moral and doctrinal issues of the day. (A crucial, contemporary instance is afforded by the *crise de conscience* occasioned by the diverse ways in which Christians of all denominations behaved under the Nazi Occupation.)

Within the churches, this centrifugal tendency is further exemplified in the consequences arising from their common efforts at liturgical change. If the church is founded on prayer, then to alter the liturgy is to disturb internal, ecclesial coherence. Yet for as long as there was some kind of cultural unity within which the Church could preserve an equilibrium, changes in church order could be contained within a stable, social and linguistic sub-structure. This is not provided by a plural society. Instead, Christians are thrown back, uncushioned by the unities of a common culture, upon the thorniest of direct theological questions; and their search for unity may be for a more secure, because more universal, foundation (cp. Towler p. 224).

What then prevents us, in such circumstances, from simple, open communion—open to all 'who love the Lord Jesus'? (Murray p. 271, Kent p. 235, Wiles p. 48). It may be urged in reply that only by giving our beliefs limits can they be given meaning, that for the sacraments (whether baptism or the eucharist) to be effective, we must first agree the meaning of the sacramental sign; and that is the particularity of Christ which constitutes the requirement of Christian membership and, thereby, the focus of its exclusiveness.

If the instances afforded by Rabbi Jacobs and Dr Sharpe are interpreted negatively, they demonstrate what is central and exclusive in Christian affirmation – that Jesus was unique, and that those who are his people become so, not by birth or by behaviour solely, but by what they say about him; and that they cease to be his people by what they unsay or deny: the Christian community is given only as it creates, maintains and re-creates itself; and for this a unity of faith has always been the crucial pre-condition.

But where is this saying and unsaying to be focused? Exegetes do not encourage us to find this in Scripture solely, or in any chosen proof texts, since this would be to diminish the irreducible pluralism, not only of the Old Testament, but less obviously of the New (Murray p.258). Fr Murray contends that the limits of an acceptable doctrinal pluralism cannot be less than those of authentic Tradition in the broadest sense, where 'heresy' has been conceived as an excess, defect or imbalance, in distinction from objectively definable limits. This suggests that the sound criteria for allowing confessing fellow-believers to intercommunicate ought not to be too restrictive verbally, but rather flexible criteria relating to the evident variety within the traditional understanding of fellow-discipleship of the Incarnate Son of God (Murray pp. 267, 272).

This brings us to what was considered to be the fundamental theological questions – how is unity of faith to be identified? Is it to be found in the agreement to use the Creed? Dr Lash argues that, as far as the intellectual element of faith is concerned, the common use of the 'great creeds' is evidence of shared beliefs sufficient to justify the celebration together of the eucharist, since to confess the Creed is to confess God's revelation in its entirety (Lash pp. 68, 70).[1] Three centuries of rationalism have certainly obscured the fact that our ability to explain the articles of the Creed in their literal and univocal sense (and thus to reduce them to statements of belief) must relate to (if it is not derived from) their *doxological* use in the life of faith, viz. in prayer, praise and worship. However much knowledge must precede and be the condition of love, God's love for us precedes our knowledge of him; and the distinction which we were led to emphasise was that between unity of faith and uniformity of belief, where the former cannot simply be reduced to or identified with the latter. Otherwise, pre-conditions might be set for mutual recognition of ministries that were conceptually more rigorous than those for common membership. Not to ask for more clarity or exactness of definition than the subject admits is always a prudent maxim. Here it is essential. To do otherwise is to widen that gap between canonical order and the evident work of the Spirit, which is at once the source of ecumenical concern and its opportunity (a point urged by Dr Oliver Tomkins, Bishop of Bristol, during the discussion).

To persist in conceiving the problems arising from our growth in unity as being between equal but incompatible alternatives – that

---

[1] Cp. J. H. NEWMAN in *Tract XC*. In referring to the *regula fidei*, he italicises the following quotation from the 17th century theologian, Archbishop Bramhall: 'The Scriptures and the Creed are not two different Rules of Faith, but *one and the same Rule dilated in Scripture, contracted in the Creed*'. *Via Media*, ii, p. 278.

what is externally unitive is internally divisive – may be to conclude
that until we have satisfactory conditions for common membership,
we cannot have mutual recognition of churches and acts of intercommunion. What the symposium shows is why these questions must
be kept distinct, if either is to be satisfactorily resolved. Nevertheless,
internal confessional membership is not static and undeveloping:
confessions live only to the extent that they revise, re-examine
and restore what may have dropped out of circulation. And the laity
survive only as they are responsive to the environment created by
industrial and technological development: this is the social reality
against which they are obliged to measure the reality-claims of
confessional membership. It demands its own unities; and in such a
society what is externally unitive may become the condition by which
what remains internally unitive can be kept alive; such may be the
necessary foundation, if members are to continue to realise and
develop with due confidence that identity which they receive from
their confessional life of prayer and obedience

Practical Considerations

The weight of the argument in Dr Lash's paper and in the symposium
generally was that, if unity of faith is a necessary condition to justify
intercommunion between separated churches, then it is sufficiently
expressed in the liturgical use and affirmation of the great Creeds.
But not only are criteria other than the purely theological involved,
but their application must itself admit of mutual balance and control.
(Fransen pp. 20, 21; Murray pp. 271, 273). As Professor Fransen
emphasises, decisions concerning eucharistic discipline are pastoral
(or prudential) judgements and, as such, ultimately the responsibility
of the holders of the apostolic office (Fransen pp. 12, 13).

Given a sufficient unity of faith, however, what would lead to the
question of intercommunion being raised on pastoral grounds?
Professor Fransen argues that it is the category of 'urgent cases' which
should be re-examined. Cases falling within this category have, in
the past, been too narrowly and juridically interpreted. It is, for
example, a matter of 'urgency' that the unity of love expressed in
what canonists call 'a mixed marriage' should be encouraged to
find its fulfilment in a unity of eucharistic devotion. As the sharing of
church buildings and the integration of Christian education increase,

so does the pressure towards common worship. Ecumenical conferences and groups working together for a particular purpose and
limited period (of which this symposium is an example) often achieve
a unity of faith which rightly seeks to express itself in worship. Are
the grounds sufficient for fellow members, in good standing with
their churches, to continue to exclude each other from communion?

Anglican contributors to the symposium pointed out that the
Church of England admits to her eucharistic communion all who
are 'in good standing' with their respective churches. It does not
'forbid' its members to communicate in other churches; but, if the
latter extend an invitation, it is left to the individual conscience
whether to accept. A further suggestion, also from Anglican sources,
is that cited by Professor Fransen (Fransen p. 31) – that of an
ecumenical concelebration, or joint celebration of the eucharist on
particular occasions and under special conditions.

The question remains, however, whether the recognition of
ministry for eucharistic purposes can be distinguished from that
of the total recognition of separated churches. It is the purpose of
Fr Coventry's note to show the grounds on which it might now be
possible for one church to regard the ministry of another as being in
some respects deficient, without being obliged to deny that the other
was not a true eucharistic ministry. His note, together with the other
papers, brings us back yet again to that distinction which it was the
main concern of the symposium to establish – it is that between the
conditions requisite for full, mutual common membership, and
those sufficient for sharing in the eucharist. In trying to see where
this distinction leads us, we should take to heart that warning first
voiced by Aristotle and repeated by Newman – that we must not
require a greater exactness of definition than the nature of the
subject admits.

A Protestant Comment

JOHN KENT

ONE CANNOT REALLY HAVE A CONSENSUS ON THE PROBLEM
of intercommunion because there are at least two quite different ways
of approaching it: first, as an end in itself, and second, as part of a
wider scheme for Christian unity. The first may be called the 'diplomatic' approach, the second the 'organic'. In the first case discussion
centres on the grounds which may exist for permitting various degrees
of intercommunion; in the second questions about intercommunion
are related, either negatively or positively, to the ecumenical cam-
paign to dissolve all existing Christian bodies in one united Church.

The 'diplomatic' approach became inevitable once Christian
institutions had split completely, as they did in fact in the period
of the so-called undivided Church, for the use of the concept of
heresy and schism only obscures the truth that the Montanists and
Donatists, for example, were still 'Christians'. The separated groups
became in effect 'high contracting parties', each with its own administration, definition of membership, and ecclesiastical foreign policy.
The gradual movement apart of Western and Eastern Christianity
made this situation permanent even after the collapse of the Roman
imperial institutions. Movement across the resulting church frontiers,
as in the case of mixed marriages, for example, or of the traveller
who found himself cut off from his own communion, caused recur-
rent problems, as did the isolated dying man for whom charity
recommended the abrogation of the rules. Looked at in this

perspective, some degree of intercommunion represents an attempt to eliminate causes of friction between ecclesiastical states. Concessions may be made on various grounds. In the earlier period of the history of the Church, admission to the sacraments of those who do not belong to one's own communion seemed possible in only very exceptional cases; at a later period the idea develops, and may be found in many contributions to this symposium, that intercommunion may be justified on broader grounds, on the ground, for example, of the essentially Christian character of another communion. Nervousness creeps in at this stage, because if these simplified conditions are made too general and are left without careful qualification it may become very difficult for the outsider to see why the two bodies should remain separate. Diplomatic approaches to the problem of intercommunion, however, do not envisage the goal of final unity but only the more limited aim of enabling groups which are separated by social as well as theological differences to co-exist tranquilly: essentially, this is done by easing individual cases. The diplomatic approach is not concerned with negotiations for reciprocal communion between churches but with widening the number of exceptions to unchanged basic rules. The very mobile character of modern society makes this increasingly necessary.

This seems to me to be the position of most of the Roman Catholic contributors to this symposium. They would like it to be much easier for non-Catholics to communicate in Catholic churches on occasion – there is nothing on the Protestant side, of course, to prevent Catholics communicating in most Protestant churches, on the occasional basis which the diplomatic approach assumes. They also feel that the Roman Catholic Church could recognise in a general sense the reality of some Protestant ministries, having in mind specifically the priesthood of the Anglican Church, which they would like to rescue from the ambiguous position in which it was landed by the blunders of late Victorian ecclesiastical statesmanship. At the level of the high contracting parties such changes would bring about a valuable relaxation of the historic tension between the Catholic and Protestant societies, though as a Methodist whose ministerial orders the Anglican Church has never been able fully to recognise officially, I do not find this Catholic anxiety for the status of the Anglican priesthood of more than minor interest.

Such a relaxation of tension, however, would remain within the bounds of the 'diplomatic' understanding of the problems of intercommunion, and it is not hard to see why. The kind of generous recognition of non-Catholic bodies suggested here could become part of an approach to organic union only if the scheme proposed answered Protestant doubts about the existence of the Papacy, about the doctrine of infallibility, and about certain aspects of Marian teaching and devotion. By keeping strictly to questions of creed and priesthood one can hope to widen the possibilities of Catholic-Protestant intercommunion, and this is the purpose of the 'diplomatic' approach as I have described it; but for intercommunion to be part of an organic relationship one has to take up these more profoundly divisive issues, which cannot be pushed into the background permanently by use of the idea of 'recognition'. In these respects membership of the Roman Catholic communion involves accepting much more than does membership of the Methodist Church, either in the United Kingdom or, in slightly varying forms, in the United States.

Nevertheless, the diplomatic method can be under-rated, especially when an ecumenical purpose informs it. In wise, but disregarded words written for *Intercommunion*, the report of a World Council of Churches Faith and Order Committee issued in preparation for the Lund Conference of 1952, the late Leonard Hodgson pleaded with his own Anglican communion to extend opportunities for reciprocal open communion services, 'so that not as individuals but as loyal representatives of our Church we may in practice recognise the equality of the sacraments of our fellow Christians from whom for the time being we are divided . . . I believe that such action would be preferable to any "concordats" involving the mutual commissioning of individual ministers by formulae of ambiguous meaning: I believe that it would do more than anything else to convince Christendom as a whole that the Anglican Church is serious in its often expressed desire for unity'.

Under the influence of the late Archbishop Fisher, Church relations in England had already turned disastrously in another direction, the pursuit of the 'organic' version of intercommunion which makes its achievement the climax of a process of unification. At the level of the high contracting parties this really means the denial of intercommunion, for first, what is allowed to individuals or small groups is understood to have no permanent theological significance, and second, by the time that the uniting Churches intercommunicate as such any distinction between them has already been removed. As developed in the Anglican–Methodist conversations, which were officially started with the aim of going forward to full communion with one another, this involved (*a*) the reconciliation of the two Churches in a service which would include integration of the existing ministries by reciprocal action; and (*b*) the acceptance by the Methodist Church of an episcopate in continuity with what is called the 'historic episcopate' and the practice of episcopal ordination for its ministers thereafter. Such a set of proposals assumed that the two Churches were divided only by their doctrines of the ecclesia and ministry, and that this problem could be solved by the Methodist Church adopting an episcopal structure, though without formal acceptance of the assertion that episcopacy is of the *esse* of the ecclesia. (It is very important, of course, that the willingness of the Methodist Church to abandon its presbyterian structure and to prepare for an episcopal substitute did not suffice to commend the proposals to an adequate Anglican majority: this failure, together with the similar Anglican–Presbyterian failure in Scotland in 1958, should be taken to heart by those tempted to think that agreements reached at the sort of level represented by the British Council of Churches matter very much.)

Roman Catholic contributors to this symposium, starting from what appears to me to be a diplomatic concept of intercommunion, are willing to say that differences about faith and order are not deep enough to prevent extensions of intercommunion *before there is any question* of moving to organic unity – though they fail to particularise, to suggest where in the multitudinous seas of Protestant denominationalism their generosity would have to stop. I am bound to sympathise, because the 'organic' method has inflamed rather than healed the wounds of the Churches.

Nevertheless, if one tries to shift from the diplomatic to the organic level, a new choice emerges. The tendency of episcopal Protestantism, typified by the Anglican Church, has been to insist that intercommunion at more than a personal level can only express an existing unity, and cannot be used as one means of searching for a unity not yet found. This position has not been sufficiently challenged. The post-war Methodist negotiators, for example, gave up the point at an early stage. In 1953 the Methodist Conference had asked to be satisfied that 'the Church of England acknowledges that our divisions are within the Christian Body which is throughout in a state of schism'. Convocation replied, in 1955, that it hesitated to use these precise words, 'but would regard all discussions between the Methodist Church and the Church of England as taking place within the Body of Christ'. The Methodist Conference of 1955 did not press the matter further, but theologically it was reasonable to suggest that if the *discussions* were taking place within the Body of Christ then both groups of Christians existed within the same Body of Christ, in which case the ground for communion was already there without imposing further demands for prior organic integration. In effect, the Methodist Church was to waste twenty years in fruitless discussion, presumably within the Body of Christ, on the kind of structural alterations which would be needed to justify denominational intercommunion.

However, just as the real Anglican answer to this would have been that reciprocal intercommunion without prior conditions would have left unresolved deep differences between the Anglican feeling for the Church as divine in origin and visible structure, and the Methodist feeling for the visible Church as historically limited in both substance and origin, so, at the 'organic' level the Protestant contributor to this symposium is driven to remind his Catholic brethren that to widen the opportunities for intercommunion between Catholic and Protestant without looking at the organic level of the problem, would be to leave unresolved deep differences between Catholic traditions about the Papacy, about infallibility and about Mary, on the one hand, and on the other, a widespread Protestant rejection of the Papacy as superfluous, of infallibility as unobtainable – and not to be made respectable by bringing in the laity in some consultative capacity, and of the Marian dogmas as unnecessary to salvation.

The question that remains is whether the Catholic symposiasts are right to ignore these issues and plead for a greater degree of intercommunion? Here my own answer would be 'yes'. The insistence that unity must proceed intercommunion as an ecumenical method has got us nowhere. If one takes 1910 as the basic date for the modern Ecumenical Movement, then two generations and two world wars later the Anglican Church and the English Free Churches remain neither reconciled nor united through a common (historic) episcopate. In England the ecumenical movement has never shown any sign of being the great new factor to which William Temple looked forward. For all the talk about the supernatural nature of the Church as the Body of Christ, what we have seen has looked very similar to secular political conflict. We need to recognise in more than words that a common Christianity exists between the English Free Church tradition, the Anglican tradition and the tradition of the Catholic Church in England, and this seems to be the major thing that the Roman Catholic contributors to this volume are trying to say. If we do not begin to intercommunicate without waiting for another generation to pass, we shall never achieve unity in the organic sense, but only witness the absorption of the stronger by the weaker, a miserable conclusion to what might have been a creative age in the history of English religion.

APPENDICES

Appendix 1

Intercommunion in England — the changing situation

JOHN KENT

NOT LONG AFTER THE SYMPOSIUM HAD ENDED THE ANGLICAN
law on admission to the Eucharist was changed by a new Canon
(B. 15A), given here as promulged on 7th July 1972:

'1. There shall be admitted to Holy Communion:

  (*a*) members of the Church of England who have been
  confirmed in accordance with the rites of that Church or
  are ready and desirous to be confirmed or who have been
  otherwise episcopally confirmed with unction or with the
  laying on of hands, except as provided by the next following
  Canon:

  (*b*) baptised persons who are communicant members of
  other Churches which subscribe to the doctrine of the Holy
  Trinity, and who are in good standing in their own Church:

  (*c*) any other baptised persons authorised to be admitted under
  regulations of the General Synod; and

  (*d*) any baptised person in immediate danger of death.

'2. If any person by virtue of sub-paragraph (*b*) above regularly
receives the Holy Communion over a long period which appears
likely to continue indefinitely, the minister shall set before him the
normal requirements of the Church of England for communicant
status in that Church.

'3. Where any minister is in doubt as to the application of this Canon, he shall refer the matter to the Bishop of the diocese or other Ordinary and follow his guidance thereon.'

This Canon was the climax of a process which had begun about forty years before. From 1933 the question of the admission of persons who did not belong to the Anglican Communion to Holy Communion in Anglican Churches had been governed by Resolutions of the Upper Houses of Convocations. These Resolutions said that the giving or withholding of permission was in the discretion of the diocesan bishop, who was to treat as special cases baptised communicant members of other Churches cut off by distance from the ministrations of their own Church; school or college chapels where services were conducted according to the rites of the Church of England and where a certain elasticity was obviously useful; and special occasions when groups of Anglicans and other Christians were joined together 'in efforts definitely intended to promote the visible unity of the Church of Christ'. It was made clear in 1933 that action under the first two heads was meant to cover individuals, not groups, and that the resolutions did not establish new laws for the Church of England, but instead confided the whole issue to the discretion of the diocesan, guided by the considerations raised above.

By the 1960's the ecumenical situation had developed so far that further action seemed necessary. The revision of Anglican Canon Law had reached a point which it was proposed to give final form to a new Canon (B. 15). Clauses 3 and 4 of the draft Canon aroused disagreement:

'3. No person shall be admitted to Holy Communion until such time as he shall be confirmed or be ready and desirous to be confirmed, except under Regulations of the Convocation of the Province made with the concurrence of the Church Assembly or under the provisions of paragraph 4 of this Canon.

'4. Nothing in these Canons shall be deemed to forbid the admission to the Holy Communion at the discretion of the Minister:

'(a) of a baptised person in instant danger of death, or
'(b) subject to the general direction of the bishop, of an

individual baptised communicant member of a Church
not in communion with the Church of England to meet
occasional and particular pastoral needs.'

The Resolutions referred to here were those which have been
outlined above. The draft Canon still reflected the cautious and rather
pre-ecumenical attitude of 1933; in an attempt to find agreement on a
better formula an Archbishops' Commission on Intercommunion was
set up in 1965, which reported in 1968 under the title *Intercommunion
Today*. The Commission's report recognised the need to provide
for the admission to Holy Communion of members of Churches
which were not in full communion with the Church of England, but
felt that this was a matter which ought not to be too precisely defined
within the necessary rigidity of a canon. The new draft canon which
the Commission put forward in 1968 proposed that the General
Synod might by regulations provide for the welcoming of such
persons, but the draft regulations which were suggested retained
much of the approach of 1933. Thus the chief new departure was a
new category of occasions: 'ones in which strong ties of family
relationship or friendship are involved, for instance when one partner
in a marriage belongs to another denomination, or when non-
Anglican relatives and friends are present at the wedding; other
similar occasions would be ordinations, religious professions or the
commissioning of departing missionaries; there is also the case of
the celebration of the Holy Communion in the room of the gravely
or chronically ill, when it may be right to administer the sacrament
also to non-Anglican relations or friends who may be present',
(*Intercommunion Today*, London 1968, p. 77). Such remedies pre-
suppose the continuance of existing ecclesiastical frontiers. The
Commission said little about the future of relations between Churches,
no doubt because, as far as England was concerned, most Anglicans
in 1968 assumed that the Anglican–Methodist negotiations were
about to create full communion between two parallel episcopal
churches pledged to go on to organic union, an event which would
have transformed the context of the proposed new canon. *Intercommunion Today* became a casualty of the internal Anglican disunity
which caused the collapse of the plan; one could no longer suppose
that the path towards full intercommunion in England would be

eased by the Free Churches taking episcopacy into their systems in the near future.

And so one comes back to the actual canon (B 15A) of 1972, whose sub-paragraph (*b*) broke away from the tradition summed up in the Regulations of 1933. The question of faith is settled by reference to the doctrine of the Trinity.

There is no question here of reciprocal intercommunion; in fact, there seems to be no official guidance to Anglicans as to the circumstances in which they may communicate at the celebrations of other Churches. In the past, most Anglicans have not taken very seriously the idea of reciprocal intercommunion with non-episcopal bodies, and *Intercommunion Today* stated that 'in Great Britain, for example, it would hardly have been possible to think of intercommunion between Anglicans and Roman Catholics in the period before the joint declaration of the Pope and the Archbishop of Canterbury in March 1966' (ibid., p. 94). The recent joint Anglican–Roman Catholic statement on the Eucharist which is discussed in the Symposium itself marks a further step towards intercommunion between the two Churches concerned. Among the English Free Churches, the union in 1972 between the Congregationalist and Presbyterian traditions hardly changed the existing situation in this respect, for the Baptist churches in the Baptist Union, the Congregationalists, the Methodists and Presbyterians had enjoyed reciprocal intercommunion with each other for many years, and the ministers of these bodies would not have regarded themselves as precluded by any official statements from admitting Anglicans to the Holy Communion if they so desired.

Nevertheless, the new Anglican canon does pave the way for further change. On the Anglican side, at any rate, the spontaneous religious action becomes possible; sacramental piety moves a stage nearer to total freedom; the eucharist itself comes closer to being freed from its embarrassing traditional role in ecclesiastical law.

Appendix 2

Those who attended the symposium or part of it are:

John A. Baker
Amelie Betton
Laurence Bright
Joseph C. Buckley
David B. Clark
Peter Coleman
John Coulson
John Coventry
John D. Crichton
Edward Crouzet
Hugh Dinwiddy
Peter Fransen
Kenneth G. Grayston
Ian Hamnett
Lady Hylton
Lord Hylton
Louis Jacobs
Philip Jebb
Patrick Kelly
John H. S. Kent
Martin King
Nicholas L. A. Lash
Johannes Lutticken
Ian McNeill
Sally McNeill

Robert Murray
Valerie Pitt
<u>Henry Rack</u>
Eric J. Sharpe
Richard Stewart
John Sullivan
Hamish Swanston
John M. Todd
Oliver Tomkins
Robert Towler
Meriol Trevor
Maurice F. Wiles
Keith R. Wilkes
Christopher Williams
Michael Williams

Index